CRITICAL READINGS
MEDIA AND AUDIENCES

Edited by
Virginia Nightingale and
Karen Ross

OPEN UNIVERSITY PRESS
Maidenhead

Open University Press
McGraw-Hill Education
McGraw-Hill House
Shoppenhangers Road
Maidenhead, Berkshire
England SL6 2QL

email: enquiries@openup.co.uk
world wide web: www.openup.co.uk

First published 2003

Copyright © Virginia Nightingale and Karen Ross, 2003

All rights reserved. Except for the quotation of short passages for the purpose of criticism and review, no part of this publication may be reproduced, stored in a retrieval system, or transmitted, in any form or by any means, electronic, mechanical, photocopying, recording or otherwise, without the prior written permission of the publisher or a licence from the Copyright Licensing Agency Limited. Details of such licences (for reprographic reproduction) may be obtained from the Copyright Licensing Agency Ltd of 90 Tottenham Court Road, London, W1T 4LP.

A catalogue record for this book is available from the British Library.

ISBN 0 335 21166 6 (pb)   0 335 21167 4 (hb)

Library of Congress Cataloging-in-Publication Data has been applied for

Typeset by YHT Ltd, London
Printed in Great Britain by Bell and Bain, Glasgow

CRITICAL READINGS: MEDIA AND AUDIENCES

ISSUES in CULTURAL and MEDIA STUDIES

Series editor: Stuart Allan

Published titles

News Culture
Stuart Allan

Modernity and Postmodern Culture
Jim McGuigan

*Sport, Culture and the Media, 2nd
edition*
David Rowe

*Television, Globalization and Cultural
Identities*
Chris Barker

Ethnic Minorities and the Media
Simon Cottle

Cinema and Cultural Modernity
Gill Branston

Compassion, Morality and the Media
Keith Tester

Masculinities and Culture
John Beynon

Cultures of Popular Music
Andy Bennett

Media, Risk and Science
Stuart Allan

Violence and the Media
Cynthia Carter and C. Kay Weaver

Moral Panics and the Media
Chas Critcher

Cities and Urban Cultures
Deborah Stevenson

Cultural Citizenship
Nick Stevenson

Culture on Display
Bella Dicks

Critical Readings: Media and Gender
Edited by Cynthia Carter and Linda
Steiner

Critical Readings: Media and Audiences
Edited by Virginia Nightingale and
Karen Ross

Media and Audiences
Karen Ross and Virginia Nightingale

*Critical Readings: Sport, Culture and
the Media*
Edited by David Rowe

Rethinking Cultural Policy
Jim McGuigan

Media, Politics and the Network Society
Robert Hassan

CONTENTS

NOTES ON CONTRIBUTORS

John Banks is Online Community Development Manager for Auran Developments and a doctoral student at the University of Queensland

Nancy Baym is an associate professor in the Department of Communication Studies at the University of Kansas, USA

S. Elizabeth Bird is Professor of Social Anthropology at the University of South Florida, USA

Jay G. Blumler is Emeritus Professor of Public Communication at the University of Leeds

David Buckingham is Professor of Education in the School of Culture, Language and Communication at the Institute of Education, UK

Ivor Crewe is Vice-Chancellor of the University of Essex, UK

(The late) **Phillip Elliott**, was Research Fellow at the Centre For Mass Communication Research, Leicester University, UK

Marie Gillespie is a senior lecturer in the Faculty of Social Sciences at the Open University, UK

Michael Gurevitch is a professor in the College of Journalism and Affiliate Faculty in the Department of Communication at the University of Maryland, USA

Stuart Hall is Professor Emeritus at the Open University, UK

James D. Halloran is Research and Emeritus Professor at the Centre for Mass Communication Research, University of Leicester, UK

Henry Jenkins is Director of the Comparative Media Studies Program at Massachusetts Institute of Technology, USA

Elihu Katz is Professor Emeritus at the Department of Sociology and Anthropology at the Hebrew University of Jerusalem, Israel

(The late) **Paul Lazarsfeld**, formerly Professor at the University of Pittsburgh

Lawrence W. Lichty is a professor in the Department of Radio and Television at Northwestern University, USA

Annette N. Markham is an assistant professor in the Department of Communication Studies at Virginia Tech University, USA

Eileen R. Meehan is Heidel Brown Chair in Media and Political Economy in the Manship School of Mass Communications at Louisiana State University, USA

David E. Morrison is Professor and Research Director for the University of Leeds Research Centres, UK

Graham Murdock is Reader in the Sociology of Culture in the Department of Social Sciences at Loughborough University, UK

Virginia Nightingale is an associate professor in the School of Communication, Design and Media at the University of Western Sydney, Australia

Patricia F. Phalen is an assistant professor in the School of Media and Public Affairs at George Washington University, USA

Karen Ross is Reader in Mass Communication at Coventry University, UK

James G. Webster is a professor and Associate Dean of the School of Speech, Department of Communication Studies at Northwestern University, USA

FOREWORD

Informing any discussion of the media in contemporary societies is likely to be some notion or other of 'the audience', whether it is rendered explicit or simply taken for granted. Indeed, it is worth noting how frequently arguments made about the media rest on certain shared assumptions about how audiences behave – assumptions that often lack any sort of evidential basis to sustain them.

Critical Readings: Media and Audiences, edited by Virginia Nightingale and Karen Ross, provides a welcome corrective to this over-reliance on broad assertions. It has been designed to work as a rich resource both on its own terms and as an accompaniment to their co-authored text, *Media and Audiences: Critical Reflections*. Like the latter text, this Reader offers a valuable overview of several key conceptual and methodological issues that have been at the heart of the field of enquiry over the years. More specifically, it traces the shift from a field dominated by mass communication studies to one increasingly preoccupied with the interactivity of diverse audience formations. Each of the chapters highlights significant insights derived from investigations conducted across a wide array of media genres in varied situational contexts. Topics explored include the complex ways in which audiences negotiate journalism, advertising, television violence, sport, talk shows and cyberspace, among other examples. Significantly, in looking across the respective chapters, it quickly becomes apparent that it is necessary to move beyond familiar conceptions of 'the audience' as a singular, cohesive totality. Indeed, the Reader demonstrates how and why competing definitions of what counts as an audience change over time and from one theoretical framework to the next. Thus in its blending of early and contemporary research studies, this collection also helps to pose new research questions for future enquiries.

The *Issues in Cultural and Media Studies* series aims to facilitate a diverse range of critical investigations into pressing questions considered to be central to current thinking and research. In light of the remarkable speed at which the conceptual agendas of cultural and media studies are changing, the series is committed to contributing to what is an ongoing process of re-evaluation and critique. Each of the books is intended to provide a lively, innovative and comprehensive introduction to a specific topical issue from a fresh perspective. The reader is offered a thorough grounding in the most salient debates indicative of the book's subject, as well as important insights into how new modes of enquiry may be established for future explorations. Taken as a whole, then, the series is designed to cover the core components of cultural and media studies courses in an imaginatively distinctive and engaging manner.

Stuart Allan
Series Editor

ACKNOWLEDGEMENTS

The editors would like to thank Stuart Allan for his tireless support of and commitment to this project and Justin Vaughan for his accommodating ways. We would also like to thank the following for giving us permission to reprint the material in this reader:

Alta Mira Press, Lanham, MD, for the extract from *Life Online: Researching Real Experience in Virtual Space*, by Annette N. Markham, pp. 191–9 and 210–16 © 1998 Alta Mira Press.

British Film Institute, for the extract from Dan Harries (ed.) *The New Media Book*, Interactive audiences? pp. 157–70, by Henry Jenkins © 2002 British Film Institute.

Hodder Arnold, London, for the extract from Roger Dickinson *et al.* (eds) *Approaches to Audiences: A Reader*, Children and television: a critical overview of the research, by David Buckingham, pp. 131–45 © 1998 Arnold.

Javnost/The Public, for the extract from *Javnost/The Public*, News we can use: an audience perspective on the tabloidisation of news in the United States, 5(3), pp. 33–50, by S. Elizabeth Bird © 1997 *Javnost/The Public*/S. Elizabeth Bird.

Lawrence Erlbaum Associates, Mahwah, NJ, for the extract from *Ratings Analysis: Theory and Practice*, Ratings analysis in avertising, pp. 158–64, 179–84, by James G. Webster, Patricia F. Phalen and Lawrence W. Lichty © 2000 Lawrence Erlbaum Associates.

McGraw-Hill/Open University Press, for the extract from Simon Cottle (ed.) *Ethnic Minorities and the Media*, Transnational communications and diaspora communities, pp. 164–78, by Marie Gillespie © 2000 McGraw-Hill/Open University Press.

Penguin Group, London, for the extract from *Demonstrations and Communication: A Case Study*, by James D. Halloran, Phillip Elliott and Graham Murdock, pp. 17–19, 238–43 © 1970 James Halloran.

Oxford University Press, for the extract from *Parliamentary Affairs*, The opinion polls: still biased to Blair, 54(4), pp. 650–65, by Ivor Crewe © 2001 Oxford University Press.

Queensland University Press, for the extract from *Australian Journal of Communication*, Improvising Elvis, Marilyn and Mickey Mouse, 21(1), pp. 5–20, by Virginia Nightingale © 1994 University of Queensland.

Queensland University Press, for the extract from Mark Balnaves, T. O'Regan and Jason Sternberg (eds) *Mobilising the Audience*, Gamers as co-creators: enlisting the virtual audience – a report from the netface, pp. 191–6, 199–211, by John Banks © 2002 Queensland University Press.

Sage Publications, Inc., Thousand Oaks, CA, for the extract from Jay G. Blumler and Elihu Katz (eds) *The Uses of Mass Communications: Current Perspectives on Gratifications Research*, Utilization of mass communication by the individual, pp. 19–32, by Elihu Katz, Jay G. Blumler and Michael Gurevitch © 1974 Sage Publications, Inc.

Sage Publications, Inc., Thousand Oaks, CA, for the extract from *Tune In, Log On: Soaps, Fandom and Online Community*, pp. 199–210, 215–18 by Nancy Baym © 2000 Sage Publications, Inc.

Sage Publications, London, for the extract from *Media, Culture & Society*, All ears: radio, reception and discourses of disability, 23(4), pp. 423–36, by Karen Ross © 2001 *Media, Culture & Society*, Sage Publications, Inc.

Taylor & Francis and CCCS, Basingstoke, for the extract from Stuart Hall, Dorothy Hobson, Andrew Lowe and Paul Willis (eds) *Culture, Media, Language*, Encoding/decoding, pp. 197–208, by Stuart Hall © 1980 Taylor & Francis/CCCS.

Extract reprinted with the permission of The Free Press, a Division of Simon & Schuster Adult Publishing Group, from *Personal Influence: The Part Played by People in the Flow of Mass Communications*, Movie Leaders, by Elihu Katz and Paul F. Lazarsfeld. Copyright © 1955 by The Free

Press; copyright renewed 1983 by Patricia Kendall Lazarsfeld and Elihu Katz.

University of Luton Enterprises Ltd, for the extract from *The Search for a Method: Focus Groups and the Development of Mass Communication Research*, pp. 207–23, by David E. Morrison © 1998 University of Luton Enterprises.

University of Minnesota Press, Minneapolis, MN, for the extract from Robert McChesney and William Solomon (eds) *Ruthless Criticism*, Heads of household and ladies of the house: gender, genre and broadcast ratings 1929–1990, pp. 204–21, by Eileen Meehan © 1993 by the Regents of the University of Minnesota.

INTRODUCTION

Audiences are unnatural phenomena. They do not exist in nature, but are created in the course of human interactions – with each other and with the technologies we invent to make our communications more enjoyable and entertaining, more powerful, fast and efficient. The twentieth-century technologies (film, radio, television) addressed masses of people simultaneously. These mass media sought to attract and control mass audiences, and they funded the development of communication forms that suited mass broadcasting and consumption – forms like the soap opera; the news broadcast; the situation comedy. Later in the century, newer technologies (the transistor radio, audio and video cassettes; CD and DVD players; games consoles) increased the range of situations where people could be audiences. The proliferation of technologies for *reproduction* and *distribution* of media forms allowed people to enjoy them in situations of their own choosing rather than at the whim of the broadcaster. By the turn of the twenty-first century, interactive digital technologies had broken the last vestiges of dependence on simultaneous mass distribution. A network and database logic capable of sustaining individual interactivity on a global scale has begun to replace the cumbersome mass media technologies of the broadcasting era.

The power of the networked audience is already causing a reorganization of the ways in which media companies control the distribution of media forms. The orchestrated world-wide release of the fifth *Harry Potter* book, for example, is a dramatic instance of mass publishing under threat. In this case, new technologies had forced world-wide release as a strategy to avoid piracy and copyright infringements that would have followed a sequential roll-out strategy, given the speed with which data can be circulated via the Internet. The controlled release of the book licensed a spectacular performance of consumption (book buying) while protecting the publisher from loss of income. From an audience perspective, the event allowed the hidden network of *Harry Potter* readers a rare opportunity to glimpse the enormous size of the reading community to which they belong, at the same time that it confirmed the conventional nature and banality of the text. The magic was less in the text than in the power of the publisher to circumvent the collective intelligence of the networked audience and yet deliver a successful media event.

The introduction of new technologies alters the underlying expectations that people bring to their engagements with media, and so the nature of audiences seems continually to change. In the broadcast era, audiences had been characterized as masses, as communities, as consumers, as markets, as niches, as targets, as individuals, as obsessed fanatics and even as vegetating couch potatoes. The Internet has fostered a new set of terms for audience modes of engagement – 'maven', 'gamers', 'lurking', for example. Because audiences are 'unnatural' they tend to be endowed with characteristics borrowed from the situations where they engage with media, and with characteristics of the media forms they enjoy. The nature of audiences is always therefore being redefined in accordance with new situations of engagement. Yet we sometimes forget that the new situations may possess parallels with past modes of media engagement.

This book therefore reproduces some of the oldest and some of the most recent writing about media audiences. It includes articles that focus on audiences for mass entertainment and for news and political commentary and provides access to studies that marked turning points in our understanding of the complexity of the social and cultural nature of being an audience. In doing so, it offers readers the opportunity to engage first hand with the language and style of academic writing from the past, and to see how those early writers thought about the relationship between media and audiences.

Because it proved impossible to put together a set of readings that could cover the last 75 years of writing about audiences and do justice to the complexity of the debates that have shaped the field, we have chosen to concentrate on the development of social and cultural accounts. We have not ventured into the terrain of psychological and psychoanalytic studies of audiences. Blackman and Walkerdine (2001) have recently addressed these fields. This Reader and its companion authored text (Ross and Nightingale 2003) are more concerned about the social, political and economic theorization of the mass media, and the gradually increasing recognition of the importance of audience activity in the media scheme of things.

Ross and Nightingale (2003) propose that there are at least five dimensions to all research about audiences. They include: the people involved; their activities; the media materials with which they engage; the media time/space in which the engagement occurs; and the media power structure that delimits the control that each stakeholder in a media event can wield. Most studies of audiences cannot address all five dimensions simultaneously and so pragmatic research decisions have to be made that lead researchers to focus on the people and/or their activities, with lesser emphasis on the media's contribution to the media/audience events. Because audience research is always informed by a theory about the media (whether explicitly or not), the readings included in this collection have been chosen for the ways in which they allow the reader to trace the impact of the social theories most commonly used in audience research on the interpretation of audience activity.

It is common when thinking about media audiences to imagine that audiences are the same as the public or society in general. Interestingly, Anderson (1991) has shown that the imagined dual identity of audience and public may have its origins in the historical impact of print capitalism. The idea that audiences are 'everybody' is linked historically to the genesis of the nation-state and to the role that print capitalism played in creating a sense of shared interests among the newly created reading publics of the eighteenth and nineteenth centuries (Ross and Nightingale 2003, chapter 2). In this sense, the reading public can be seen to have been the first really significant audience formation, and to have been the model for democratic organization. The reading public also provided a prototype for understanding the even larger and more inclusive audience formations that characterized the age of broadcasting.

In introducing her history of radio in America, Susan Smulyan has pointed out that when radio was first introduced, 'no one knew how to make money from broadcasting' (1994: 1). She also notes that the form that American broadcasting subsequently took was influenced by three factors, 'the desire for *national* radio; the choice of a particular technology – wired *networks* – to provide radio service to the entire nation; and dislike and distrust of radio advertising on the part of both listeners and businesses' (1994: 2, our emphasis). Clearly there was an early appreciation in the USA of the link between mass audiences and making a profit from broadcasting. But there was also a strong undercurrent of concern about the use of advertising to finance broadcasting. It is therefore far from surprising that early audience research was first devoted to establishing how many people were listening and to which of the available alternatives they were tuned

(Beville 1988). Nor is it surprising that many governments decided to finance independent academic research into broadcasting and its socio-cultural impact as an expression of public responsibility and to provide information needed for the development of broadcasting policy.

Radio had, after all, added an unprecedented level of immediacy to national mass communications and, in doing so, created suitable conditions for the emergence of mass audiences as researchable, socio-cultural phenomena. Just as businesses had not known how to make money from broadcasting, there were few precedents for researchers to call on to develop strategies for researching, analysing and measuring audiences. The radio era established two forms of audience research: (a) measurement and ratings analysis, and (b) functionalist studies of propaganda and mass persuasion as communicative and mediated events (Katz and Lazarsfeld in this collection is an example: see Chapter 1).

By the mid-1950s, television broadcasting had been introduced in virtually all developed nations. Television consolidated the research preoccupation with mass audiences, with measuring audience size and composition, and with statistical analysis. The information produced by the early audience measurement and public opinion research produced commercially exploitable information, and during the television era such research was institutionalized as syndicated research services funded by the commercial television networks. Measures of audiences like 'ratings', 'share', 'reach' and 'frequency' were developed in the early days of broadcasting and are still used today. The methods of audience measurement have also changed little: the telephone interview, the diary method, call out research, through-the-book techniques – all continue to appear in the commercial research repertoire, even though they disappeared from the academic research agenda years ago. As saleable (and expensive) commodities in their own right, ratings and other syndicated research products were co-opted by the commercial research sector. Webster, Phalen and Lichty (Chapter 11) provide a valuable account of the models and assumptions that inform contemporary ratings analysis.

Still, on the domestic front, television prompted parents to notice the amount of time that children spent watching television. Television immobilized children in front of the small screen, but mobilized educators and researchers to investigate the impact of television viewing on homework and the types of activities displaced by television (Himmelweit *et al.* 1958; Halloran 1970; Noble 1975). Many adults too were content to sit, mesmerized by the box, for hours on end. As a result, television prompted widespread community concern about the effects and possible social consequences – for human health, psychological well-being and public safety –

of television viewing in general and of heavy viewing in particular (see, for example, Gerbner and Gross 1976).

And then there was the question of *what* was viewed. Where radio research had focused primarily on public opinion and studies of persuasion and propaganda, television shifted concern about audiences onto media content. Vigorous debates began in the media and among academic researchers about the prevalence and influence of sexual and violent content on the small screen (Eysenck and Nias 1978). In spite of protestations to the contrary by some media campaigners (Postman 1985), the research methods and strategies devised for mass audience research proved unreliable when applied to questions of the impact of entertainment media. The nature of television, a continuous stream of programming fragments, forced researchers to consider what it means to be an audience, when people start and stop being audiences, and whether being an audience is an active or passive pastime (Williams 1974; Morley 1980; Nightingale 1984).

Mass society theories and approaches to audience measurement had assumed audience passivity. The assumption of a passive audience had been incorporated into the techniques used to measure and analyse mass audiences and public opinion research (Webster, Phalen and Lichty – Chapter 11), but these theories could not account for the interpretative work of audiences, nor answer questions about the long-term impact of the materials (programmes, ideas, information, opinions) with which people become acquainted as a consequence of their audience activities. By the 1980s, therefore, attention shifted to the differential effects of mass broadcasting – to the impact, as it were, of the global on the local, and to detailed ethnographic studies of the deployment by localized audience groups of globally available materials. The abstract approach of mass audience theories had masked key differences within the mass audience and systematically obliterated evidence of audience diversity, especially if that diversity was culture specific. Cultural researchers tried to redress this neglect by turning their attention to analysing mass broadcasting from the perspective of particular, situated audience groups (Ross – Chapter 8; Gillespie – Chapter 9).

This cultural turn in audience research had also been prompted by earlier calls for the development of a theory of popular culture as a context for audience studies (Carey and Kreiling 1974), and by a recognition that audience studies could provide evidence of the meaning and cultural significance of media texts (Hall – Chapter 4). The dramatic nature of the change in audience research that occurred from the mid-1970s is captured by Neuman's assessment that it was comparable to a paradigm shift, reflecting the inability of mass audience/mass society debates to continue producing interesting questions. He suggests that the mass audience/mass society debates had simply run out of steam (Neuman 1991: 12). But this assessment fails to recognize that the cultural approach configured the mass audience differently, seeing it as an expression of multiple and overlapping groups and identities, rather than as a representation of a uniform national culture. The cultural approach had simply turned itself upside down and begun exploring broadcasting's superstructure from the perspective of audiences.

The process whereby interest in the mass gave way to interest in the particular in audience research is evident in the older readings reproduced in this book. Halloran, Elliott and Murdock (Chapter 2), for example, challenged the prevailing mass communication models by proposing that audiences are not independent observers of media events, but are culturally connected to the events – implicated in the events by virtue of shared cultural participation. This study was one of the first to explicitly investigate the *cultural* basis of mass communication, and in a sense the authors fired the opening shots in a struggle between culture theorists and functionalist researchers.

Carey and Kreiling (1974: 233) played a pivotal role in this struggle. They complained that, 'faced with making some explicit statements about cultural forms, social scientists retreat into obscurantism and reduce their subject matter to social structures or psychological needs'. Their comments were directed primarily at the researchers who advocated the 'uses and gratifications' approach. 'Uses and gratifications' was an extremely influential functionalist approach to studying audiences (see Katz, Blumler and Gurevitch – Chapter 3), but it investigated audience activity as an expression of human needs, particularly individual or psychological needs which, in the end, possess very low explanatory power as accounts of audience choices. While asserting the importance of audience activity and individual needs, the 'uses and gratifications' approach nevertheless failed to integrate a sense of identity, an understanding that people are formed in culture, into the approach. Carey and Kreiling correctly argued that without such an understanding, 'uses and gratifications' would not be able to deliver a cogent analysis of the processes of mass communication.

Stuart Hall (Chapter 3) had already sketched a model of audience research based in a theory of culture – his encoding/decoding model. The model, based on the Marxist premise of hegemony, assumed that the analysis of media texts and discourses would elucidate the struggle between encoders and decoders over the production and control of cultural meaning. As a result, many of the researchers who took up the cultural approach were diverted from the course mapped by Hall, and instead sought evidence of 'resistance' to dominant texts rather than to map both conformity and resistance (Nightingale 1996). The dynamic nature of Hall's model therefore was lost in a celebration of the diversity of audience response, and the confusion of the search for dominant meanings with textual criticism. The cultural approach to audience research reached the height of its popularity in the 1990s, and produced a wealth of important documentation of audience diversity, even if, as Nightingale has argued recently, this also involved focusing on exotic or extreme audiences at the expense of mainstream experiences (Nightingale 2003).

One of the more interesting aspects of contemporary thinking and writing about media audiences is the re-emergence of an interest in the mass audience (Morrison – Chapter 7; Webster, Phalen and Lichty – Chapter 11). There appear to be several reasons for this. First, audience measurement and ratings analysis were not touched by the cultural turn in audience research. Until recently they could ignore questions about whether the audiences they measured and projected might one day disappear. For the duration of the television era, the assumptions on which they had been based remained inviolate. Generously funded by entrepreneurial and commercially driven media corporations, and safe in their protected world of syndicated reports and continuous and consistent findings, commercial researchers had no need to consider the changing media landscape in which they operated.

During the 1980s, as mass audiences grew larger, it became statistically possible to identify and address target and niche audiences. This allowed advertisers to spend less on advertising and achieve the same or better results since advertising could target only potential customers. Even as cultural researchers sought to demonstrate how audiences resist dominant ideas and maintain their local cultures, marketers developed a parallel interest in audience cultures – but to better exploit particular formations within the mass audience (Turow 1997; Robinson 1999). The audience orientation of cultural research was matched, in effect, by the emergence of a customer orientation in marketing.

Today television is losing market share to new media, and audiences are on the move. Television is being squeezed by the new media mix. It is forced to fight off competition for advertising revenue from computer games, mobile media and the Internet – even from radio which is suddenly more attractive because of its mobility. At the same time, new media have provided advertisers with the capacity to solicit, store and mine databases of consumer choices in unprecedented detail for themselves. The customer relationship approaches to marketing increase the options for manufacturers to approach customers directly, thus avoiding the expense of brand advertising on television. Manufacturers and their customers are starting to expect more than the 'exposure' model of audience response can deliver, in terms of immediacy of sales decisions and interaction between manufacturer and consumer. Television and radio stations are less important in the marketing mix than they have previously been.

There are thus a range of philosophically diverse approaches to understanding and researching audiences. In Part II we have tried to demonstrate these differences by the juxtaposition of readings and by introducing a range of articles that introduce qualitative and ethnographic methods. Morrison (Chapter 7) discusses the research method most frequently used in academic audience research, the focus group, providing guidelines for good practice. The value positions that inform the work of Ross (Chapter 8), Gillespie (Chapter 9) and Buckingham (Chapter 10) contrast starkly with the abstract statistical methods proposed by Webster, Phalen and Lichty (Chapter 11), and Eileen Meehan's critical evaluation of ratings analysis (Chapter 12) helps to make this contrast even clearer. The readings in this section should also alert the reader to the relevance of information presented here for the discourse on globalization. On the one hand, local audiences confront global media that encourage intensification of local and global ties at the expense of national and regional affiliations (Gillespie – Chapter 9). On the other, global product is increasingly designed with the more lucrative segments of the mass audience in mind. The middle ground, where national identities and interests should be consolidated, thus starts to look quite shaky.

The final piece in the interplay between audiences and media to be noted here concerns the issue of new media and audience interactions with them. The convergence of old technologies and the development of new media enable people to be audiences in a greater variety of contexts than was possible previously. People are able to shape and vary their media engagements in more satisfying ways. Audiences have always borrowed, poached, improvised and collected snippets of useful media 'stuff'. The looks, body shapes, hairstyles or voices of others – especially famous others – can be useful for purposes of identity development, or for creating a stylistically charged cultural intervention in an otherwise tedious everyday world. Studying the ecology of media bric-à-brac among audiences has been particularly prevalent in the study of fans and fan communities (Nightingale – Chapter 13). But fans have also been open to the possibilities that new media offer for improving their interactions with others (Baym – Chapter 14; Markham – Chapter 15). They have been among the first to create opportunities to meet online, talk, and share ideas, information, images and creative work, and to establish links for the purpose of trade in memorabilia and cult objects. Banks (Chapter 16) and Jenkins (Chapter 17) have recognized the expression of 'intelligent community' (Levy 1997) in such fan activities, and see fans as the explorers of the productive dimensions of cyberspace.

Of course, cyberspace is itself a contested space where commerce and culture collide and compete. The contemporary struggles over copyright and intellectual property focused on the Web but also expressed in legal contestation over product names and patents is evidence that the rights of audiences can never be taken for granted and are in a process of continual dispute and contestation. By radically transforming the nature of the media event (from broadcasting to interactivity), the *new media* of the twenty-first century – digital, converged, infinitely variable, and interchangeable as sources of information – and the *activist* audiences they call into being have precipitated a reconsideration of the *mass media* of the early twentieth century and their *reactive* audiences. The so-called *passive* audiences for mass broadcasting are fast becoming not *active* but *activist* audiences for interactive media. While currently the media are both broadcast and interactive, we should not imagine that they will always remain this way.

In selecting the readings reprinted in this book, we have tried to recognize the changing nature of both audiences and audience research, and in doing so, to demonstrate that contemporary culture is a *mediated* culture. More media mean people spend more time in mediated activities – in other words, *being audiences*. The more mediated engagements and activities that people spend time on and with, the greater the range and diversity of audience research that could be undertaken. By including some less readily available readings from significant research of the past and the present, we have tried to provide an opportunity for readers to assess for themselves the competing theories about what it means to be an audience and what it is about being an audience that could be investigated in the future.

References

Anderson, B. (1991) *Imagined Communities: Reflections on the Origin and Spread of Nationalism* (rev. edn). London: Verso.

Beville, H.M. Jr (1988) *Audience Ratings: Radio, Television, and Cable*. Mahwah, NJ: Lawrence Erlbaum & Associates.

Blackman, L. and Walkerdine, V. (2001) *Mass Hysteria: Critical Psychology and Media Studies*. Houndmills: Palgrave.

Carey, J. and Kreiling, A. (1974) Popular culture and uses and gratifications: notes towards an accommodation, in J. Blumler and E. Katz (eds) *The Uses of Mass*

Communications: Current Perspectives on Gratifications Research. London: Sage.

Eysenck, H. and Nias, D.K.B. (1978) *Sex, Violence and the Media*. London: Maurice Temple Smith.

Gerbner, G. and Gross, L. (1976) Living with television: the violence profile, *Journal of Communication*, 26(2): 173–99.

Halloran, J.D. (1970) *The Effects of Television*. London: Panther.

Himmelweit, H.T., Oppenheim, A. and Vince, P. (1958) *Television and the Child*. Oxford: Oxford University Press.

Levy, P. (1997) *Collective Intelligence: Mankind's Emerging World in Cyberspace* (trans. Robert Bononno). Cambridge, MA: Perseus Books.

Morley, D. (1980) *The 'Nationwide' Audience: Structure and Decoding*. London: British Film Institute.

Neuman, W.R. (1991) *The Future of the Mass Audience*. Cambridge: Cambridge University Press.

Nightingale, V. (1984) Media audiences – media products? *Australian Journal of Cultural Studies*, 2(1): 23–35.

Nightingale, V. (1996) *Studying Audiences: The Shock of the Real*. London: Routledge.

Nightingale, V. (2003) The cultural revolution in audience research, in A. Valdivia, (ed.) *Blackwell's Media Studies Reader* (in press). London: Blackwell.

Noble, G. (1975) *Children in Front of the Small Screen*. London: Constable and Sage.

Postman, N. (1985) *Amusing Ourselves to Death*. New York: Viking.

Robinson, J. (1999) *The Manipulators*. London: Simon & Schuster/Pocket Books.

Ross, K. and Nightingale, V. (2003) *Media and Audiences: Critical Reflections*. Buckingham: Open University Press.

Smulyan, S. (1994) *Selling Radio: The Commercialization of American Broadcasting 1920–1934*. Washington: Smithsonian Institution Press.

Turow, J. (1997) *Breaking Up America: Advertisers and the New Media World*. Chicago: University of Chicago Press.

Williams, R. (1974) *Television: Technology and Cultural Form*. London: Fontana.

THE STUDY OF ACTIVE
AUDIENCES

By the late 1940s, two approaches to audience research had been firmly established. Robert Merton, Paul Lazarsfeld and their associates had pioneered 'content and response' analysis (Merton 1968). They maintained that content production should to be devised with a solid appreciation of the information and experiential backgrounds that audiences are likely to bring to the interpretation of media messages and investigated how people use the media to cement their social status and peer recognition (Merton 1968; Ross and Nightingale 2003, chapter 2). The alternative approach, against which Merton and Lazarsfeld had defined their practice, was audience measurement and campaign research. Audience measurement and campaign analysis constituted the first 'effects' research, where the information sought by researchers consisted only of how many people were viewing. The effectiveness of a media campaign was judged by the number of viewers who tuned in or were aware of the message. How people interpreted the message was (and remains) of less interest for those who plan media campaigns, and this lack of interest in what audiences do with media messages created the view that audiences are passive. The apparent 'passivity' of mass audiences encouraged political economists and others to develop theories that portrayed audiences as helpless, addicted, overwhelmed by the volume of media information (Neuman 1991: 82), and therefore incapable of understanding where their real interests might lie. This 'pessimistic' view of mass audiences remains influential, but outside the focus of this Reader.

The articles chosen for this section instead trace the development of our understanding of audience activity, and the ways in which it is linked to people's engagement in social and political action. Creating an informed basis for analysis of the ways that people engage with media for such purposes is one of the main foci of this Reader and its companion text (Ross and Nightingale 2003). The section begins therefore with an example of audience research which explored how people in the early 1950s used the media to establish new ways to interact with others (Katz and Lazarsfeld – Chapter 1). Katz and Lazarsfeld understood audiences to be influenced not just by media content but also by the special interests that people they knew took in the media. The example included here, of 'movie leaders', documents how people with special interests in film were considered to be experts by their friends and their opinions of new films were sought. Katz and Lazarsfeld's study focused on how people with specialized media interests were recognized as experts or 'influence leaders' by their peers, who subsequently sought their advice as to whether to see a film. Such opinion leaders were able to interpret the social significance of media materials to others in their communities. The emphasis in this and other early research by the functionalists of the 1940s and 1950s was on the ways in which the media functioned as a facilitator of connectivity between people and society.

Later researchers, investigating the political economy of the media from various Marxist perspectives, focused on how the structures and processes of media production (particularly of news production) alienated people from the production process and trivialized their capacity to participate actively in the production of their culture. Neuman (1991: 82) has usefully summarized the range of theories that depicted the 'helpless audience' as disabled by 'information overload', by 'audience segmentation', by the nature of media formats designed to address mass audiences, by the global nature of communication flows, by 'addiction' to the media and by the ways in which media formats manipulate audiences – as much by the stories never told as by those that are. The 'helpless' audience theories have been described as 'pessimistic' because they suggest that there is no hope for audiences to escape from the tyranny of the media.

By the 1970s, however, a new generation of researchers with more specialized interest in the study of audiences began to question such pessimistic evaluations of audience passivity, and again to integrate studies of news production with studies of people's responses to particular media events (see Halloran, Elliott and Murdock – Chapter 2). While the Halloran, Elliott and Murdock research coupled analysis of news production with its reception (just as earlier functionalist research had done), its theoretical underpinning was radically different in that it recognized that audiences are socio-cultural formations, actively structured by their positions in the society. In this case people's interpretation of media information was shown to be strongly influenced by audience membership of the occupational categories (police, student) chosen for inclusion in the research. The study also focused attention on the professional practice of journalists and news production teams rather than on the message only.

At the same time, in the USA, the functionalist social theory of Merton and Lazarsfeld (Merton 1968) had been radically changed by the mid-twentieth-century infatuation with individualism – a climate that produced the 'uses and gratifications' approach (see Katz, Blumler and Gurevitch – Chapter 3). 'Uses and gratifications' shifted away from social and cultural theorization of audience formations altogether, preferring a theory of audiences as driven by their individual needs and wants. It shifted the understanding of the 'active audience' forward, by proposing that audiences were psychologically active in choosing the media that interested them, but side-stepped acknowledging that audiences bring a history of socio-cultural experience to their engagements with the media. While 'uses and gratifications' was extremely influential in its day, it paved the way for a powerful anti-individualist argument which positioned media research within a theory of popular culture, and proposed that audiences are culturally constructed and their interpretations of media texts informed by socio-cultural experiences rather than by individual whim. This position was most forcefully articulated by Hall (see Hall – Chapter 4).

Hall's encoding/decoding theory proposed that both textual production and audience interpretation are part of the same cultural process – the production of discourses and ideas. Like the political economy models of the 'passive' audience, it saw the media as a regulatory regime for maintaining social control, but it recognized the necessity for such a regime to create discursive spaces where contested ideas could be explored so that the repressive nature of the media machine was covered over. The model proposed that the media produce three types of discourses: dominant, negotiated and resistant. It was hypothesized that audiences could accept media messages, negotiate them (partially accept and partially resist), or they could resist them completely. Interestingly, much of the research inspired by the encoding/decoding model focused on audience resistance and negotiation of the media's control of media discourses and programmes (Fiske 1992). According to Bird (Chapter 5), over-estimation of the capacity of audiences to 'read critique of the status quo into all kinds of popular journalistic texts' demonstrates that resistance studies sometimes fail to understand accurately the nature of popular texts, and the true nature of audience dependence on such texts.

Elizabeth Bird therefore took issue with the celebration of 'tabloidization' and set out to explore how audiences for tabloid news actually view the news they regularly use. Her aim was to provide guidelines for the production of news 'that could embrace the tabloid style, while still inviting audiences to participate more fully in a civic democracy'. Bird shared control of the research situation with her research participants, and this makes the inclusion of segments of verbatim discussion that took place between her and her interviewees of particular interest.

Just as Bird has shown better ways of investigating audience engagement with mass media forms, other researchers have started to critically appraise the use of abstract statistical information based on audience surveys, such as audience ratings and opinion polls, for their capacity to influence mass audiences by misrepresenting the state of public opinion. Ivor Crewe (Chapter 6) discusses the relative importance of opinion polls as both barometers of public opinion and as influences on actual voting behaviour in the context of a general election. What Crewe argues is that, far from being accurate reflections of actual public's views, opinion polls can, on the contrary, provide a misleading reading of the nation's pulse. This essay thus cautions against too much reliance on the opinion poll as a reliable instrument to gauge public opinion, largely because most sampling methods have so many inherent biases and the opinion poll has shown itself to be of decreasing value as an instrument for prediction of election results. We return to this issue at the end of Part II, in the discussion of ratings analysis.

The development of our understanding of audience activity and its relevance for critical appraisal of the media has a long history in media research. While some early studies were preoccupied with the cynical appropriation of the media by powerful elites as a propagandist tool to dupe the masses, other researchers increasingly focused their interests on audience autonomy, both individual and communal, and began to emphasize what audiences do *with* media rather than what media do *to* audiences. The debate about 'effects' continues apace, with some researchers insisting on the sophisticated media consumer knowingly using the media to suit their own desires. Others insist equally strongly that the media need to be more strictly controlled, because the promotion of violent and sexual images, support of particular political candidates or endorsement of specific branded commodities consistently present one-sided arguments. The increasing deregulation of media ownership laws has also provoked a return to the emphasis on the exercise of social control by the media. In the face of these fears, cultural researchers continue to place their faith in the primacy and mediating power of community and communal interaction as the true mediators of media effects. This is the type of audience research explored in Part II.

References

Fiske, J. (1992) The cultural economy of fandom, in L. Lewis (ed.) *The Adoring Audience: Fan Culture and Popular Media*. London: Routledge.

Merton, Robert K. (1968) *Social Theory and Social Structure*. New York: The Free Press and Collier Macmillan.

Neuman, W.R. (1991) *The Future of the Mass Audience*. Cambridge: Cambridge University Press.

Ross, K. and Nightingale, V. (2003) *Media and Audiences: Critical Reflections*. Maidenhead: Open University Press.

1 MOVIE LEADERS

Elihu Katz and Paul Lazarsfeld

Approximately 60 per cent of our respondents said that they go to the movies once a month or more; 40 per cent go less often than once a month or do not go at all. In view of this fact, we have decided to confine our analysis of the flow of influence about movies only to those who may be considered active participants in the movie arena – that is, to those who go to the movies at least once a month.

From previous research, we know that there is a strong relationship between movie-going and age.[1] Our data confirm this: it is the young people who go to the movies:

Table 1.1 Young people constitute the major element in the movie market

Frequency of attendance	Under 25	25–34	35–44	45 and over
Once a week or more	68%	49%	34%	19%
One to three times per month	20	31	35	27
Less than once a month	7	14	26	37
Never	5	6	5	17
Total (= 100%)	(141)	(157)	(148)	(271)

While 88 per cent of the youngest age group goes to the movies once a month or more, Table 1.1 reveals that each succeeding age group shows a

Elihu Katz and Paul Lazarsfeld (1955) Movie leaders, *Personal Influence*. New York: The Free Press, pp. 296–308. Reprinted by kind permission of The Free Press.

marked decline, so that by the time women reach the age of 45, more than half of them go to the movies less often than once a month.

'Youth culture': movie leadership and the life-cycle

Judging from this distribution of participation in the movie arena, we shall certainly expect to find that the concentration of opinion leadership is among the girls. But our curiosity extends further. We do not know, for example, how marriage and motherhood affect a woman's chances for movie leadership, if they do at all. Let us look, then, at the relationship between the life-cycle and movie leadership.

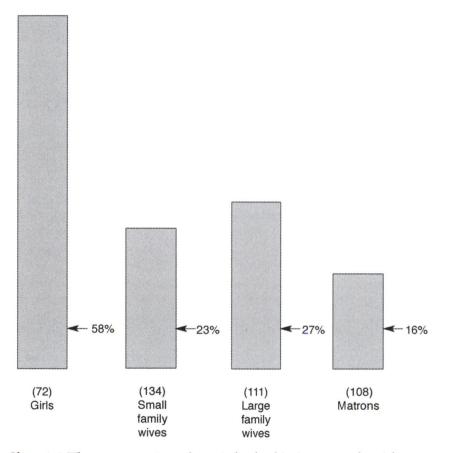

← 58%	←23%	←27%	← 16%
(72) Girls	(134) Small family wives	(111) Large family wives	(108) Matrons

Chart 1.1 The concentration of movie leadership is among the girls

Overwhelmingly, even more than in the fashion arena, the movie leaders can be found among the girls – the young, single women with fewest family responsibilities. Well over half of the girls say that they have recently been asked their opinions about current movie fare.[2] Of course, it is not age alone that makes the difference. The difference between the movie leadership rates of the girls and the wives is so very sharp (58% to 23%) and the difference among the three types of married women so very small (23%, 27%, 16%) that it is evident that the fact of being married or single is as important as age in being a predisposing factor in movie leadership. Obviously, the pattern of social activities and responsibilities in the one case is entirely different than it is in the other. The unmarried girl is not only younger than the small or large family wife; she is also freer. The difference between the girls and the wives, then, is the difference between a woman relatively unburdened with family responsibility, and a mother with a full load of family responsibility; more than that, it is the difference between an unmarried girl and the role of movie-going in her social affairs, and a young woman who has 'settled down.'

While being young and unmarried is associated both with more frequent movie-going and more frequent leadership chances, within each age group the very frequent movie-goers are more likely to be leaders than those who go less often.

Table 1.2 The more frequent movie-goers among both young and old are more likely to be movie leaders

| | UNDER 25 | | 25 AND OVER | |
	Frequent goers	Occasional goers	Frequent goers	Occasional goers
Leaders	55%	32%	28%	13%
Non-leaders	45	68	72	87
Total (= 100%)	(87)	(28)	(165)	(157)

Among the women under 25 years of age, the table indicates those who are frequent goers (once a week or more) are considerably more likely to be movie leaders than those who go only occasionally (one to three times a month); and the same thing is true for the older age group.

Now that we know something about the relationship between the life-cycle and movie leadership, we should ask – as we have done in the previous sections – about the flow of influence within and between age groups. We shall expect, as in the other areas, to find considerable homogeneity of age between influential and influencee. But at the same time – in view of the striking concentration of movie leadership among the girls – we shall expect, too, that in addition to influence exchanges among age peers, there is a flow from young to old. Rather than enter into that discussion at this point, however, we should like first to introduce a finding which complicates our analysis of the movie arena in a very interesting way and has important bearing, too, on the character of the flow of movie influence. That finding can be most clearly perceived by considering the relationship between movie leadership and our index of gregariousness.

Movie leadership and gregariousness: a special case

In every other arena we have examined so far, we have found gregariousness to be an attribute of the opinion leader. As a matter of fact, it is reasonable to posit that some greater-than-average degree of contact with other people is a requirement for any kind of informal leadership. Yet, we find that in the case of movie leadership, there is virtually no relationship between the incidence of leadership and our index of gregariousness.

In other words, we are forced to explain why leadership in the fields of marketing, fashions and public affairs is so much more highly related to our measure of gregariousness than leadership in the arena of movie-going. And we think we have an answer.

In fact, we have three answers. One answer should be apparent from the relationship which we reported ... between the life-cycle and gregariousness. There we found, it will be recalled, that the girls – by virtue of their relatively low level of organizational affiliation but relatively large number of friends – tended to fall into our category of 'medium gregariousness.' And since we have observed that the ranks of movie leadership are filled to an overwhelming degree with girls, it is easy to understand why the movie leaders tend to be concentrated somewhat more among women of medium gregariousness than among women of high and low gregariousness.

A second factor which undoubtedly plays a part in explaining why women of high gregariousness are not more likely to be leaders in this arena is that women of high gregariousness – those who have many organizational contacts and a large number of personal friends – may have reason to be less interested in the movies than women whose social lives are less full.

But there is a third answer, too, one which is very important for an understanding of what goes on in this sphere of influence. For even if we explain that the women of highest gregariousness are less interested in movies, and that the girls are concentrated in the medium gregariousness level, we still must understand how it is that the proportion of leaders even

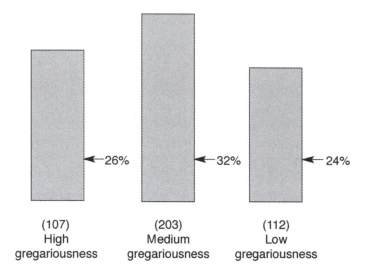

26%   32%   24%

(107)   (203)   (112)
High   Medium   Low
gregariousness gregariousness gregariousness

Chart 1.2 Movie leadership does not parallel gregariousness

among the least gregarious women – the women with fewest friends and fewest organizational contacts – is virtually as high as it is among the much more gregarious women. And the answer, we think, is that the act of movie-going itself is a gregarious activity, although one which our index of gregariousness cannot measure. Here is our explanation:

Upon examining the context for decision-making in the movie arena – that is, the conditions under which people decide to go to one movie rather than another – we find that virtually no one of our respondents goes to the movies alone.[3] Unlike public affairs, or more strictly speaking, the holding of opinions on public affairs, movie-going is an activity which is shared in a direct way with other people. Almost nine out of ten of our respondents stated that they had attended their last motion picture exhibition accompanied by someone else. This shared movie-going is almost unanimous among women under 25, and it is almost so among older women as well. There is no significant difference in shared attendance between married and unmarried women, nor is there any between movie leaders and non-leaders.

Since movie-going is so strongly characterized by its group nature, it seems highly reasonable to suppose that it is within the movie-attending groups themselves that most of the give-and-take about movies and the movie world goes on. The movie leader finds her following immediately at hand among her movie-going companions; to lead, she does not require the audience of many friendships and organizational affiliations which are characteristic of the more gregarious leaders in the other areas. In the realm of the movies, there are no isolates; if you find a movie-goer, the chances are you have found a movie-going group. The act of movie-going, therefore, is more properly studied as a product of group decision rather than of individual decision; and in such decisions, presumably, our movie leaders should have the upper hand.[4] But the point here is that movie leaders are 'gregarious' in the very special sense that movie-going itself is a gregarious enterprise.

Shared movie-going and the flow of influence

If we are correct, it should follow that the flow of influence in this realm is concentrated in these movie-going groups. But, since we did not anticipate this problem sufficiently in advance we can only hint at the possibility that this is the case.[5] Evidence that might lend circumstantial weight to our argument is that there is a similarity between the kind of people women report as influential in their movie decisions and those whom they say (in answer to another question) are their steady movie companions. Compare the movie companions and the movie leaders[6] named by married and single women, for example:

Table 1.3 Movie-going companions and movie leaders seem to be somewhat the same sort of people

| | SINGLE WOMEN | | MARRIED WOMEN | |
	Their companions	Their leaders	Their companions	Their leaders
Non-family (friends, neighbors, others)	67%	76%	15%	40%
Family (parents, husbands, children, others)	33	23	85	60
Total (= 100%)	(66)	(35)	(316)	(132)

It is quite clear from Table 1.3 that the single women, the girls, name as their movie-going companions, and as their movie leaders, individuals who are not members of their families; the wives, on the other hand, seek the advice as well as the companionship of their kin. Closer scrutiny of the details of the table reveals that both groups, but particularly the wives, seek non-family advice in somewhat greater proportion than non-family companions. This disparity is probably a reflection of the fact that the family is more readily available and, for the wives, more socially acceptable as a movie-going group. Although one might prefer to be escorted by a non-family companion, either the unavailability of other people or the demands of family loyalties and obligations objectively restrict this possibility. In this connection, it is very interesting to note that even among women of equivalent age and marital status, leaders are more likely than non-leaders to go to the movies with non-family companions.

Table 1.4 Leaders go to the movies with non-family members more often than do non-leaders

| | PER CENT WHO GO WITH NON-FAMILY MEMBERS | |
	Leaders	Non-leaders
Under 25	53% (57)	38% (58)
25 or older	31% (66)	15% (249)
Unmarried	70% (42)	52% (30)
Married	26% (78)	12% (275)

One way to explain this phenomenon might be as follows: the women who go to the movies in the company of non-family members would be more likely to remember having been asked advice than those who go with family members; in the family situation, that is, it would be more usual for advice to have been a give-and-take affair and not to recall it when interviewed. If this is the case, then Table 1.4 is not of great moment. It simply means that the non-family movie-goers are more likely to designate themselves as movie leaders.

Another explanation is possible, however: it may be that going to the movies with non-family members has something special about it which is more directly connected with movie leadership. Specifically, our guess is that attending with the family may be a somewhat more ritualistic activity – and, therefore, one involving less careful choosing – than attending with non-family companions. The husband-wife attendance unit, say, or the child-parent unit may tend more toward seeing whatever film is playing in the local theater on their usual day of attendance, while non-family units may be less ritualistic.

As a matter of fact, we have some evidence which tends to support this speculation. All the movie-goers were asked: 'When are you most likely to go to a movie?' with several possibilities provided for, among them 'When there are pictures which especially interest you.' Our expectation is that the leaders – who go more often with non-family attendance units than with the family units – would indicate this motive more strongly than the non-leaders, and this is indeed the case:

Table 1.5 Movie leaders are more likely to go to the movies when there is a film which especially interests

| | PER CENT WHO GO WHEN THE PICTURE SOUNDS INTERESTING | | | |
| | FREQUENT GOERS | | OCCASIONAL GOERS | |
	Under 25	25 & Older	Under 25	25 & Older
Leaders	70% (48)	76% (46)	89% (9)	71% (20)
Non-leaders	56% (39)	57% (112)	58% (19)	73% (137)

Among both frequent and occasional goers in the younger groups, and among the older, more frequent goers, leaders are much more likely than non-leaders to go when the picture sounds interesting. Conversely, only 19 per cent of the leaders as compared with 27 per cent of the non-leaders report that they go when they have 'a free evening.'

There is further evidence of interest in the particular picture itself. In the first interview these women were asked, regarding the last movie they had seen: 'Did you go primarily just to go to a movie, to see a certain picture, or for both reasons?' Again we find that more of the leaders were interested in the picture itself:

Table 1.6 Leaders make particular choices more than non-leaders

| | PER CENT WHO WENT TO SEE A CERTAIN PICTURE | | | |
| | FREQUENT GOERS | | OCCASIONAL GOERS | |
	Under 25	25 & Older	Under 25	25 & Older
Leaders	57% (48)	63% (46)	78% (9)	81% (20)
Non-leaders	54% (39)	57% (112)	26% (19)	68% (137)

Although the difference is relatively small between those leaders and non-leaders who are young and go frequently, the differences are larger in the other categories and are consistent throughout.

Compared with non-leaders, then, movie leaders are more likely to pick out a particular picture to see; this is true 'usually,' as well as for the most recent movie attended. This finding probably means two things: first of all, it suggests that the companions of the movie leaders may be less particular than their leaders; secondly, it lends weight to our suggestion that movie-going groups composed of non-family members may, as groups, be more choosy than groups made up of family members. In any event, this is an interesting matter for further investigation.

Despite these important considerations, however, we must not allow ourselves to lose sight of the fundamental point which was established earlier. This was the finding that, *in general*, the norm for married women is to seek both the companionship and leadership of members of their families, while the norm for the girls is to share these things with their friends.

Age and the flow of influence

This basic difference in the movie habits of the young, unmarried girl and the older, married woman has important implications for the flow of influence among the several age groups in the arena of movie-going. It will be recalled that our discussion of this topic was intentionally postponed, so that the social setting of movie-going could be presented first. Our contention has been that the kind of advice-giving which is reflected in movie leadership and in our data on the flow of influence probably takes place within the framework of these movie-going groups. Just as we saw that a woman's movie leaders and her companions seem to be the same kinds of people, now we will see that advice-giving is most likely to flow among people of more or less the same age:

Table 1.7 The flow of movie influence among age groups[7]

| Her movie leader's age is | INFLUENCEE'S AGE IS | | | |
	15–24	25–44	45+	Totals
15–24	30	9	4	43
25–44	11	36	6	53
45+	2	8	11	21
Totals	43	53	21	117

Our respondents report having influenced people of pretty much the same ages as themselves. Thus 70 per cent (30 out of 43) of the 15–24 age group were influenced by age-peers and the same holds true for 68 per cent (36 out of 53) of the 25–44 age group and 52 per cent (11 out of 21) of the women over 45. In sum, putting together what we have learned so far, girls are most likely to have been influenced by age peers and older women by other adults; the girls, of course, were influenced by friends, and older, married women primarily by age-peers within the family.

The role of the movie expert

The picture we get from the reports in Table 1.7 of the actual incidents of influence seems to indicate a sharp demarcation between the 'youth culture' and the world of adults as far as movie influence, attendance and decisions are concerned. But if, as has been suggested, the kind of movie leader we have described thus far is typically part of a movie-going group (whose companions, when she is young, are age-peers and when she is older are adult family members) and if the influence flow we have described takes place within such groups, then it may be that we have not yet told the entire story of the flow of movie influence. For it may be that a different type of influence transaction typically takes place *outside* these groups.

One way of getting at such an influence flow, if it exists, is by means of another of the questions we asked our respondents: 'Do you know anybody around here who usually knows something about the movies and can tell what's a good picture to see?'[8] About 40 per cent of our respondents said they did know such a person. Predominantly, these respondents were people who go more frequently to the movies and who were more likely to say that the last time they went to the movies, they went 'to see a certain picture' rather than 'just to go to the movies.'

In any event, our interest here is in whether the relationships between these movie 'experts' – the 'general influentials' – and their advisees are any different from those of the specific influentials and their influencees which we have seen up to now. If, as we suspect, the specific influentials are part of the movie-going group which they lead but that these 'experts' are not, perhaps we shall be able to round out our picture of the flow of movie influence. Let us duplicate the table we just examined, substituting the 'expert' for the specific influential.

Table 1.8 The flow of expert advice about movies among age groups

	RESPONDENT'S AGE IS			
Her movie expert is	15–24	25–44	45+	Totals
15–24	24	27	12	63
25–44	5	42	17	64
45+	5	9	9	23
Totals	34	78	38	150

The table indicates, quite clearly, that there is a major difference between the two types of opinion leadership. While the movie 'experts' of the youngest group are still people like themselves, the older groups have substituted younger women as experts in far greater proportion than they name such people as specific influentials. This can best be seen by comparing the row and the column of 'totals.' Whereas 23 per cent of all respondents are below 25 years of age, 42 per cent of the experts they designate belong in this age group.

An examination of the relationships between these respondents and their movie experts reveals that the category of children seems to make the major difference. For women 35 years of age or over, children – that is, their own children – account for almost a third of the experts they designate.

If this 'general influential' question is a good indication, then, it appears that both younger and older women seek out movie experts among the young, although the final decision may often be modified by primary influentials in the movie-going groups who are more likely to be in the same age bracket as their groups.

Social status and movie leadership

Of the three factors which we are employing to locate and describe opinion leaders – life-cycle, social status and gregariousness – only the life-cycle is relevant in the realm of movie-going. Our measure of gregariousness, we have seen, is not associated with movie leadership and, now we may add, neither is our index of social status. This, of course, is what might have been expected. There was no reason to suppose, say, that girls of any given status level would produce fewer movie leaders than girls of any other level, and the same holds true for wives and matrons. On each status level, approximately one person in four is a movie leader, and of the four arenas of leadership with which we are concerned in this study, status level is least relevant to that of movie leadership.

The flow of influence about movies: a summary

In sum, it is evident that movie-going is a main theme of American youth culture and that the influentials in this realm arise from the ranks of the young and carefree. What's more, within every life-cycle bracket, the leader is the more frequent movie-goer, more particular about what she sees and more exogamous in the choice of her movie companions.

Movie-going, we have seen, is not a solitary activity; people go to the movies in groups. The flow of influence in this realm, we think, takes place largely within these movie-going groups which are usually made up of age peers. But when it comes to consulting a movie 'expert,' people of all ages turn to the girls.

Notes

1   See, for example, Lazarsfeld and Kendall (1948) and Handel (1950).
2   As in the other arenas movie leaders are (a) those women who told us twice that they had recently been asked their advice about what picture to see, and (b) those women who reported only one incident of advice-giving but who considered themselves 'more likely' than others to be sought out for advice about movies.
3   This is reported also by Handel (1950), who cites a study which indicates that 86% of women and 70% of men were accompanied by another person the last time they went to the movies. The typical attendance unit consists of two people.
4   The marketing arena is the only one of the other three arenas we are considering which can be characterized by some degree of shared decisions. We have treated this possibility only very briefly in our chapter on marketing leaders, but see, for example, Riley (1953) for the suggestion that joint decisions of mother and child govern choice of breakfast cereals.
5   Had we planned for this possibility and asked explicitly about the joint movie-going decision, we would have obtained many more affirmative replies. As it is, most people, we think, simply did not associate our question, 'Did you hear someone talk about it?' with the everyday give-and-take which they carry on with movie-going companions.
6   When women answered that they 'heard someone talk about it,' they were asked to name this influential and state their relationship to her. These are the people we are here calling 'their leaders.'
7   This table is based on respondents' designations of influencees. Hence, the leaders are sample members and those whom they advised are not.
8   This question was asked in each of the other areas as well, but we have not reported it except here and in the case of public affairs.

References

Handel, L.A. (1950) *Hollywood Looks at its Audience*. Urbana, IL: University of Illinois Press.

Lazarsfeld, P.F. and Kendall, P.L. (1948) *Radio Listening in America*. New York: Prentice Hall.

Riley, M.W. (1953) An interpersonal approach to opinion research. Paper delivered at the annual meeting of the American Association for Public Opinion Research.

② VIEWERS' REACTIONS

James D. Halloran, Phillip Elliott and Graham Murdock

Introduction

The event and how the media dealt with it have been described and analysed and we can now examine the reactions of some of those who actually watched the television portrayal of the October demonstration. Although, as was mentioned earlier, it was possible to attempt only tentative explorations in several general areas, it was clearly necessary to make some attempt to examine what may be regarded as the final stage in the selection process and to see what links, if any, there were between the various stages in the process. For example, the concept of 'news value' is central to much of the work discussed in the preceding chapters, so it is important to attempt to assess viewers' reactions to what they considered to be news and to see amongst other things if they felt that incidents and personalities had been over-employed, and explanations and background neglected, in the news coverage of the demonstration. The wider repercussions of unwitting bias and the use of narrow perspectives could also be examined.

The study was concerned with an event which could be reasonably accurately described in terms of declared aims and purposes, preparation, background, those taking part, their motivations and what actually took place; consequently it was thought that it would be worth while trying to

James D. Halloran, Phillip Elliott and Graham Murdock (1970) Viewers' reactions, *Demonstrations and Communication: A Case Study*. Harmondsworth: Penguin Books, pp. 17–19, 238–43. Reprinted by kind permission of James Halloran.

find out what viewers knew and thought about these matters, after they had been exposed to the media coverage of the event. In the background were two major questions. First, do the media in general and does television in particular present an accurate, meaningful and adequate picture of the events covered? Second, what are the consequences for general knowledge and for social and political attitudes of the methods adopted by the media in selecting the events to be covered and in presenting these events, i.e. in covering the news?

It is appreciated that this is not the first time these questions have been asked, although to date not many useful answers have been forthcoming. It was also appreciated from the outset of this exercise that this limited inquiry could not possibly go far beyond a preliminary exploration of the general problem area. In the event, as will be seen, the leads produced by the exploration suggest approaches that, if pursued, could take us a considerable way towards answering not only the questions referred to above but perhaps also the more fundamental one which asks whether or not the media are providing us with the material necessary for us to act as informed citizens in a participatory democracy.

Research carried out on behalf of the two broadcasting institutions in this country suggests that they have different public images and that they are regarded in different ways by the viewing public. It was felt that there might also be differences between them in how they set about covering the news. The anticipated relationship between these differences on the one hand and differences in viewers' reactions on the other was another question, which was reflected in this audience study. In this connexion, viewers' perceptions of bias was one area which it was decided to examine. Other questions were asked in the hope that some evidence might be forthcoming to support or refute the oft-repeated claim that on the whole the mass media serve to maintain and reinforce the status quo.

That different people may use the same television programme in different ways, attending, perceiving, retaining, interpreting and recalling selectively, is well known. In a manner of speaking, people see what they want to see. They often use the information provided by the media not so much to learn new things but to reinforce existing attitudes and elaborate old experiences. In any given situation, those more involved are likely to be more narrow and extreme in their reactions to the media portrayal of that situation than those less involved. Perceptions and attitudes will be influenced accordingly. The study of viewers' reactions was planned with this phenomenon in mind.

Finally, the study dealt with one other important area of interest and concern: namely, reactions to the media portrayal of violence and aggression.

We have already seen how the news story of the demonstration came to focus on the question of violence, but the audience study takes us beyond the reactions to this particular phenomenon. One of the demonstrators ... stated that the demonstration was about violence in Vietnam. Alistair Burnet, in the *Protest* programme, asked whether the use of violence was ever justified in the support of any cause. The reactions of the audience to some of these wider questions were also explored. Needless to say, there was no attempt to measure the influence of specific aspects of the news coverage. However, it was hoped that it might be possible to obtain a clearer idea of what particular incidents, events etc. different people regarded as violent. We know from other work that what is seen as violent by one person is not necessarily seen as violent by another.

Moreover, the research effort in this field has been handicapped because quite often a single concept, 'violence', has been used to cover extremely complex sets of factors with regard both to stimulus (e.g. media content) and to response (e.g. behaviour after viewing). Clarification was sought in this area too – although it should be emphasised that here as elsewhere in the study the overall orientation was essentially exploratory.

It was decided to administer questionnaires to viewers selected from three separate groups – police, students and 'neutrals'. These groups were selected on the basis of assumed involvement with the 'contending parties' in the demonstration. The nature, degree and implication of this involvement will be discussed later.

The actual recruitment of the samples was determined, to a very large degree by sheer availability and accessibility. Who would be able and willing to cooperate at such short notice was the overriding question. The subjects had to be in a position where they could watch the television news bulletins on Sunday evening, so police duties and student accommodation and viewing facilities had to be taken into account in the recruitment. Thanks to the cooperation of the Leicestershire and Rutland Constabulary, and the Presidents of Junior Common Rooms and Student Societies within the University of Leicester, questionnaires were completed and returned by 91 police and 182 students.[1] They were asked to complete the questionnaire after watching the news bulletins at 9.35 p.m. (BBC) and 10.10 p.m. (ITN) on Sunday 27 October. The 'neutral' sample was selected at random from lists of adult students attending classes at two university extra-mural centres. This sample was asked to watch the same news bulletins and complete the same questionnaire as the others but, in addition, they were given another, extended questionnaire in the week preceding the demonstration, which they were asked to complete and return by post before Sunday the twenty-seventh. It was not found possible to administer a pre-demonstration questionnaire to students and police, 189 'neutrals' completed and returned both questionnaires.[2]

Apart from the possibility of a slight under-representation of radical students in the student sample (many were actually taking part in the demonstration), there is no reason to believe that the police and students who completed the questionnaire were markedly different from their fellows. However, it must be emphasised that in the strict sense these cannot be regarded as representative of their groups, still less of the population at large. The neutral sample was quite heavily skewed towards a higher than average terminal education age, and away from the lower socio-economic and occupational categories.[3] Perhaps it should be stressed that reaction to the television portrayal of a situation by those differently involved in the situation, and not statements about police and students as such, is one of the main foci of this study.

All three samples were questioned not only on their general reactions to and criticisms of the television news coverage of the demonstration, but also on their opinions on such matters as biased reporting, differences in presentation between the two channels, incidents disapproved, incidents which should not have been shown, and those which were seen as violent and disturbing. They were also asked to describe the behaviour of both police and demonstrators, as they had seen it portrayed on television, to state if they felt the behaviour of the police and demonstrators had been influenced in any way by the presence of television cameras, and to comment on the identity and motivations of those taking part in the demonstrations. Attitudes on some relevant issues or topics (e.g. the war in Vietnam, students, the value of demonstrations) were assessed, and questions were also asked about interest in political affairs.[4]

In the pre-demonstration questionnaire, in addition to being asked to answer questions which would make it possible for comparison to be made between pre- and post-viewing responses in some of the relevant areas, the neutrals were also asked to give an account of what they had heard about the demonstration, and to indicate the source of this information.

Questionnaire approaches such as the one outlined above have their uses, but they also have clear limitations. They are not the most suitable instruments for probing at depth, for evoking answers to 'why' questions, for extending the range of possible response – still less for following up leads which may emerge in the course of an exploration.

As this audience study was seen primarily as an exploratory piece of work, it was felt that the information obtained from the answers to the questionnaire might be elaborated, insights gained into the nature and complexity of the reported reactions, and leads obtained for future research, if another more open – less structured – method could be used in conjunction with the questionnaire.

With this in mind, it was decided to recruit six discussion groups: two groups each of students, police and neutrals, with ten people in each group.[5] These groups came to the University during the evening of Sunday 27 October and watched both late evening news bulletins (9.35 p.m. BBC and 10.10 p.m. ITN). The groups met in six different rooms and, immediately after the ITN bulletin, they each took part in a discussion session, which lasted, on average, about one hour. The discussion was tape-recorded. A staff member was allocated to each group, as discussion group leader. The chief task of the leaders was to ensure wide participation and adequate discussion of the main areas covered in the questionnaire. They were given plenty of scope, should the situation merit it, to develop specific points, to probe at depth, and to extend the range of discussion within the broadly defined areas. Thus, in addition to assessing general reactions and criticisms, and examining the broad differences between the three samples, it was possible to go beneath these surface responses (although in a non-quantitative manner) and obtain some idea of other possible areas of application and of the underlying motivations, predispositions and value orientations. People can express concern about an issue, or even about a specific aspect of an issue (e.g. dissatisfaction at pro-authority bias in news bulletins) for very different reasons, at different levels of involvement, and have widely different solutions or remedies in mind. The mere expression of satisfaction or dissatisfaction which is sometimes reported by surveys in this field does not necessarily tell us very much about the nature and range of this feeling. The discussion groups, however, provided some interesting ideas in this connexion, and gave clear indications for future research.

Notes

1   This represents response rates of police: 91 per cent and students: 52 per cent.
2   This represents a response rate of 54 per cent. Initially, it had been hoped to recruit policewomen or police wives to the 'police' sample. This could not be done. In the account which follows, the returns from female students and female neutrals are not included in the analyses. Unless otherwise stated, the bases throughout are as follows: police 91, neutrals 90, students 137 (all males).
3   As far as age is concerned, 98 per cent of the students were under the age of 25 yrs. Twenty-two per cent of the police and 11 per cent of the neutrals were in this category. Eight per cent of the police and 28 per cent of the neutrals were

over 45 yrs. The remainder in both samples were in the category 26 to 45 yrs.

4   On formulating the questions social scientific considerations were not the only ones that had to be borne in mind. It would not have been appropriate to ask the police to answer certain questions (e.g. about actual political affiliation). In drawing up the questionnaire, we were glad to have the advice of the Chief Constable and his senior colleagues.

5   These groups were recruited in the same way as the main group.

UTILIZATION OF MASS COMMUNICATION BY THE INDIVIDUAL

3

Elihu Katz, Jay G. Blumler and Michael Gurevitch

Suppose that we were studying not broadcasting-and-society in mid-twentieth-century America but opera-and-society in mid-nineteenth-century Italy. After all, opera in Italy, during that period, was a 'mass' medium. What would we be studying? It seems likely, for one thing, that we would find interest in the attributes of the medium – what might today be called its 'grammar' – for example, the curious convention that makes it possible to sing contradictory emotions simultaneously. For another, we would be interested in the functions of the medium for the individual and society: perceptions of the values expressed and underlined; the phenomena of stardom, fanship, and connoisseurship; the festive ambience which the medium created; and so on. It seems quite unlikely that we would be studying the effects of the singing of a particular opera on opinions and attitudes, even though some operas were written with explicit political, social, and moral aims in mind. The study of short-run effects, in other words, would not have had a high priority, although it might have had a place. But the emphasis, by and large, would have been on the medium as a cultural institution with its own social and psychological functions and perhaps long-run effects.

We have all been over the reasons why much of mass communication research took a different turn, preferring to look at specific programs as

Elihu Katz, Jay G. Blumler and Michael Gurevitch (1974) Utilization of mass communication by the individual, in Jay G. Blumler and Elihu Katz (eds) *The Uses of Mass Communications: Current Perspectives on Gratifications Research*. Beverley Hills and London: Sage Publications, pp. 19–32. Reprinted by kind permission of Sage Publications, Inc.

specific messages with, possibly, specific effects. We were social psychologists interested in persuasion and attitude change. We were political scientists interested in new forms of social control. We were commissioned to measure message effectiveness for marketing organizations, or public health agencies, or churches, or political organizations, or for the broadcasting organizations themselves. And we were asked whether the media were not causes of violent and criminal behavior.

Yet even in the early days of empirical mass communication research this preoccupation with short-term effects was supplemented by the growth of an interest in the gratifications that the mass media provide their audiences. Such studies were well represented in the Lazarsfeld-Stanton collections (1942, 1944, 1949); Herzog (1942) on quiz programs and the gratifications derived from listening to soap operas; Suchman (1942) on the motives for getting interested in serious music on radio; Wolfe and Fiske (1949) on the development of children's interest in comics; Berelson (1949) on the functions of newspaper reading; and so on. Each of these investigations came up with a list of functions served either by some specific contents or by the medium in question: to match one's wits against others, to get information or advice for daily living, to provide a framework for one's day, to prepare oneself culturally for the demands of upward mobility, or to be reassured about the dignity and usefulness of one's role.

What these early studies had in common was, first, a basically similar methodological approach whereby statements about media functions were elicited from the respondents in an essentially open-ended way. Second, they shared a qualitative approach in their attempt to group gratification statements into labelled categories, largely ignoring the distribution of their frequency in the population. Third, they did not attempt to explore the links between the gratifications thus detected and the psychological or sociological origins of the needs that were so satisfied. Fourth, they failed to search for the interrelationships among the various media functions, either quantitatively or conceptually, in a manner that might have led to the detection of the latent structure of media gratifications. Consequently, these studies did not result in a cumulatively more detailed picture of media gratifications conducive to the eventual formulation of theoretical statements.

The last few years have witnessed something of a revival of direct empirical investigations of audience uses and gratifications, not only in the United States but also in Britain, Sweden, Finland, Japan, and Israel. These more recent studies have a number of differing starting points, but each attempts to press toward a greater systematization of what is involved in conducting research in this field. Taken together, they make operational many of the logical steps that were only implicit in the earlier work. They are concerned with (1) the social and psychological origins of (2) needs, which generate (3) expectations of (4) the mass media or other sources, which lead to (5) differential patterns of media exposure (or engagement in other activities), resulting in (6) need gratifications and (7) other consequences, perhaps mostly unintended ones. Some of these investigations begin by specifying needs and then attempt to trace the extent to which they are gratified by the media or other sources. Others take observed gratifications as a starting point and attempt to reconstruct the needs that are being gratified. Yet others focus on the social origins of audience expectations and gratifications. But however varied their individual points of departure, they all strive toward an assessment of media consumption in audience-related terms, rather than in technological, aesthetic, ideological, or other more or less 'elitist' terms. The convergence of their foci, as well as of their findings, indicates that there is a clear agenda here – part methodological and part theoretical – for a discussion of the future directions of this approach.

Some basic assumptions of theory, method and value

Perhaps the place of 'theory' and 'method' in the study of audience uses and gratifications is not immediately apparent. The common tendency to attach the label 'uses and gratifications approach' to work in this field appears to virtually disclaim any theoretical pretensions or methodological commitment. From this point of view the approach simply represents an attempt to explain something of the way in which individuals use communications, among other resources in their environment, to satisfy their needs and to achieve their goals, and to do so by simply asking them. Nevertheless, this effort does rest on a body of assumptions, explicit or implicit, that have some degree of internal coherence and that are arguable in the sense that not everyone contemplating them would find them self-evident. Lundberg and Hultén (1968) refer to them as jointly constituting a 'uses and gratifications model.' Five elements of this model in particular may be singled out for comment:

1   The audience is conceived of as active, that is, an important part of mass media use is assumed to be goal directed (McQuail *et al.* 1972). This assumption may be contrasted with Bogart's (1965) thesis to the effect that 'most mass media experiences represent pastime rather than purposeful activity, very often [reflecting] chance circumstances

within the range of availabilities rather than the expression of psychological motivation or need.' Of course, it cannot be denied that media exposure often has a casual origin; the issue is whether, in addition, patterns of media use are shaped by more or less definite expectations of what certain kinds of content have to offer the audience member.

2   In the mass communication process much initiative in linking need gratification and media choice lies with the audience member. This places a strong limitation on theorizing about any form of straight-line effect of media content on attitudes and behavior. As Schramm *et al.* (1961) said:

> In a sense the term 'effect' is misleading because it suggests that television 'does something' to children. ... Nothing can be further from the fact. It is the children who are most active in this relationship. It is they who use television rather than television that uses them.

3   The media compete with other sources of need satisfaction. The needs served by mass communication constitute but a segment of the wider range of human needs, and the degree to which they can be adequately met through mass media consumption certainly varies. Consequently, a proper view of the role of the media in need satisfaction should take into account other functional alternatives – including different, more conventional, and 'older' ways of fulfilling needs.

4   Methodologically speaking, many of the goals of mass media use can be derived from data supplied by individual audience members themselves – that is, people are sufficiently self-aware to be able to report their interests and motives in particular cases, or at least to recognize them when confronted with them in an intelligible and familiar verbal formulation.

5   Value judgments about the cultural significance of mass communication should be suspended while audience orientations are explored on their own terms. It is from the perspective of this assumption that certain affinities and contrasts between the uses and gratifications approach and much speculative writing about popular culture may be considered.

State of the art: theoretical issues

From the few postulates outlined above, it is evident that further development of a theory of media gratification depends, first, on the clarification of its relationship to the theoretical traditions on which it so obviously draws and, second, on systematic efforts toward conceptual integration of empirical findings. Given the present state of the art, the following are priority issues in the development of an adequate theoretical basis.

Typologies of audience gratifications

Each major piece of uses and gratification research has yielded its own classification scheme of audience functions. When placed side by side, they reveal a mixture of shared gratification categories and notions peculiar to individual research teams. The differences are due in part to the fact that investigators have focused on different levels of study (e.g., medium or content) and different materials (e.g., different programs or program types on, say, television) in different cultures (e.g., Finland, Israel, Japan, Sweden, the United Kingdom, the United States, and Yugoslavia).

Unifunctional conceptions of audience interests have been expressed in various forms. Popular culture writers have often based their criticisms of the media on the ground that, in primarily serving the escapist desires of the audience, they deprived it of the more beneficial uses that might be made of communication (McDonald 1957). Stephenson's analysis (1967) of mass communication exclusively in terms of 'play' may be interpreted as an extension, albeit in a transformed and expanded expression, of this same notion. A more recent example has been provided by Nordenstreng (1970), who, while breaking away from conventional formulations, still opts for a unifunctional view when he claims that, 'It has often been documented (e.g., during television and newspaper strikes in Finland in 1966–67) that perhaps the basic motivation for media use is just an unarticulated need for social contact.'

The wide currency secured for a bifunctional view of audience concerns is reflected in Weiss' (1971) summary, which states that, 'When ... studies of uses and gratifications are carried out, the media or media content are usually viewed dichotomously as predominantly fantasist-escapist or informational-educational in significance.' This dichotomy appears, for example, in Schramm's (1949) work (adopted subsequently by Schramm *et al.* 1961; Pietila 1969; and Furu 1971), which distinguishes between sets of 'immediate' and 'deferred' gratifications, and in the distinction between informational and entertainment materials. In terms of audience gratifications specifically, it emerges in the distinction between surveillance and escape uses of the media.

The four-functional interpretation of the media was first proposed by Lasswell (1948) on a macro-sociological level and later developed by

Wright (1960) on both the macro- and the mirco-sociological levels. It postulated that the media served the functions of surveillance, correlation, entertainment, and cultural transmission (or socialization) for society as a whole, as well as for individuals and subgroups within society. An extension of the four-function approach can also be found in Wright's suggestive exploration of the potential dysfunctional equivalents of Lasswell's typology.

None of these statements, however, adequately reflects the full range of functions, which has been disclosed by the more recent investigations. McQuail *et al.* (1972) have put forward a typology consisting of the following categories: diversion (including escape from the constraints of routine and the burdens of problems, and emotional release); personal relationships (including substitute companionship as well as social utility); personal identity (including personal reference, reality exploration, and value reinforcement); and surveillance.

An effort to encompass the large variety of specific functions that have been proposed is made in the elaborate scheme of Katz, *et al.* (1973). Their central notion is that mass communication is used by individuals to connect (or sometimes to disconnect) themselves – via instrumental, affective, or integrative relations – with different kinds of others (self, family, friends, nation, etc.). The scheme attempts to comprehend the whole range of individual gratifications of the many facets of the need 'to be connected.' And it finds empirical regularities in the preference for different media for different kinds of connections.

Gratification and needs

The study of mass media use suffers at present from the absence of a relevant theory of social and psychological needs. It is not so much a catalogue of needs that is missing as a clustering of groups of needs, a sorting out of different levels of need, and a specification of hypotheses linking particular needs with particular media gratifications. It is true that the work of Schramm *et al.* (1961) draws on the distinction between the reality and pleasure principles in the socialization theories of Freud and others, but more recent studies suggest that those categories are too broad to be serviceable. Maslow's (1954) proposed hierarchy of human needs may hold more promise, but the relevance of his categories to expectations of communication has not yet been explored in detail. Lasswell's (1948) scheme to specify the needs that media satisfy has proven useful, and it may be helpful to examine Lasswell and Kaplan's (1950) broader classification of values as well.

Alternatively, students of uses and gratifications could try to work backwards, as it were, from gratifications to needs. In the informational field, for example, the surveillance function may be traced to a desire for security or the satisfaction of curiosity and the exploratory drive; seeking reinforcement of one's attitudes and values may derive from a need for reassurance that one is right; and attempts to correlate informational elements may stem from a more basic need to develop one's cognitive mastery of the environment. Similarly, the use of fictional (and other) media materials for 'personal reference' may spring from a need for self-esteem; social utility functions may be traced to the need for affiliation; and escape functions may be related to the need to release tension and reduce anxiety. But whichever way one proceeds, it is inescapable that what is at issue here is the long-standing problem of social and psychological science: how to (and whether to bother to) systematize the long lists of human and societal needs. Thus far, gratifications research has stayed close to what we have been calling media-related needs (in the sense that the media have been observed to satisfy them, at least in part), but one wonders whether all this should not be put in the broader context of systematic studies of needs.

Sources of media gratifications

Studies have shown that audience gratifications can be derived from at least three distinct sources: media content, exposure to the media per se, and the social context that typifies the situation of exposure to different media. Although recognition of media content as a source of gratifications has provided the basis for research in this area from its inception, less attention has been paid to the other sources. Nevertheless, it is clear that the need to relax or to kill time can be satisfied by the act of watching television, that the need to feel that one is spending one's time in a worthwhile way may be associated with the act of reading (Waples *et al.* 1940; Berelson 1949), and that the need to structure one's day may be satisfied merely by having the radio 'on' (Mendelsohn 1964). Similarly, a wish to spend time with one's family or friends can be served by watching television at home with the family or by going to the cinema with one's friends.

Each medium seems to offer a unique combination of (a) characteristic contents (at least stereotypically perceived in that way); (b) typical attributes (print vs. broadcasting modes of transmission, iconic vs. symbolic representation, reading vs. audio or audio-visual modes of reception); and (c) typical exposure situations (at home vs. out-of-home, alone vs. with others, control over the temporal aspects of exposure vs. absence of such control). The issue, then, is what combinations of attributes may render different media more or less adequate for the satisfaction of different needs (Katz *et al.* 1973).

Gratifications and media attributes

Much uses and gratifications research has still barely advanced beyond a sort of charting and profiling activity: findings are still typically presented to show that certain bodies of content serve certain functions or that one medium is deemed better at satisfying certain needs than another. The further step, which has hardly been ventured, is one of explanation. At issue here is the relationship between the unique 'grammar' of different media – that is, their specific technological and aesthetic attributes – and the particular requirements of audience members that they are then capable, or incapable, of satisfying. Which, indeed, are the attributes that render some media more conducive than others to satisfying specific needs? And which elements of content help to attract the expectations for which they apparently cater?

It is possible to postulate the operation of some kind of division of labor among the media for the satisfaction of audience needs. This may be elaborated in two ways: taking media attributes as the starting point, the suggestion is that those media that differ (or are similar) in their attributes are more likely to serve different (or similar) needs; or, utilizing the latent structure of needs as a point of departure, the implication is that needs that are psychologically related or conceptually similar will be equally well served by the same media (or by media with similar attributes).

To illustrate the first approach, Robinson (1972) has demonstrated the interchangeability of television and print media for learning purposes. In the Israeli study, Katz *et al.* (1973) found five media ordered in a circumplex with respect to their functional similarities: books–newspapers–radio–television–cinema–books. In other words, books functioned most like newspapers, on the one hand, and like cinema, on the other. Radio was most similar in its usage to newspapers, on the one hand, and to television, on the other. The explanation would seem to lie not only with certain technological attributes that they have in common, but with similar aesthetic qualities as well. Thus, books share a technology and an informational function with newspapers, but are similar to films in their aesthetic function. Radio shares a technology, as well as informational and entertainment content, with television, but it is also very much like newspapers – providing a heavy dose of information and an orientation to reality.

An illustration of the second aspect of this division of labor may also be drawn from the same study. Here, the argument is that structurally related needs will tend to be serviced by certain media more often than by others. Thus, books and cinema have been found to cater to needs concerned with self-fulfilment and self-gratification: they help to 'connect' individuals to themselves. Newspapers, radio, and television all seem to connect individuals to society. In fact, the function of newspapers for those interested in following what is going on in the world may have been grossly underestimated in the past (Lundberg and Hultén 1968; Edelstein 1973). Television, however, was found to be less frequently used as a medium of escape by Israeli respondents than were books and films. And a Swedish study of the 'functional specialities of the respective media' reported that, 'A retreat from the immediate environment and its demands – probably mainly by the act of reading itself – was characteristic of audience usage of weekly magazines' (Lundberg and Hultén 1968).

Media attributes as perceived or intrinsic

When people associate book-reading, for example, with a desire to know oneself, and newspapers with the need to feel connected to the larger society, it is difficult to disentangle perceptions of the media from their intrinsic qualities. Is there anything about the book as a medium that breeds intimacy? Is there something about newspapers that explains their centrality in socio-political integration? Or, is this 'something' simply an accepted image of the medium and its characteristic content?

In this connection, Rosengren (1972) has suggested that uses and gratifications research may be profitably connected with the long-established tradition of enquiry into public perceptions of the various media and the dimensions according to which their respective images and qualities are differentiated (cf. especially Nilsson (1971) and Edelstein (1973) and the literature cited therein). A merger of the two lines of investigation may show how far the attributes of the media, as perceived by their consumers, and their intrinsic qualities are correlated with the pursuit of certain gratifications. So far, however, this connection has only been partially discussed in the work of Lundberg and Hultén (1968).

The social origins of audience needs and their gratifications

The social and environmental circumstances that lead people to turn to the mass media for the satisfaction of certain needs are also little understood as yet. For example, what needs, if any, are created by routine work on an assembly line, and which forms of media exposure will satisfy them? What motivates some people to seek political information from the mass media and others to actively avoid it? Here one may postulate that it is the combined product of psychological dispositions, sociological factors, and environmental conditions that determines the specific uses of the media by members of the audience.

At certain levels it should not prove unduly difficult to formulate discrete hypotheses about such relationships. For example, we might expect 'substitute companionship' to be sought especially by individuals with limited opportunities for social contacts: invalids, the elderly, the single, the divorced or widowed living alone, the housewife who spends much time at home on her own, and so on.

At another level, however, it is more difficult to conceive of a general theory that might clarify the various processes that underlie any such specific relationships. A preliminary structuring of the possibilities suggests that social factors may be involved in the generation of media-related needs in any of the following five ways (each of which has attracted some comment in the literature):

1   Social situation produces tensions and conflicts, leading to pressure for their easement via mass media consumption (Katz and Foulkes 1962).
2   Social situation creates an awareness of problems that demand attention, information about which may be sought in the media (Edelstein 1973).
3   Social situation offers impoverished real-life opportunities to satisfy certain needs, which are then directed to the mass media for complementary, supplementary, or substitute servicing (Rosengren and Windahl 1972).
4   Social situation gives rise to certain values, the affirmation and reinforcement of which is facilitated by the consumption of congruent media materials (Dembo 1972).
5   Social situation provides a field of expectations of familiarity with certain media materials, which must then be monitored in order to sustain membership of valued social groupings (Atkins 1972).

The versatility of sources of need satisfaction

Before becoming too sanguine about the possibility of relating social situations to psychological needs to media/content gratifications, it is important to bear in mind that gratifications studies based on specific media contents have demonstrated that one and the same set of media materials is capable of serving a multiplicity of needs and audience functions.

Presumably, that is why Rosengren and Windahl (1972) have drawn attention to 'a growing consensus that almost any type of content may serve practically any type of function.' For example, Blumler *et al.* (1970) have found that the television serial *The Saint* serves functions of personal reference, identification with characters, and reality-exploration, in addition to its more obvious diversionary function. Similarly, their study of the gratifications involved in news viewing referred not only to the expected surveillance motive but also to functions of social utility, empathy, and even escape. In summarizing the implications of their evidence, McQuail *et al.* (1972) point out that:

> the relationship between content categories and audience needs is far less tidy and more complex than most commentators have appreciated. ... One man's source of escape from the real world is a point of anchorage for another man's place in it.

Gratifications and effects

Pioneers in the study of uses and gratifications were moved chiefly by two aspirations. The first, which has largely been fulfilled, was to redress an imbalance evident in previous research: audience needs, they said, deserved as much attention in their own right as the persuasive aims of communicators with which so many of the early 'effects' studies had been preoccupied. The second major aim of uses and gratifications research, however, was to treat audience requirements as intervening variables in the study of traditional communication effects. Glaser's (1965) formulation offers a typical expression of the rationale behind this prospect:

> Since users approach the media with a variety of needs and predispositions ... any precise identification of the effects of television watching ... must identify the uses sought and made of television by the various types of viewers.

Despite this injunction, hardly any substantial empirical or theoretical effort has been devoted to connecting gratifications and effects. Some limited evidence from the political field suggests that combining functions and effects perspectives may be fruitful (Blumler and McQuail 1969). But there are many other foci of traditional effects studies for which no detailed hypotheses about gratifications/effects interactions have yet been framed.

One obvious example is the field of media violence. Another might concern the impact on inhabitants of developing countries of exposure to television serials, films, and popular songs of foreign (predominantly

American) origin. Yet another might relate to the wide range of materials, appearing especially in broadcast fiction, that purport simultaneously to entertain and to portray more or less faithfully some portion of social reality – e.g., the worlds of law enforcement, social work, hospital life, trade unionism, working-class neighborhoods, and ways of life at the executive level in business corporations and civil service departments.

Hypotheses about the cumulative effects of exposure to such materials on audience members' cognitive perceptions of these spheres of activity, and on the individuals engaged in them, might be formulated in awareness of the likely fact that some individuals will be viewing them primarily for purposes of escape, while others will be using them for reality-exploring gratifications. In these circumstances should we expect a readier acceptance of portrayed stereotypes by the escape seekers – the thesis of Festinger and Maccoby (1964) on persuasion via distraction might be relevant here – or by those viewers who are trusting enough to expect such programs to offer genuine insights into the nature of social reality?

A similar body of recently analyzed materials may be found in the television soap opera, with its postulated capacity to 'establish or reinforce value systems' (Katzman 1972). In fact one cluster of gratifications that emerged from an English study of listeners to a long-running daytime radio serial (*The Dales*) centered on the tendency of the program to uphold traditional family values (Blumler *et al.* 1970). This suggests that an answer to Katzman's 'key question' ('to what degree do daytime serials change attitudes and norms and to what extent do they merely follow and reinforce their audience?') might initially be sought by distinguishing among the regular followers of such programs those individuals who are avowedly seeking a reinforcement of certain values from those who are not.

In addition, however, the literature refers to some consequences of audience functions that conventional effects designs may be unable to capture. First, there is what Katz and Foulkes (1962) have termed the 'feedback' from media use to the individual's performance of his other social roles. Thus, Bailyn (1959) distinguished child uses of pictorial media that might 'preclude more realistic and lasting solutions' to problems from those that, at one level, were 'escapist' but that should more properly be categorized as 'supplementation.' Similarly, Schramm *et al.* (1961) maintained that child uses of the mass media for fantasizing might either drain off discontent caused by the hard blows of socialization or lead a child into withdrawal from the real world. And Lundberg and Hultén (1968) have suggested that for some individuals the substitute companionship function may involve use of the media to replace real social ties, while for others it may facilitate an adjustment to reality.

Second, some authors have speculated on the connection between functions performed by the media for individuals and their functions (or dysfunctions) for other levels of society. This relationship is particularly crucial for its bearing on evaluative and ideological controversies about the role of mass communication in modern society. Thus, Enzenberger (1972) suggests that the 8 millimeter camera may satisfy the recreational and creative impulses of the individual and help to keep the family together while simultaneously atomizing and depoliticizing society. Or news viewing may gratify the individual's need for civic participation; but if the news, as presented, is a disjointed succession of staccato events, it may also leave him with the message that the world is a disconnected place. Similarly, many radical critics tend to regard television as part of a conspiracy to keep people content and politically quiescent – offering respite, para-social interaction with interesting and amusing people, and much food for gossip – while propagating a false social consciousness.

Implications for research policy and media policy

In reviewing the state of the art of gratifications research, we have focused on issues – theoretical, methodological, and ideological – rather than on systematized findings. We have also tried to make manifest our assumptions. Thus, we have confronted the image of the beery, house-slippered, casual viewer of television with the notion of a more 'active' audience – knowing that both images are true. We have asked whether a methodology based on respondents' introspection can be adequate. We have indicated the absence of satisfactory bridging concepts between the constraints arising from social situations and the gratifications sought from the media; or between particular patterns of use and likely effect.

These issues bear not only on the direction of future research, but also, echoing Nordenstreng (1970), on the relationship between research policy and media policy. Thus, we have raised the question of the extent to which the media create the needs that they satisfy. Even more fundamentally, we ask whether the media do actually satisfy their consumers – an assumption that radical critics of the media take more for granted than do gratification researchers (cf., Emmett, 1968–69). To assert that mass communication is a latter-day opiate of the masses presupposes a media-output audience-satisfaction nexus that gratifications research treats as hypothesis rather than fact.

In other words, our position is that media researchers ought to be studying human needs to discover how much the media do or do not contribute to their creation and satisfaction. Moreover, we believe it is our job to clarify the extent to which certain kinds of media and content favor certain kinds of use – to thereby set boundaries to the over-generalization that any kind of content can be bent to any kind of need. We believe it is part of our job to explore the social and individual conditions under which audiences find need or use for program material aimed at changing their image of the status quo or 'broadening their cultural horizons' (Emmett 1968–69).

From the point of view of media policy, then, we reject the view that an application of the uses and gratifications approach to policy questions must inevitably support or exonerate the producers of junk or the status quo of media content. That belief seems to require the acceptance of one or both of two other assumptions: existing patterns of audience needs support the prevailing patterns of media provision and no other; and audience concerns are in fact trivial and escapist. For reasons that should now be plain, we find both these propositions dubious.

Though audience oriented, the uses and gratifications approach is not necessarily conservative. While taking account of what people look for from the media, it breaks away from a slavish dependence of content on audience propensities by bringing to light the great variety of needs and interests that are encompassed by the latter. As McQuail *et al.* (1972) have argued, uses and gratifications data suggest that the mass media may not, after all, be as 'constrained as the escapist theory makes out from performing a wider range of social functions than is generally assigned to them in western societies today.' In other words, instead of depicting the media as severely circum-scribed by audience expectations, the uses and gratifications approach highlights the audience as a source of challenge to producers to cater more richly to the miltiplicity of requirements and roles that it has disclosed.

Authors' Note

A more extended version of this essay was first prepared for presentation in May 1973 to a conference at Arden House, Harriman, New York, on Directions in Mass Communication Research, which was arranged by the School of Journalism of Columbia University and supported by a grant from the John and Mary Markle Foundation. It may be consulted in full in W. Phillips Davison and Frederick T.C. Yu (eds) (1974) *Mass Communication Research: Major Issues and Future Directions* New York: Praeger. The present text is a modified version of an abridgment that originally appeared in *Public Opinion Quarterly* Winter 1973–74.

References

Atkin, C.K. (1972) Anticipated communication and mass media information-seeking. *Public Opinion Quarterly*, 36.

Bailyn, L. (1959) Mass media and children, *Psychological Monographs*, 71.

Berelson, B. (1949) What missing the newspaper means, in P.F. Lazarsfeld and F.N. Stanton (eds.) *Communications Research, 1948–9*. New York: Duell, Sloan & Pearce.

Blumler, J.G., Brown, J.R. and D. McQuail (1970) The social origins of the gratifications associated with television viewing. Leeds: The University of Leeds. (mimeo)

Blumler, J.G. and McQuail, D. (1969) *Television in Politics*. Chicago: University of Chicago Press.

Bogart, L. (1965) The mass media and the blue-collar worker, in A. Bennett and W. Gomberg (eds.) *Blue-Collar World: Studies of the American Worker*. Englewood Cliffs, N.J.: Prentice-Hall.

Dembo, R. (1972) Life style and media use among English working-class youths, *Gazette*, 18.

Edelstein, A. (1973) An alternative approach to the study of source effects in mass communication, *Studies of Broadcasting*, 9.

Emmett, B. (1968–69) A new role for research in broadcasting, *Public Opinion Quarterly*, 32.

Enzenberger, H. M. (1972) Constituents of a theory of the media, in D. McQuail (ed.) *Sociology of Mass Communications*. Harmondsworth: Penguin.

Festinger, L. and Maccoby, N. (1964) On resistance to persuasive communication, *Journal of Abnormal and Social Psychology*, 60.

Furu, T. (1971) *The Function of Television for Children and Adolescents*. Tokyo: Sophia University.

Glaser, W.A. (1965) Television and voting turnout, *Public Opinion Quarterly*, 29.

Herzog, H. (1942) Professor quiz: a gratification study, in P. F. Lazarsfeld and F. N. Stanton (eds) *Radio Research, 1941*. New York: Duell, Sloan & Pearce.

Katz, E. and Foulkes, D. (1962) On the use of the mass media for 'escape': clarification of a concept, *Public Opinion Quarterly*, 26.

Katz, E., Gurevitch, M. and Haas, H. (1973) On the use of mass media for important things. *American Sociological Review*, 38.

Katzman, N. (1972) Television soap operas: what's been going on anyway? *Public Opinion Quarterly*, 36.

Lasswell, H. (1948) The structure and function of communications in society, in L. Bryson (ed.) *The Communication of Ideas*. New York: Harper.

Lasswell, H. and Kaplan, A. (1950) *Power and Society*. New Haven: Yale Univ. Press.

Lazarsfeld, P.F. and Stanton, F.N. (eds) (1942) *Radio Research, 1941*. New York: Duell, Sloan & Pearce.

Lazarsfeld, P.F. and Stanton, F.N. (eds) (1944) *Radio Research, 1942–3*. New York: Duell, Sloan & Pearce.

50 | CRITICAL READINGS: MEDIA AND AUDIENCES

Lazarsfeld, P.F. and Stanton, F.N. (eds) (1949) *Communications Research, 1948–49*. New York: Harper.
Lundberg, D. and Hultén, O. (1968) *Individen och Massmedia*. Stockholm: EFL.
McDonald, D. (1957) A theory of mass culture, in D.M. White and B. Rosenberg (eds) *Mass Culture: The Popular Arts in America*. Glencoe: Free Press.
McQuail, D., Blumler, J.G. and Brown, J.R. (1972) The television audience: a revised perspective, in D. McQuail (ed.) *Sociology of Mass Communications*. Harmondsworth: Penguin.
Maslow, A.H. (1954) *Motivation and Personality*. New York: Harper.
Mendelsohn, H. (1964) Listening to radio, in L.A. Dexter and D.M. White (eds) *People, Society and Mass Communications*. Glencoe: Free Press.
Nilsson, S. (1971) Publikens upplevelse av tv-program. Stockholm: Sveriges Radio PUB. (mimeo)
Nordenstreng, K. (1970) Comments on 'gratifications research' in broadcasting, *Public Opinion Quarterly*, 34.
Pietila, V. (1969) Immediate versus delayed reward in newspaper reading, *Acta Sociologica*, 12.
Robinson, J.P. (1972) Toward defining the functions of television, *Television and Social Behavior*. Vol. 4. Rockville, MD.: National Institute of Mental Health.
Rosengren, K.E. (1972) Uses and gratifications: an overview. Sweden: University of Lund. (mimeo)
Rosengren, K.E. and Windahl, S. (1972) Mass media consumption as a functional alternative, in D. McQuail (ed.) *Sociology of Mass Communications*. Harmondsworth: Penguin.
Schramm, W. (1949) The nature of news, *Journalism Quarterly*, 26.
Schramm, W., Lyle J. and Parker, E.B. (1961) *Television in the Lives of Our Children*. Stanford: Stanford University Press.
Stephenson, W. (1967) *The Play Theory of Mass Communication*. Chicago: University of Chicago Press.
Suchman, E. (1942) An invitation to music, in P.F. Lazarsfeld and F.N. Stanton (eds) *Radio Research, 1941*. New York: Duell, Sloan & Pearce.
Waples, D., Berelson, B. and Bradshaw F.R. (1940) *What Reading Does to People*. Chicago: University of Chicago Press.
Weiss, W. (1971) Mass communication. *Annual Review of Psychology*, 22.
Wolfe, K.M. and Fiske M. (1949) Why children read comics, in P.F. Lazarsfeld and F.N. Stanton (eds) *Communications Research, 1948–9*. New York: Harper.
Wright, C. (1960) Functional analysis and mass communication, *Public Opinion Quarterly*, 24.

4 | ENCODING/DECODING *

Stuart Hall

Traditionally, mass-communications research has conceptualized the process of communication in terms of a circulation circuit or loop. This model has been criticized for its linearity – sender/message/receiver – for its concentration on the level of message exchange and for the absence of a structured conception of the different moments as a complex structure of relations. But it is also possible (and useful) to think of this process in terms of a structure produced and sustained through the articulation of linked but distinctive moments – production, circulation, distribution/consumption, reproduction. This would be to think of the process as a 'complex structure in dominance', sustained through the articulation of connected practices, each of which, however, retains its distinctiveness and has its own specific modality, its own forms and conditions of existence. This second approach, homologous to that which forms the skeleton of commodity production offered in Marx's *Grundrisse* and in *Capital*, has the added advantage of bringing out more sharply how a continuous circuit – production-distribution-production – can be sustained through a 'passage of forms'.[1] It also highlights the specificity of the forms in which the product of the process 'appears' in each moment, and thus what distinguishes discursive 'production' from other types of production in our society and in modern media systems.

Stuart Hall (1980) *Encoding/decoding*, in Stuart Hall, Dorothy Hobson, Andrew Lowe and Paul Willis (eds) *Culture, Media, Language*. London: Hutchinson/CCCS, pp. 197–208. Reprinted by kind permission of Taylor & Francis and CCCS.
* This article is an edited extract from 'Encoding and Decoding in Television Discourse'. CCCS Stencilled Paper no. 7.

The 'object' of these practices is meanings and messages in the form of sign vehicles of a specific kind organized, like any form of communication or language, through the operation of codes within the syntagmatic chain of a discourse. The apparatuses, relations and practices of production thus issue, at a certain moment (the moment of 'production/circulation') in the form of symbolic vehicles constituted within the rules of 'language'. It is in this discursive form that the circulation of the 'product' takes place. The process thus requires, at the production end, its material instruments – its 'means' – as well as its own sets of social (production) relations – the organization and combination of practices within media apparatuses. But it is in the *discursive* form that the circulation of the product takes place, as well as its distribution to different audiences. Once accomplished, the discourse must then be translated – transformed, again – into social practices if the circuit is to be both completed and effective. If no 'meaning' is taken, there can be no 'consumption'. If the meaning is not articulated in practice, it has no effect. The value of this approach is that while each of the moments, in articulation, is necessary to the circuit as a whole, no one moment can fully guarantee the next moment with which it is articulated. Since each has its specific modality and conditions of existence, each can constitute its own break or interruption of the 'passage of forms' on whose continuity the flow of effective production (that is, 'reproduction') depends.

Thus while in no way wanting to limit research to 'following only those leads which emerge from content analysis',[2] we must recognize that the discursive form of the message has a privileged position in the communicative exchange (from the viewpoint of circulation), and that the moments of 'encoding' and 'decoding', though only 'relatively autonomous' in relation to the communicative process as a whole, are *determinate* moments. A 'raw' historical event cannot, *in that form*, be transmitted by, say, a television newscast. Events can only be signified within the aural-visual forms of the televisual discourse. In the moment when a historical event passes under the sign of discourse, it is subject to all the complex formal 'rules' by which language signifies. To put it paradoxically, the event must become a 'story' before it can become a *communicative event*. In that moment the formal sub-rules of discourse are 'in dominance', without, of course, subordinating out of existence the historical event so signified, the social relations in which the rules are set to work or the social and political consequences of the event having been signified in this way. The 'message form' is the necessary 'form of appearance' of the event in its passage from source to receiver. Thus the transposition into and out of the 'message form' (or the mode of symbolic exchange) is not a random 'moment', which we can take up or ignore at our convenience. The 'message form' is a determinate moment; though, at another level, it comprises the surface movements of the communications system only and requires, at another stage, to be integrated into the social relations of the communication process as a whole, of which it forms only a part.

From this general perspective, we may crudely characterize the television communicative process as follows. The institutional structures of broadcasting, with their practices and networks of production, their organized relations and technical infrastructures, are required to produce a programme. Using the analogy of *Capital*, this is the 'labour process' in the discursive mode. Production, here, constructs the message. In one sense, then, the circuit begins here. Of course, the production process is not without its 'discursive' aspect: it, too, is framed throughout by meanings and ideas: knowledge-in-use concerning the routines of production, historically defined technical skills, professional ideologies, institutional knowledge, definitions and assumptions, assumptions about the audience and so on frame the constitution of the programme through this production structure. Further, though the production structures of television originate the television discourse, they do not constitute a closed system. They draw topics, treatments, agendas, events, personnel, images of the audience, 'definitions of the situation' from other sources and other discursive formations within the wider socio-cultural and political structure of which they are a differentiated part. Phillip Elliott has expressed this point succinctly, within a more traditional framework, in his discussion of the way in which the audience is both the 'source' and the 'receiver' of the television message. Thus – to borrow Marx's terms – circulation and reception are, indeed, 'moments' of the production process in television and are reincorporated, via a number of skewed and structured 'feedbacks', into the production process itself. The consumption or reception of the television message is thus also itself a 'moment' of the production process in its larger sense, though the latter is 'predominant' because it is the 'point of departure for the realization' of the message. Production and reception of the television message are not, therefore, identical, but they are related: they are differentiated moments within the totality formed by the social relations of the communicative process as a whole.

At a certain point, however, the broadcasting structures must yield encoded messages in the form of a meaningful discourse. The institution-societal relations of production must pass under the discursive rules of language for its product to be 'realized'. This initiates a further differentiated moment, in which the formal rules of discourse and language are in dominance. Before this message can have an 'effect' (however defined), satisfy a 'need' or be put to a 'use', it must first be appropriated as a meaningful discourse and be meaningfully decoded. It is this set of decoded meanings which 'have an effect', influence, entertain, instruct or persuade, with very complex perceptual, cognitive, emotional, ideological or behavioural consequences. In a 'determinate' moment the structure employs a code and yields a 'message': at another determinate moment the 'message', via its decodings, issues into the structure of social practices. We are now fully aware that this re-entry into the practices of audience reception and 'use' cannot be understood in simple behavioural terms. The typical processes identified in positivistic research on isolated elements – effects, uses, 'gratifications' – are themselves framed by structures of understanding, as well as being produced by social and economic relations, which shape their 'realization' at the reception end of the chain and which permit the meanings signified in the discourse to be transposed into practice or consciousness (to acquire social use value or political effectivity).

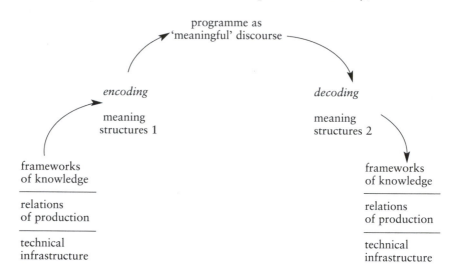

Clearly, what we have labelled in the diagram 'meaning structures 1' and 'meaning structures 2' may not be the same. They do not constitute an 'immediate identity'. The codes of encoding and decoding may not be perfectly symmetrical. The degrees of symmetry – that is, the degrees of 'understanding' and 'misunderstanding' in the communicative exchange – depend on the degrees of symmetry/asymmetry (relations of equivalence) established between the positions of the 'personifications', encoder-producer and decoder-receiver. But this in turn depends on the degrees of identity/ non-identity between the codes which perfectly or imperfectly transmit, interrupt or systematically distort what has been transmitted. The lack of fit between the codes has a great deal to do with the structural differences of relation and position between broadcasters and audiences, but it also has something to do with the asymmetry between the codes of 'source' and 'receiver' at the moment of transformation into and out of the discursive form. What are called 'distortions' or 'misunderstandings' arise precisely from the *lack of equivalence* between the two sides in the communicative exchange. Once again, this defines the 'relative autonomy', but 'determinateness', of the entry and exit of the message in its discursive moments.

The application of this rudimentary paradigm has already begun to transform our understanding of the older term, television 'content'. We are just beginning to see how it might also transform our understanding of audience reception, 'reading' and response as well. Beginnings and endings have been announced in communications research before, so we must be cautious. But there seems some ground for thinking that a new and exciting phase in so-called audience research, of a quite new kind, may be opening up. At either end of the communicative chain the use of the semiotic paradigm promises to dispel the lingering behaviourism which has dogged mass-media research for so long, especially in its approach to content. Though we know the television programme is not a behavioural input, like a tap on the knee cap, it seems to have been almost impossible for traditional researchers to conceptualize the communicative process without lapsing into one or other variant of low-flying behaviourism. We know, as Gerbner has remarked, that representations of violence on the TV screen 'are not violence but messages about violence':[3] but we have continued to research the question of violence, for example, as if we were unable to comprehend this epistemological distinction.

The televisual sign is a complex one. It is itself constituted by the combination of two types of discourse, visual and aural. Moreover, it is an iconic sign, in Peirce's terminology, because 'it possesses some of the properties of the thing represented'.[4] This is a point which has led to a great deal of confusion and has provided the site of intense controversy in the study of visual language. Since the visual discourse translates a three-dimensional world into two-dimensional planes, it cannot, of course, *be* the referent or concept it signifies. The dog in the film can bark but it cannot bite! Reality exists outside language, but it is constantly mediated by and through language: and what we can know and say has to be produced in and through discourse. Discursive 'knowledge' is the product not of the transparent representation of the 'real' in language but of the articulation of language on real relations and conditions. Thus there is no intelligible discourse without the operation of a code. Iconic signs are therefore coded signs too – even if the codes here work differently from those of other signs.

There is no degree zero in language. Naturalism and 'realism' – the apparent fidelity of the representation to the thing or concept represented – is the result, the effect, of a certain specific articulation of language on the 'real'. It is the result of a discursive practice.

Certain codes may, of course, be so widely distributed in a specific language community or culture, and be learned at so early an age, that they appear not to be constructed – the effect of an articulation between sign and referent – but to be 'naturally' given. Simple visual signs appear to have achieved a 'near-universality' in this sense: though evidence remains that even apparently 'natural' visual codes are culture-specific. However, this does not mean that no codes have intervened; rather, that the codes have been profoundly *naturalized*. The operation of naturalized codes reveals not the transparency and 'naturalness' of language but the depth, the habituation and the near-universality of the codes in use. They produce apparently 'natural' recognitions. This has the (ideological) effect of concealing the practices of coding which are present. But we must not be fooled by appearances. Actually, what naturalized codes demonstrate is the degree of habituation produced when there is a fundamental alignment and reciprocity – an achieved equivalence – between the encoding and decoding sides of an exchange of meanings. The functioning of the codes on the decoding side will frequently assume the status of naturalized perceptions. This leads us to think that the visual sign for 'cow' actually *is* (rather than *represents*) the animal, cow. But if we think of the visual representation of a cow in a manual on animal husbandry – and, even more, of the linguistic sign 'cow' – we can see that both, in different degrees, are *arbitrary* with respect to the concept of the animal they represent. The articulation of an arbitrary sign – whether visual or verbal – with the concept of a referent is the product not of nature but of convention, and the conventionalism of discourses requires the intervention, the support, of codes. Thus Eco has argued that iconic signs 'look like objects in the real world because they reproduce the conditions (that is, the codes) of perception in the viewer'.[5] These 'conditions of perception' are, however, the result of a highly coded, even if virtually unconscious, set of operations – decodings. This is as true of the photographic or televisual image as it is of any other sign. Iconic signs are, however, particularly vulnerable to being 'read' as natural because visual codes of perception are very widely distributed and because this type of sign is less arbitrary than a linguistic sign: the linguistic sign, 'cow' possesses *none* of the properties of the thing represented, whereas the visual sign appears to possess *some* of those properties.

This may help us to clarify a confusion in current linguistic theory and to define precisely how some key terms are being used in this article. Linguistic theory frequently employs the distinction 'denotation' and 'connotation'. The term 'denotation' is widely equated with the literal meaning of a sign: because this literal meaning is almost universally recognized, especially when visual discourse is being employed, 'denotation' has often been confused with a literal transcription of 'reality' in language – and thus with a 'natural sign', one produced without the intervention of a code. 'Connotation', on the other hand, is employed simply to refer to less fixed and therefore more conventionalized and changeable, associative meanings, which clearly vary from instance to instance and therefore must depend on the intervention of codes.

We do *not* use the distinction – denotation/connotation – in this way. From our point of view, the distinction is an *analytic* one only. It is useful, in analysis, to be able to apply a rough rule of thumb which distinguishes those aspects of a sign which appear to be taken, in any language community at any point in time, as its 'literal' meaning (denotation) from the more associative meanings for the sign which it is possible to generate (connotation). But analytic distinctions must not be confused with distinctions in the real world. There will be very few instances in which signs organized in a discourse signify *only* their 'literal' (that is, near-universally consensualized) meaning. In actual discourse most signs will combine both the denotative and the connotative *aspects* (as redefined above). It may, then, be asked why we retain the distinction at all. It is largely a matter of analytic value. It is because signs appear to acquire their full ideological value – appear to be open to articulation with wider ideological discourses and meanings – at the level of their 'associative' meanings (that is, at the connotative level) – for here 'meanings' are *not* apparently fixed in natural perception (that is, they are not fully naturalized), and their fluidity of meaning and association can be more fully exploited and transformed.[6] So it is at the connotative *level* of the sign that situational ideologies alter and transform signification. At this level we can see more clearly the active intervention of ideologies in and on discourse: here, the sign is open to new accentuations and, in Vološinov's terms, enters fully into the struggle over meanings – the class struggle in language.[7] This does not mean that the denotative or 'literal' meaning is outside ideology. Indeed, we could say that its ideological value is strongly *fixed* – because it has become so fully universal and 'natural'. The terms 'denotation' and 'connotation', then, are merely useful analytic tools for distinguishing, in particular contexts, between not the presence/absence of ideology in language but the different levels at which ideologies and discourses intersect.[8]

The level of connotation of the visual sign, of its contextual reference and positioning in different discursive fields of meaning and association, is the point where *already coded* signs intersect with the deep semantic codes of a culture and take on additional, more active ideological dimensions. We might take an example from advertising discourse. Here, too, there is no 'purely denotative', and certainly no 'natural', representation. Every visual sign in advertising connotes a quality, situation, value or inference, which is present as an implication or implied meaning, depending on the connotational positioning. In Barthes's example, the sweater always signifies a 'warm garment' (denotation) and thus the activity/value of 'keeping warm'. But it is also possible, at its more connotative levels, to signify 'the coming of winter' or 'a cold day'. And, in the specialized sub-codes of fashion, sweater may also connote a fashionable style of *haute couture* or, alternatively, an informal style of dress. But set against the right visual background and positioned by the romantic sub-code it may connote 'long autumn walk in the woods'.[9] Codes of this order clearly contract relations for the sign with the wider universe of ideologies in a society. These codes are the means by which power and ideology are made to signify in particular discourses. They refer signs to the 'maps of meaning' into which any culture is classified; and those 'maps of social reality' have the whole range of social meanings, practices, and usages, power and interest 'written in' to them. The connotative levels of signifiers, Barthes remarked, 'have a close communication with culture, knowledge, history, and it is through them, so to speak, that the environmental world invades the linguistic and semantic system. They are, if you like, the fragments of ideology'.[10]

The so-called denotative *level* of the televisual sign is fixed by certain, very complex (but limited or 'closed') codes. But its connotative *level*, though also bounded, is more open, subject to more active *transformations*, which exploit its polysemic values. Any such already constituted sign is potentially transformable into more than one connotative configuration. Polysemy must not, however, be confused with pluralism. Connotative codes are *not* equal among themselves. Any society/culture tends, with varying degrees of closure, to impose its classifications of the social and cultural and political world. These constitute a *dominant cultural order*, though it is neither univocal nor uncontested. This question of the 'structure of discourses in dominance' is a crucial point. The different areas of social life appear to be mapped out into discursive domains, hierarchically organized into *dominant or preferred meanings*. New, problematic or troubling events, which breach our expectancies and run counter to our 'common-sense constructs', to our 'taken-for-granted' knowledge of social structures, must be assigned to their discursive domains before they can be said to 'make sense'. The most common way of 'mapping' them is to assign the new to some domain or other of the existing 'maps of problematic social reality'. We say *dominant*, not 'determined', because it is always possible to order, classify, assign and decode an event within more than one 'mapping'. But we say 'dominant' because there exists a pattern of 'preferred readings'; and these both have the institutional/political/ideological order imprinted in them and have themselves become institutionalized.[11] The domains of 'preferred meanings' have the whole social order embedded in them as a set of meanings, practices and beliefs: the everyday knowledge of social structures, of 'how things work for all practical purposes in this culture', the rank order of power and interest and the structure of legitimations, limits and sanctions. Thus to clarify a 'misunderstanding' at the connotative level, we must refer, *through* the codes, to the orders of social life, of economic and political power and of ideology. Further, since these mappings are 'structured in dominance' but not closed, the communicative process consists not in the unproblematic assignment of every visual item to its given position within a set of prearranged codes, but of *performative rules* – rules of competence and use, of logics-in-use – which seek actively to *enforce* or *pre-fer* one semantic domain over another and rule items into and out of their appropriate meaning-sets. Formal semiology has too often neglected this practice of *interpretative work*, though this constitutes, in fact, the real relations of broadcast practices in television.

In speaking of *dominant meanings*, then, we are not talking about a one-sided process which governs how all events will be signified. It consists of the 'work' required to enforce, win plausibility for and command as legitimate a *decoding* of the event within the limit of dominant definitions in which it has been connotatively signified. Terni has remarked:

> By the word *reading* we mean not only the capacity to identify and decode a certain number of signs, but also the subjective capacity to put them into a creative relation between themselves and with other signs: a capacity which is, by itself, the condition for a complete awareness of one's total environment.[12]

Our quarrel here is with the notion of 'subjective capacity', as if the referent of a televisional discourse were an objective fact but the interpretative level were an individualized and private matter. Quite the opposite seems to be the case. The televisual practice takes 'objective' (that is, systemic) responsibility precisely for the relations which disparate signs contract with one another in any discursive instance, and thus continually rearranges, delimits and prescribes into what 'awareness of one's total environment' these items are arranged.

This brings us to the question of misunderstandings. Television producers who find their message 'failing to get across' are frequently concerned to straigten out the kinks in the communication chain, thus facilitating the 'effectiveness' of their communication. Much research which claims the objectivity of 'policy-oriented analysis' reproduces this administrative goal by attempting to discover how much of a message the audience recalls and to improve the extent of understanding. No doubt misunderstandings of a literal kind do exist. The viewer does not know the terms employed, cannot follow the complex logic of argument or exposition, is unfamiliar with the language, finds the concepts too alien or difficult or is foxed by the expository narrative. But more often broadcasters are concerned that the audience has failed to take the meaning as they – the broadcasters – intended. What they really mean to say is that viewers are not operating within the 'dominant' or 'preferred' code. Their ideal is 'perfectly transparent communication'. Instead, what they have to confront is 'systematically distorted communication'.[13]

In recent years discrepancies of this kind have usually been explained by reference to 'selective perception'. This is the door via which a residual pluralism evades the compulsions of a highly structured, asymmetrical and non-equivalent process. Of course, there will always be private, individual, variant readings. But 'selective perception' is almost never as selective, random or privatized as the concept suggests. The patterns exhibit, across individual variants, significant clusterings. Any new approach to audience studies will therefore have to begin with a critique of 'selective perception' theory.

It was argued earlier that since there is no necessary correspondence between encoding and decoding, the former can attempt to 'pre-fer' but cannot prescribe or guarantee the latter, which has its own conditions of existence. Unless they are wildly aberrant, encoding will have the effect of constructing some of the limits and parameters within which decodings will operate. If there were no limits, audiences could simply read whatever they liked into any message. No doubt some total misunderstandings of this kind do exist. But the vast range must contain *some* degree of reciprocity between encoding and decoding moments, otherwise we could not speak of an effective communicative exchange at all. Nevertheless, this 'correspondence' is not given but constructed. It is not 'natural' but the product of an articulation between two distinct moments. And the former cannot determine or guarantee, in a simple sense, which decoding codes will be employed. Otherwise communication would be a perfectly equivalent circuit, and every message would be an instance of 'perfectly transparent communication'. We must think, then, of the variant articulations in which encoding/decoding can be combined. To elaborate on this, we offer a hypothetical analysis of some possible decoding positions, in order to reinforce the point of 'no necessary correspondence'.[14]

We identify *three* hypothetical positions from which decodings of a televisual discourse may be constructed. These need to be empirically tested and refined. But the argument that decodings do not follow inevitably from encodings, that they are not identical, reinforces the argument of 'no necessary correspondence'. It also helps to deconstruct the common-sense meaning of 'misunderstanding' in terms of a theory of 'systematically distorted communication'.

The first hypothetical position is that of the *dominant-hegemonic position*. When the viewer takes the connoted meaning from, say, a television newscast or current affairs programme full and straight, and decodes the message in terms of the reference code in which it has been encoded, we might say that the viewer *is operating inside the dominant code*. This is the ideal-typical case of 'perfectly transparent communication' – or as close as we are likely to come to it 'for all practical purposes'. Within this we can distinguish the positions produced by the *professional code*. This is the position (produced by what we perhaps ought to identify as the operation of a 'metacode') which the professional broadcasters assume when encoding a message which has *already* been signified in a hegemonic manner. The professional code is 'relatively independent' of the dominant code, in that it applies criteria and transformational operations of its own, especially those of a technico-practical nature. The professional code, however, operates *within* the 'hegemony' of the dominant code. Indeed, it serves to reproduce the dominant definitions precisely by bracketing their hegemonic quality and operating instead with displaced professional codings which foreground such apparently neutral-technical questions as visual quality, news and presentational values, televisual quality, 'professionalism' and so on. The hegemonic interpretations of, say, the politics of Northern Ireland, or the Chilean *coup* or the Industrial Relations Bill are principally generated by political and military elites: the particular choice of presentational occasions and formats, the selection of personnel, the choice of images, the staging of debates are selected and combined through the operation of the professional code. How the broadcasting professionals are able *both* to operate with 'relatively autonomous' codes of their own *and* to act in such a way as to reproduce (not without contradiction) the hegemonic signification of events is a complex matter which cannot be further spelled out here. It must suffice to say tht the professionals are linked with the defining elites not only by the institutional position of broadcasting itself as an 'ideological apparatus',[15] but also by the structure of *access* (that is, the systematic 'over-accessing' of selective elite personnel and their 'definition of the situation' in television). It may even be said that the professional codes serve to reproduce hegemonic definitions specifically by *not overtly* biasing their operations in a dominant direction: ideological reproduction therefore takes place here inadvertently, unconsciously, 'behind men's backs'.[16] Of course, conflicts, contradictions and even misunderstandings regularly arise between the dominant and the professional significations and their signifying agencies.

The second position we would identify is that of the *negotiated code* or position. Majority audiences probably understand quite adequately what has been dominantly defined and professionally signified. The dominant definitions, however, are hegemonic precisely because they represent definitions of situations and events which are 'in dominance', (*global*). Dominant definitions connect events, implicitly or explicitly, to grand totalizations, to the great syntagmatic views-of-the-world: they take 'large views' of issues: they relate events to the 'national interest' or to the level of geo-politics, even if they make these connections in truncated, inverted or mystified ways. The definition of a hegemonic viewpoint is (a) that it defines within its terms the mental horizon, the universe, of possible meanings, of a whole sector of relations in a society or culture; and (b) that it carries with it the stamp of legitimacy – it appears coterminous with what is 'natural', 'inevitable', 'taken for granted' about the social order. Decoding within the *negotiated version* contains a mixture of adaptive and oppositional elements: it acknowledges the legitimacy of the hegemonic definitions to make the grand significations (abstract), while, at a more restricted, situational (situated) level, it makes its own ground rules – it operates with exceptions to the rule. It accords the privileged position to the dominant definitions of events while reserving the right to make a more negotiated application to 'local conditions', to its own more *corporate* positions. This negotiated version of the dominant ideology is thus shot through with contradictions, though these are only on certain occasions brought to full visibility. Negotiated codes operate through what we might call particular or situated logics: and these logics are sustained by their differential and unequal relation to the discourses and logics of power. The simplest example of a negotiated code is that which governs the response of a worker to the notion of an Industrial Relations Bill limiting the right to strike or to arguments for a wages freeze. At the level of the 'national interest' economic debate the decoder may adopt the hegemonic definition, agreeing that 'we must all pay ourselves less in order to combat inflation'. This, however, may have little or no relation to his/her willingness to go on strike for better pay and conditions or to oppose the Industrial Relations Bill at the level of shop-floor or union organization. We suspect that the great majority of so-called 'misunderstandings' arise from the contradictions and disjunctures between hegemonic-dominant encodings and negotiated-corporate decodings. It is just these mismatches in the levels which most provoke defining elites and professionals to identify a 'failure in communications'.

Finally, it is prossible for a viewer perfectly to understand both the literal and the connotative inflection given by a discourse but to decode the message in a *globally* contrary way. He/she detotalizes the message in the preferred code in order to retotalize the message within some alternative framework of reference. This is the case of the viewer who listens to a debate on the need to limit wages but 'reads' every mention of the 'national interest' as 'class interest'. He/she is operating with what we must call an *oppositional code*. One of the most significant political moments (they also coincide with crisis points within the broadcasting organizations themselves, for obvious reasons) is the point when events which are normally signified and decoded in a negotiated way begin to be given an oppositional reading. Here the 'politics of signification' – the struggle in discourse – is joined.

Notes

1 For an explication and commentary on the methodological implications of Marx's argument, see S. Hall (1974) A reading of Marx's 1857 *Introduction to the Grundrisse*, *WPCS*, 6.
2 J.D. Halloran (1973) Understanding television. Paper for the Council of Europe Colloquy on Understanding Television, University of Leicester.
3 G. Gerbner *et al.* (1970) *Violence in TV Drama: A Study of Trends and Symbolic Functions*. Pennsylvania: The Annenberg School, University of Pennsylvania.
4 Charles Peirce (1931–58) Speculative grammar, *Collected Papers*. Cambridge, MA: Harvard University Press.
5 Umberto Eco, Articulations of the cinematic code, *Cinemantics*, No. 1.
6 See the argument in S. Hall (1972) Determinations of news photographs, *WPCS*, 3.
7 Vološinov (1973) *Marxism and the Philosophy of Language*. The Seminar Press.
8 For a similar clarification, see Marina Camargo Heck, Ideological dimensions of media messages.
9 Roland Barthes (1971) Rhetoric of the image, *WPCS* 1.
10 Roland Barthes (1967) *Elements of Semiology*. Cape.
11 For an extended critique of 'preferred reading', see Alan O'Shea, Preferred reading. Unpublished paper, CCCS, University of Birmingham.
12 P. Terni (1973) Memorandum, Council of Europe Colloquy on Understanding

Television, University of Leicester.

13 The phrase is Habermas's (1970) in Systematically distorted communications, in P. Dretzel (ed.) *Recent Sociology 2*. Collier-Macmillan. It is used here, however, in a different way.

14 For a sociological formulation which is close, in some ways, to the positions outlined here but which does not parallel the argument about the theory of discourse, see Frank Parkin (1971), *Class Inequality and Political Order*. Macgibbon and Kee.

15 See Louis Althusser (1971). Ideology and ideological state apparatuses, *Lenin and Philosophy and Other Essays*. New Left Books.

16 For an expansion of this argument, see Stuart Hall (1972). The external/internal dialectic in broadcasting, *4th Symposium on Broadcasting*. University of Manchester, and (1976) Broadcasting and the state: the independence/impartiality couplet, AMCR Symposium, University of Leicester, CCCS unpublished paper.

NEWS WE CAN USE
AN AUDIENCE PERSPECTIVE ON THE TABLOIDISATION OF NEWS IN THE UNITED STATES

5

S. Elizabeth Bird

Tabloidisation and the audience

Critics often place the blame for tabloidisation on the journalism profession itself. Thus Krajicek (1998, 3) writes: 'Initially, tabloidization occurred not by conscious decision but by collective assent among reporters and editors. It happened because too many journalists like me were willing to acquiesce to a series of breaches of the traditional values of our occupation.' These critics often seem to overlook the impetus coming not from journalists, but from the audience. Krajicek does ask an important question: 'Does society define news or does news define society? Do the media condition reality or reflect it?' (p. 12). While critics agree that the audience has a role in determining the direction in which journalism is going, limited empirical work has been done on how audiences actually view news, how they define it, and what they do with it. These are the questions I wish to address here.

In fact in most cases, with the obvious exception of such studies as Morley (1980) and Jensen (1990), analyses of news make assumptions about the audience from the texts themselves. Some critics have applied psychological explanations for the preference for sensational stories,

S. Elizabeth Bird (1997) News we can use: an audience perspective on the tabloidisation of news in the United States, *Javnost/The Public*, 5(3): 35–49. Reprinted by kind permission of *Javnost/The Public*/S. Elizabeth Bird.

defining the audience as 'sensation seekers' who need increasing doses of exposure (Zuckerman 1984), or as 'morbidly curious' (Haskins 1984). These explanations have the effect of neuroticising the audience as sick or abnormal if they are attracted to unwholesome news. Or if the audience is considered at all, it is often to condemn them as lacking in taste and judgement, as Langer (1992) discusses. In more recent developments, cultural studies scholars have discovered the active audience for sensational news. Thus Fiske (1992) and Glynn (1990) celebrate the tabloid style in print and television, arguing that audiences may epitomise De Certeau's 'textual poachers' (1984), characterised by 'sceptical reading competencies that are equivalent of the social competencies by which the people control the immediate conditions of their everyday lives' (Fiske 1992: 54). From this perspective, tabloid news, with its mocking, irreverent style, is actually subversive, allowing the 'people' to challenge the hegemony of the 'power bloc.' However, as Sparks (1992) ably points out, there is little evidence that readers and viewers of news actually take the ironic stance that Fiske celebrates, and empirical work on American tabloid readers challenges Fiske's assertions (Bird 1992). Fiske posits an active, critical audience which is able to read critique of the status quo into all kinds of popular journalistic texts, but as Sparks suggests, most popular news actually reflects a reactionary stance.

As I have written elsewhere (Bird 1992), I am also unconvinced that the sceptical, carnivalesque reading of tabloid style is actually typical of most consumers of this kind of news. I do not see tabloid consumption as essentially subversive or transgressive, but neither do I see enjoyment of tabloid-style news as a symptom of mindlessness either. Rather, I am more inclined to see audiences as active, selective readers, who approach all kinds of news with the unstated question: 'What can I get from this information, or this story. How does it apply to my life, and why should I pay attention?' Journalists and critics fret about what people *should* want to know, and readers and viewers are also frequently torn between what they ought to be interested in and what actually captures their attention. Perhaps if we can understand what does capture attention, we might be able to develop a journalism that could embrace tabloid style, while still inviting audiences to participate more fully in a civic democracy.

Following from my earlier work on supermarket tabloids, a preliminary, small-scale study has been an attempt to throw some light on the role that news stories play in everyday life. What kinds of stories do people find memorable? What do they do with them? How does an understanding of what readers and viewers actually do with news help us in understanding both the value and the dangers of the tabloidisation trend. In this study, I used a two-phase, somewhat experimental technique, aimed at eliciting data that tried to approximate everyday experience. For the study, I prepared a videotape made up of excerpts from the Rupert Murdoch tabloid TV show, *A Current Affair*, the reality show *Unsolved Mysteries*, and an episode of ABC's *World News Tonight*. Copies were lent to a small sample of people (22), who watched the tapes in their homes with a family member or friend, and then discussed the tapes, recording the conversation with a small audio tape recorder. Some guiding questions were included, asking, for example, which stories they found most memorable and why. Later, I interviewed the same people by phone, asking them a range of similar questions, such as what the idea of 'news' meant to them; which kind of news stories they paid attention to, and so on. Through all of this, I was trying to get a sense of how news fits into people's lives on an ongoing basis.[1]

At this point, I wish to focus on some of the aspects of the study that speak directly to the issue of tabloidisation. Although there is no single, clear definition of the term, some themes are consistent. Among them are the rise of a 'storytelling' news style, focusing on personal narratives about individuals. Indeed, Sparks (1992: 39) suggests that one of the hallmarks of popular journalistic style is that, The popular conception of the personal becomes the explanatory framework within which the social order is presented as transparent. Second, we see the increasing predominance of the visual image over analysis and rational description, a trend remarked upon by countless cultural and media critics, and certainly not confined to the genre of news (see, for example, Jhally 1987; Ewen 1988). Related to both points is the growing use of dramatic techniques, such as photo enhancement and re-enactments.

News and storytelling

Journalism's emphasis on the personal, the sensational and the dramatic is, of course, not new. Street literature, ballads, and oral gossip and rumour have all contributed to the development of news as we know it (Bird and Dardenne 1988; Stephens 1988; Bird 1992). Critics have been pontificating about the salacious excesses of newspapers for generations; even mainstream news has always been torn between what practitioners see as a duty to inform, and their need to entertain and engage their audience. The human interest story in itself is not to so much a symptom of tabloidisation, which is better characterised as the triumph of the human interest story as the *central* component of news. My study does suggest that the growing personalisation of the news is indeed audience driven, although there are other factors involved.

Existing surveys confirm the preference for human interest stories, while at the same time describing many people's feelings of guilt about this preference (see, for example, Price and Czilli 1996). The Pew Research Center for the People and the Press concluded that in 1997, Americans were happier with their own lives, felt more religious conviction and were less attentive to the news than at any time in recent years (1998: 1). From 1986–96, 25 percent of respondents closely followed the news stories tracked by Pew, while only 19 percent did in 1997. The death of Princess Diana was the only story that attracted the close attention of a majority of people surveyed, while for the second consecutive year, not one domestic policy story made the annual list of top 10 news stories (p. 1). Parker and Deane (1997) write that although only small percentages of people claim to follow stories about scandal and entertainment, the data suggest that the public *knows more* about these types of stories than it does about virtually any other category of news. On average the public answered 60 percent of the questions dealing with scandal, entertainment and crime correctly (p. 6), a percentage far higher than any other category.

Critics often seem baffled by this. How can people spend so much time thinking about such obviously 'trivial' topics? Part of that bafflement comes from a difference in the way journalists/critics and audiences define news and how it is used. Journalism critics tend to define news in terms of how effective the texts of news stories are at conveying information about the world to readers and viewers. They assume that readers consume news in order to learn facts about the world around them and be informed. In that respect, they follow what Carey (1975) calls a 'transmission' view of communication. Audience definitions also include this 'informing' function, although I believe the cultural pressure to be informed is felt less and less today. But everyday definitions of news focus more on how these stories are inserted in people's daily lives, growing and becoming the subjects of speculation and discussion. As Dahlgren writes: 'Audiences can take the stories and 'run' with them, in many directions' (1992: 15). Much of the news that readers and viewers are exposed to is either ignored or forgotten almost immediately; from the audience perspective, relevant news consists of stories that take on a life of their own outside the immediate context of the newspaper or television broadcast.

Stories that do take on life tend to be dramatic and personal – these are the stories that people actually remember, as I shall show. This is not necessarily a bad thing; the rise of talk shows, tabloid news, and other forums has allowed concerns to be raised that otherwise would not be.

Showing the personal side of public events is probably the most effective way to make people understand the impact of those events. And people want personal stories because they are memorable. Anthropologist John Rayfield showed quite convincingly years ago that the kind of stories people remember are chronological narratives, with a clear structure, a moral point, and vivid imagery. Traditional inverted pyramid news stories, with the standard 'who, what, where' – format, were the most difficult to remember.

My research bears this out. Invariably, the stories the participants recalled and wanted to talk about were the *Current Affair* and *Unsolved Mysteries* ones, even those people who said they despised such shows. By contrast, most respondents found it hard to remember any of the *World News* stories, even though they had just sat through them. Respondents aged over 35 were far more likely to say the more traditional *World News* approach was better, more accurate, and what news was about. For these viewers, being informed was a value in itself, yet even they were not moved to talk with enthusiasm about hard news. Compare, for example, these two exchanges between a middle-aged (40s), married couple. First, they discuss the *World News* segment:

Wife: Oh yes, there was something about the economy

Husband: They were discussing the economics, where Clinton says he's going to do something about it, and the Republicans say, well, don't fix it if it ain't broke. And more or less to that effect...

Wife: Well the Republicans kept saying things were getting better, and the Democrats kept saying they weren't...

Husband: Yeah.

Wife: And then the growth for the last three months of the quarter were 3.8, which is a pretty good...

Husband: Which is a pretty good growth, yeah.

Wife: Growth, Umm...

Later, the same couple talks about the segment on *Unsolved Mysteries*, which involved a story about a purported UFO landing. The difference in their tone is clear:

Wife: I think the show about the UFO was interesting in that there are so many unanswered questions.

Husband: Yes, why did the guy get burned? Was he burned because of the radiation that was in the ground, apparently there before?

Wife: But why in circles? Or buttons, as he called them himself...

Husband: Where he got burned. Yeah, I don't know.

Wife: And I was surprised...

Husband: Yeah, and why did his shirt catch on fire when that ship took off? How does that, how did that occur, it looked like he was a decent distance away from it.

Wife: Oh, he was running away from it, though. They didn't show that they found the burned shirt, that's, I wondered if that was anywhere around...

Husband: And why did the compass go bonkers? There's lots of questions...

The couple went on to discuss the story animatedly for several more minutes, returning to it later. In contrast, participants generally found it difficult to discuss hard news stories at all, except in terms of their personal interests. This applied especially to those who expressed a clear disdain for news as 'boring,' the word used most by as younger respondents. Males in their twenties were more negative about *World News Tonight* than any other group, reacting strongly to its lack of dramatic appeal. Even the perceived importance of a story did not change that, as this exchange between a college student and his friend illustrates:

Respondent: The, uh, all the ABC *World News Tonight*, that sucked.

Friend: Yeah, they were lame.

Respondent: Waiting for those verdicts in the LA riots. That was kinda interesting. I mean, 'cause that was such a big national deal. But the story wasn't that great.

Friend: Yeah, not that interesting.

It was only when a story actually hit a personal chord that these young men conversed about the program at all. For example, a segment on the Clinton policy on permitting gay people in the military, which tended to be ignored or dismissed by older respondents and women, made for a few minutes of conversation:

Respondent: Do you think it's bad that they're gonna maybe be in there?

Friend: I mean it's just like, I mean there's gay guys ... you know, military and everyone's close and your showering together and stuff.

Respondent: I'd hate it.

Friend: I mean, yeah, you never know if some gay guy's looking at you.

Respondent: Pick up that soap for me man.

Friend: Yeah, you're in the shower, you ain't gonna be pickin' up no soap.

This pattern continued throughout the taped conversations. Older people expressed a concern for being informed, while younger people often aggressively rejected the very notion, but both groups became engaged when stories spoke to their personal interests or convictions. In follow-up interviews, this preference for the personal story came over just as strongly. Thus a woman in her 50s says:

Well, I'm interested in people. I just like people and I like to know about them ... That little girl that fell down the well in Texas ... The boy that had his arms got caught in the threshing machine ... I'm very interested to see how things come out on those kind of cases.

A male college student explains his preference for talk shows:

This is the actual people talking about their problems, and you get questions from a bunch of people, instead of, you know, three or four ideas from producers or whatever, so you get all these people asking questions from different angles.

A woman in her 30s likes to see

people living their lives, and what's happening in their lives, and how they're bettering their lives, or how they're screwing up their lives ... I guess I'm just more interested in that type of thing ... It is very important to know what's going on ... in a larger perspective, too, but I guess I just find it more interesting.

As another late-30s woman puts it, she likes emotional stories because, 'life without emotion is life without feeling, life without forethought, and life without good results. You've got to feel in order to react.' She continues, 'there's a lot of reasons why things happen, a lot of reasons why people do the things they do, and if a person understands the story behind it, they can have a better idea and a better awareness to avoid being in that situation themselves ...' These comments point to the way that news stories are applied to a person's life, an issue to which I will return. A female college student explicitly describes the value of the story:

> They (tabloid shows) seem to start from the beginning, like if they do have a person on who is in this big news event, they'll, like, start from them when they were real little, and them growing up, and them getting married, and you find out stuff, ... and they just make the whole ordeal sound like something that could happen to anybody ... Then they give a nice little conclusion about what's going on with them now, and on *Current Affair*, they give every little news item, like, a little name ... That kind of makes it seem more of a good story.

A cardinal rule of journalism has long been to learn how to put a human face on current events. I would not quarrel with that, tending to agree with John Tomlinson (1997: 77) that 'Personalization can be read here not as trivialisation but as achieving greater imaginative proximity to the lifeworld of the audience.' There is certainly a case for seeing the increasing move to the personal as a democratisation of news, a chance for all voices to be heard, and thus an opening up of public discourse. Feminist theorists have argued that forums like talk shows allow the private, female realm to enter the public sphere, so that feminine discourse about the personal is seen as a valuable part of public debate. Indeed, Grindstaff, while she has mixed feelings about mainstream conventions in journalism: 'If talk shows are to be criticised for turning the experiences of ordinary people into a circus sideshow, then the so-called respectable media must also be taken to task for rendering these people so completely invisible in the first place that daytime talk is their best or only option for public exposure' (Grindstaff 1997: 196). While journalists and media critics wring their hands because the public 'needs' to be informed and is apparently perversely resisting this need, people themselves say, 'why do I need to know this; what difference does it make to *my* life?'

Furthermore, elite definitions of news and popular definitions are often at odds, in that news that would be dismissed as salacious gossip by critics may be perceived as useful information by audiences, helping them discuss and deal with issues of morality, law and order, and so on, in their daily lives. A case in point is a story that became almost synonymous with 'tabloidisation' in the United States in the 1992–93 Amy Fisher/Joey Buttafuoco saga, which chronicled the trial and imprisonment of 16-year-old Fisher for the attempted murder of her middle-aged lover's wife. Amy Fisher drove critics to despair. Pointing out that indexed clippings of the story topped 100,000 by 1996, Krajicek (1998: 15) writes: 'For most of the 1990s Buttafuoco's every belch appeared as news in hundreds of newspapers and on scores of television news programs in the United States, Canada, and abroad ... he was covered relentlessly, beyond all reason.' Each of the three network television stations produced a movie about the case, and a survey showed that by January 1993, 40 percent of Americans had seen at least one of them (Parker and Deane 1997). Buttafuoco was given massive coverage again in December 1995 when he violated his parole. 'Since 1992 the mass media had been attached to Buttafuoco like barnacles. If I had chosen to do so, I could have had informed conversations about Buttafuoco with friends in California, relatives in Nebraska and Florida, and colleagues in Toronto' (Krajicek 1998, 137).

Of course, that was exactly the point. People were indeed conversing about Amy and Joey all over the country, and greatly enjoying it. A snippet of conversation between a mother and her teenage daughter in my study points to the conscious way in which people participated in the story, which was open to range of interpretations:

Daughter: As many people as watched the Super Bowl watched the Amy Fisher story on all three networks. It was on all the talk shows, it was on all the news head lines. *Current Affair, Inside Edition.* And that was how America lived for four weeks, or however long.

Mother: And didn't we like it because we could be the judge?

Daughter: Well, yeah.

Mother: Didn't we like it because we were being the judge of that? We could point our fingers which ever way we wanted it. We could make it Joey's fault, we could make it Amy's fault, we could make it her folks' fault. We could make it anybody's fault we wanted. We could be the jury.

As people speculate, they tend to look for answers from within their own experience. What would I do if this happened to me? How can I prevent this happening to someone I know? During the period of my interviews, the Amy Fisher/Joey Buttafuoco scandal was at its height. Although the story was not on the tape, several participants raised it as an example of distasteful sensationalism, yet were almost irresistibly drawn to discuss it. From an audience point of view, the best stories are those that leave room for speculation, for debate, and for a degree of audience 'participation.'[2] It was clear that people of different ages and backgrounds applied the story differently in their lives. Thus, a 67-year-old woman said:

Oh, I think it's rather creepy. Let me tell you, I'm retired now, but I was a social worker. And I ... worked with a lot of people ... a little bit lower in morals, and so forth ... and I guess I'm kind of hoping he gets his, too ... I think we all know things like that go on, and again you can look at it from several standpoints as the woman is blamed, although certainly she was wrong, and I just have an idea that he probably egged her on ... so I think he's equally guilty. And I think she was, oh, you know, just a young gal who thought everything would be OK if she just got rid of the wife. Naive. Even though she was well-versed in sexual matters.

A second woman, age 39, stresses different elements in the story:

It was just an amazingly huge story, and it was this young girl, older man, and I think what made it kind of interesting was the wife being so strong behind her husband, and I found that kind of fascinating myself, because everything just seemed to stack against him ... And Amy steadfastly stands behind her story, too, they all do. And it's, I guess it's whatever you want to believe, and everybody takes it their own way ... And to think that a young girl would actually, you know, shoot another woman in a love affair, I guess...

A 21-year-old woman perhaps reflects on her closer sense of identification with the teenage Amy Fisher:

It's a thing I could never imagine happening to me, being involved in a murder, or having this big love triangle or something ... I mean, how did Amy get into that situation, that she had to shoot that sleazy guy's wife, I mean you'd have to be desperate, and he must have had some kind of hold on her – he was just slime, don't you think? I mean really, his wife didn't deserve that ... If I ever thought my life was bad, at least I'm not this person.

Finally, a woman in her forties saw the story as a vehicle for speculation that led into a consideration of what sort of circumstances throw ordinary people into these extraordinary events:

You know we watched a couple of 'em here, my kids and I. Because, I don't know why we did, I think because we had read so much about it, and then they had the different sides, and it was sort of like, we watched it and then we decided who we really thought was the guilty person, and who gave us the facts and who didn't, and ... but it's garbage, I mean, really, it's garbage.

When asked why this story was so interesting, she continued:

Just maybe human nature, I guess ... like when I hear about stuff like that, what I always ask myself is how, you know, how could they get to that point ... it's, you know, you cannot relate at all to what this person has done or why they've done it, and so you want this explanation ... And maybe that's because you're afraid that your next door neighbor could end up like that, you know.

Human interest stories are clearly integrated into this woman's life, allowing her to interrogate boundaries, questions of motivation, and issues that seem much more relevant to her life than, say, economic news. An important aspect of this process is that it is participatory. As we struggle to make sense of a story, we involve others in the negotiation of meaning. Thus a 21-year-old man says: 'When you watch by yourself, a lot of times you have ideas that you have unsolved because you can't converse with other individuals ...' A 37-year-old woman agrees: 'I feel that in order to really be a good conversationalist, you can't be self-centred, and I want to hear everyone's opinion about what's going on in the news. There's something in their view that I can use, and hopefully there's something in my view that can contribute to making theirs better.' She considers *Unsolved Mysteries* to be important news because 'it helps others in the community feel a part of the news world ... The community or the listeners get to contribute to the story and make the news effective and be part of the results.'

The power of the image

Another thing that makes stories memorable, and thus worth paying attention to, is the vivid verbal or visual image. Television news has always had the advantage of the visual image, and has long been criticised for misusing or sensationalising it, as was print journalism before it. The debate over what images are appropriate continues, but one often-cited symptom of tabloidisation is the way the image has crowded out rational analysis. For television, the existence of an image will actually determine whether a story is used or not, especially on that most ratings-driven genre, local news, which is watched by far more Americans than national news. As Krajicek (1998: 24) writes, 'Today the possession of any 'hot' video means there *will* be a story, whether it rates a story or not.' American local news is a litany of unconnected, usually violent images, often of events that have no immediate relevance to the region in which they're shown – freeway pileups, fires, police chases and stand-offs. A 1995 survey by Rocky Mountain Media Watch of 100 local television broadcasts found that 42 percent of air-time was devoted to such 'mayhem' (Krajicek 1998: 27). In addition, local news anchors are encouraged to display visual aids whenever possible – not just the traditional charts and graphs, but such items as cans of beans to illustrate a consumer story: 'I began to wonder how many of the day's stories were selected not on the basis of traditional news values ... but on the basis of prop value: how quickly and cheaply the broadcasters could find a prop to go with the story' (Heider 1998: B8). The trend in local news is exemplified perfectly in a recent promotional campaign for a Tampa Bay ABC affiliate station, comprising a series of 30-second spots that began airing in the summer of 1997. The most frequently-shown spot was shot in slow-motion with sepia colours. It began with images of local scenes and people, moving into images of the flag raising at Iwo Jima; John Kennedy Jr. saluting at his father's funeral; and the wedding of Charles and Diana, before ending with more local images and finally the faces of the two news anchors. The voice-over went as follows:

Female Anchor: The best news is always about people. The look in somebody's eyes will tell you much more about what's happening than a million pages of news copy ever will.

Male Anchor: Think about the images that will always be in your mind. They are the faces of history, faces that show in a glance what something feels like. The news is made by people, and the news should be about people.

Female Anchor: I'm Marty Tucker.

Male Anchor: And I'm Brendan McLaughlin. And we're part of something real. 28 Tampa Bay News. Real people, real news.

The final sentence became the signature slogan that now appears on the channel throughout the day.

Going one step further than the visually-obsessed local news channels, tabloid TV shows from their beginning were not even constrained by the availability of actual news footage. Instead, they have developed the art of the re-enactment, or dramatisation, in which actual events are recreated by actors for the cameras. According to Krajicek (1998: 42), the re-enactment was probably first used in August 1986 when *A Current Affair* aired a dramatisation of events leading up to what became known as the 'Preppy Murder,' a widely-publicised case in which a wealthy young man, Robert Chambers, was accused of killing student Jennifer Levin. In the following decade, the technique became a stock feature of reality shows and syndi-cated news magazines, and is widely cited as one of the key elements in tabloidisation. Indeed, it seemed for a while that the re-enactment was one of the few features that separated tabloid news from serious news. But recently, dramatisations have started to creep into network news magazines such as *Dateline NBC, 20/20*, and *Turning Point*, as well as in local news, particularly in crime re-enactments that mimic national shows like *America's Most Wanted*. Gradually the dramatisation is beginning to be seen as just another way to enhance the story, to bring it to life.

In my research, I was interested in how people perceive such techniques. While it would be unsafe to draw major conclusions from a small project, I was intrigued by a generational difference that emerged. Middle-aged and older people did not like re-enactments, seeing them as somehow cheating, as detracting from the reality of the news, probably a view shared by most journalism critics. Typical was a women in her 40s who appreciates the dramatic value of the technique, while clearly distrusting the effects:

Well, it's a great tactic, you know, because there's nothing that sticks in a person's mind longer than the picture of something. ... Visual effects like that are very effective, but you know my thought is ... how do they really know? ... I mean, were these people unkept and unshaven, or were they really pretty and sexy-looking, and smelled like Aramis? I don't know ... if I'm just looking at it and not thinking about it, it would make it more real because of the visual effects. But my mind always goes back and says, how do they know?

This woman points to the fact that the dramatisation can actually seem 'more real,' unless the viewer actively works against seeing it that way. Younger people, however, seemed much less bothered by the technique – in fact it may enhance their appreciation. Thus a male college student comments:

It's sometimes hard to visualise how things happen, and when they do re-cap 'em, it does help ... For example, I was watchin' (*Rescue*) *911* one time, and an ambulance was following a car, and the car that they were following, the mother had a seizure and she fell asleep at the wheel, and there was a baby in the front seat, and they totally recapped this, the story, and the thing was, she was like bouncin' off curbs, and swervin', and one of the ambulance drivers got out and tried to run and catch the car. You know, the story went on and on and on, and just how they showed it, I mean you're like, wow, that really can happen. And I'd say somethin' like that was really beneficial to understand the story. Kind of like a movie ... I mean people want to see what happened and how it happened, and when you're watchin' the regular news, I mean, they just tell you what happened.

Later in the interview, this young man was talking about how he now believed that the government is hiding things from the people When did this come to him? 'Oh, yeah, after I saw *JFK*. That really changed my view.' Once again, we see how something that is actually a recreation, told for dramatic purposes, is perceived as more convincing than either traditional news or history. Another male college student agreed. 'I like it because it lets you know exactly what's going on ... whereas words you can still, you know, imagine things.' When asked if this might create a danger that the audience might not be seeing what actually happened, he replied, 'No ... They have no reason to really lie.'

If there really is a generational difference, is it because younger people are indeed the visual generation? Are they more easily persuaded by the truth of visual images, which are seen as somehow transparent, obvious, unmediated? Perhaps the 'realness' of something may be more tied up with the impact of the images, rather than whether those images correspond to any outside reality. If that is true, it is a worrying thought, particularly as we get deeper into an era where technology makes image manipulation more and more sophisticated, and where constructed images and documentary images become more seamlessly intertwined. For at the same time, the younger people in my study were also the most likely to be cynical and untrusting of *any* news or any 'facts' generally, reflecting a kind of relativism that is often seen as the hall-mark of the postmodern age. From this perspective, any viewpoint, any 'fact' is as likely to be as 'true' as any other. Perhaps it is the fact that is presented with most drama and visual impact, the one that can 'break through the clutter' as advertisers say, that in the end wins out.

Reality does seem to be an important value for viewers. If something is real, and happening to actual people, it carries a ring of authenticity about it. The enormous popularity of shows like *Cops, America's Funniest Home Videos*, and the endless video compilations aired by Murdoch's Fox network, such as *When Animals Attack*, attests to this. Producers can get away with poor production values if the effect is 'real.' Yet at the same time, young viewers seem happy to accept the ability of producers to stage or re-enact events to make them more real than real. Like the young man quoted above, a young woman in the study argued that 'everything that was said (on the re-enactment) was things that really came out of one of the people's mouth at one time during the case ... I mean, like ... they can't twist it too much because they have to give people rights.'

Grindstaff (1997: 192) describes how talk shows respond to the very audience demands I have been discussing: 'Producers want 'real' people to provide first-hand testimony about their personal experience as it relates to the topic at hand, the more emoting the better. They do not want distanced analysis, or complicated discussions of politics or law.' Yet at the same time these real people can be hard to handle: 'these are the guests who, in some ways, pose the greatest challenge to producers because the very qualities that make them 'real' make them more difficult to manage in routine ways. The pressure of deadlines, the nature of the topics, and the performances required of guests actually push producers toward people who *are* media savvy, have had prior talk-show experience, and may even be actors faking their stories' (p.189).

What does it all mean?

So we know that news audiences generally prefer lively, dramatic, human interest stories over news about political and economic issues, and this is not necessarily a terrible thing. As Dahlgren (1992: 16) writes, news can and should be pleasurable, even though 'the discourses of journalism cannot admit this.' He goes on to argue that 'journalism ... often *does* foster ... feelings of collective belonging ... yet this is rarely recognized and even more seldom praised' (p. 17). The conversations that viewers and readers have about news stories serve to bind people together, and given them common topics of conversation in a world in which common ties are getting fewer and fewer. News stories of scandals, even of such trivial tales as Amy Fisher and Joey Buttafuoco, offer an entry point to everyday discussions of morality, boundaries, and appropriate behaviour (see essays in Lull and Hinerman 1997).

A common line of argument against this is, of course, that knowledge of trivia prevents people from learning about important issues. As Krajicek (1998: 137) puts it, 'We all knew too much about Joey, which told me that we knew less than we should have about something else.' The Pew Research Center even suggests that human interest stories *cause* viewers to be ignorant: 'Not surprisingly, we found that knowledge about what was happening in Bosnia decreased with the number of Amy Fisher movies watched' (Pew Research Center 1997: 3). Unfortunately, 'there is little evidence to suggest that if people were not discussing Amy and Joey, they would necessarily be discussing the situation in Bosnia.'

In other words, audiences do make active choices about the news they can use, and berating them about what they should be interested in is unlikely to have much effect. However, audiences can only run with the stories they are given; as Sparks (1992: 37) comments, 'the sense which people can make of newspapers depends at least in part on what the journalists have actually written in the first place.' The current climate of tabloidisation in news is a product of the dynamic between audiences, journalists, and economic forces. Stories like Amy Fisher are demonstrably popular, and earn ratings. But they are also cheap and easy for news outlets all over the country to run they are delivered on the wires, and they can fill hours and inches of news space profitably, for very little reporting effort. A newspaper or broadcast that is full of Amy Fisher stories does not have a staff digging to uncover financial mismanagement or corruption. In that respect, the human interest story, especially the big, national story, *is* pushing out diversity of information from the news media. And if stories are not placed on the agenda by the media, the audience cannot discuss them.

The danger as I see it, is not the personalisation of news in itself. The best kind of human interest stories do indeed increase our knowledge and understanding of important events – it may have taken John Hersey's *Hiroshima* to make many Americans understand the human devastation of the atomic bomb. Tomlinson (1997: 73) is optimistic about the power of the personal story to have impact and genuinely inform: 'Those experiences that penetrate deepest into our lifeworld are the ones that can be imaginatively incorporated into this on-going narrative of self-identity.' He argues that journalists must try harder to interpret important national and global issues in personal terms in order to engage audiences. Indeed, that does happen. We may recall a famous photograph of two lovers in the former Yugoslavia, who died under gunfire while trying to reach safety. It was certainly emotional and sensational, yet that photo and the explanatory story probably introduced many Americans to the reality of a situation of which they had only been vaguely aware. People talked about that story in their leisure time, just as they talked about famine in Somalia once they had noticed the heart-wrenching pictures and stories of dying children.

But even this kind of fairly superficial reporting requires resources and the will to try. It is cheaper and easier to buy wire stories and pictures that do not require interpretation or analysis, or to focus on shocking or heart-warming tales generated locally. The real danger of tabloidisation is the trend toward personalisation becoming the *only* way to tell a story, and that these stories themselves become more and more disconnected. Sparks (1992: 41) rightly criticises popular journalistic techniques on the grounds that 'they offer the experiences of the individual as the direct and unmediated key to the understanding of the social totality,' arguing further that 'the simple reality is that the nature of the social totality is neither constituted through immediate individual experience nor entirely comprehensible in its terms.' And, as Sparks suggests, popular journalism is headed in directions where even 'the urge to extrapolate from the individual experience to the social totality is declining. More and more, the tabloidised U.S. media offer stories whose aim is simply to engage our emotions, with no other purpose in mind, and where indeed the 'personal' obliterates the 'political' as a factor for human behavior' (Sparks 1992: 40).

The talk shows and magazine shows, and more and more the mainstream news, are becoming a stream of apparently random stories about individual lives, making it difficult to make connections to larger issues. Important issues become reduced to personal stories – the plight of the homeless becomes one woman's story, corruption in an industry becomes one guy pitted against each other, the complexity of the Gulf War becomes Bush vs. Saddam, and good vs. evil. The pressure toward the personal, as Hallin (1992: 22) puts it, 'heightens emotion and makes black and white what is in fact more ambiguous.'

And in a climate that validates personal experience over logic and reasoned argument, it becomes equally valid to pay attention to any and all personal views, no matter how uninformed, bigoted, or irrational. So in the United States we have seen a proliferation of shows in which people share their experiences with fatalities and fetishes, apparitions and angels, all without context or comment. The *Jerry Springer show*, a talk show in which foul-mouthed guests come to blows under the auspices of themes like 'I Slept with Three Brothers,' or 'Men who Dress Like Babies' has become the top-rated daytime talk show, proving immensely popular with young people, who egg the guests on with chants of 'Jerr-y, Jerr-y.' The show only reached the boundaries of acceptability when producers cancelled a program on guests who practice bestiality, titled, 'I Married a Horse' (Deggans 1998: B2).

Springer's core audience also points to another troublesome trend. Younger audiences are especially unlikely to pay attention to news. A 1996 Gallup Poll showed that people under 50 were far more able to identify sports and entertainment figures than politicians and international figures (for example, 15 percent could name the prime minister of Israel, while 75 percent could name the host of the *Tonight Show*). Older Americans were still relatively ignorant (only 70 percent could name the Vice-President), but their recognition of popular and hard news figures was much more even (Newport 1996). Parker and Deane (1997: 4) reached similar conclusions: 'Those over 50 are almost twice as likely as members of Generation X to say they follow national politics and domestic policy very closely, and 10 percentage points more likely to follow election campaigns and international politics.' The Pew Research Center reported in 1996 that news viewership had declined among people under 30 more than among any other group, with only around 20 percent watching either network or cable news. Some of this may simply be a difference in life-stage; older people may have more time to pay attention to the news.

But more likely it both a reflection and a cause of the tabloidisation process. In the United States today, there has been an astonishing proliferation of news outlets – talk shows, TV magazines, TV 'tabloids,' cable networks, and most recently, the Internet. All are fighting for audiences and competing to meet the proven demand for spectacle and drama. Many of the younger generation, with access to an incredible array of entertainment, appear to have given up even the pretence that 'being informed' is useful and necessary. In fact they seem to be becoming more and more unreachable by any message; even beer advertisers are struggling to find ways to break through the noise and reach college-age consumers: 'It's a combination of their short attention span and the information glut,' complains the editor of *Beer Marketer's Insights* (Hays 1998).

And U.S. journalism itself sometimes seems to be giving up making an effort to do anything but tell stories and provide spectacle. Instead, they have plunged headlong into the competition. Mainstream newspapers now routinely use tabloids as sources, as in April, 1992, when *A Current Affair* declard Britain's Prince Edward to be gay. Based on that information alone, newspapers like *Newsday*, The *Boston Globe*, The *Atlanta Journal and Constitution*, and the *Orlando Sentinel* ran the story (Krajicek 1998: 32). The effect of competition was also demonstrated in the saturation coverage of the death of Princess Diana, and the initial coverage of the sex scandal involving President Bill Clinton and Monica Lewinsky. Spurred on by countless rumours emanating from the Internet and elsewhere, the press published information without attribution, much of it later proved wrong. Although many more responsible media then stepped back and issued a *mea culpa* (see, for example, Dahl 1998), in some respects the damage was done.

For the audience relationship with the press is a complicated and ambivalent one. Although the taste for sensational news is clear, at least for now the public is still torn between that taste and a perception that the press should be more than amusing storytellers. The Pew Research Center (1998) reported this year that public criticism of the press for inaccuracy, unfairness, intrusiveness, and sensationalism is at an all time high. More than half those surveyed think news stories are often inaccurate, up 20 percent since 1985. Only a third say the news media help society solve problems, while 54 percent say the news media get in the way of society solving its problems. Krajicek (1998: 198) argues that journalists 'have lost their grip on respect, trust, and confidence, their most valuable occupational commodities. Journalists may know that they are viewed as manipulative enemies by the public, but they seem not to understand what that means.'

So what does it mean? Many have argued that the explosion of news outlets has democratised news, making it more responsive to what people want, even if at least the older generation feels uncomfortable about it all. People like personal stories with high visual impact. They like talk shows with their personal revelations. Many do not care if the images are faked, and the talk shows are scripted. It is certainly true that the older news style tended to present a very institutional picture, where representatives of government and the *status quo* monopolised most of the time.

But the apparent deluge of new information is in many ways an illusion. It only appears to offer variety, when it is the same old stories going round and round all the time. Cultural theorists who argue that greater popularisation leads to more democracy may be right in a way, but inherent in their theories is the notion that as more people's voices are heard, they will gain access to the wider political process. That hope appears illusory; Grindstaff (1997) suggests for example that while talk shows love to use 'ordinary people,' who are all too eager to air their grievances on national television, the forum they are given is guaranteed to encourage emotionalism and volatility, actually further marginalising them as entertaining but freakish 'trash.' We saw the illusory 'more voices, less information' effect in the massive media coverage of the Gulf War, which gave us thousands of hours of discussion and countless personal stories about soldiers, their families, the personality of Bush and Saddam, spectacular computer imagery of smart bombs, and so on (Hallin and Gitlin 1994). It gave us little coverage of what was actually going on in the war, because the government censors forbade such coverage, and because journalists were too worried about competition to take a stand. Nor was there public outrage about censorship, perhaps because journalists are so widely seen as sleazemongers rather than courageous spokespeople for truth.

John Tomlinson (1997: 81) argues that 'it does not follow that because people so readily involve themselves in the 'personalised' morality of scandals, they therefore lack the capacity or the innate motivation to engage with more 'serious' moral issues. It may be a question of how these issues are presented to them.' I believe this is true, and this closer look at how audiences actually use news tends to support the idea that potentially people will pay attention to stories about important issues when or if they are presented to them effectively, and in a form they want, rather than as bitter pill to 'improve' them. The challenge to journalism is how to do this, and how to respond to the demand of the audiecne for 'news we can use,' while showing them the connections between their lives and the larger social and political world. If journalism cannot rise to that challenge, it may be that in the whirling, tabloidised environment of the American news media, 'the battle for large-scale,' serious public discourse is already lost.

Notes

1   Throughout this paper, I quote from transcripts of these interviews, carried out in the Spring of 1993. In selecting quotations. I attempt to choose comments that seem representative of a point of view shared by others. Space limitations preclude the extensive use of numerous quotations that make the same general point.
2   Elsewhere, I have discussed in more detail the relationship of scandalous stories to melodrama, and the role of the audience in participating in development of the story (Bird 1997).

References

Bird, S.E. (1987) What a story! Understanding the audience for scandal, in J. Lull and S. Hinerman (eds) *Media Scandals: Morality and Desire in the Popular Culture Marketplace*. Cambridge: Polity Press.

Bird, S.E. (1992) *For Enquiring Minds: A Cultural Study of Supermarket Tabloids*. Knoxville: University of Tennessee Press.

Bird, S.E. and Dardenne, R.W. (1988) Myth, chronicle and story: exploring the narrative qualities of news, in J.W. Carey (ed.) *Media, Myths, and Narratives*. Newbury Park: Sage.

Carey, J.W. (1975). A cultural approach to communication, *Communication* 2: 50–68.

Dahl, D. (1998) In race to be first, truth often suffers, *St. Petersburg Times*, 31 January, 1A: 5A.

Dahlgren, P. (1992) Introduction, in P. Dahlgren and C. Sparks (eds) *Journalism and Popular Culture*. Newbury Park: Sage.

De Certeau, M. (1984) *The Practice of Everyday Life*. Berkeley: University of California Press.

Deggans, E. (1998) *Springer* officials decide bestiality episode is unfit, *St. Petersburg Times*, 23 May, B2.

Ewen, S. (1988) *All Consuming Images: The Politics of Style in Contemporary Culture*. New York: Basic Books.

Fiske, J. (1992) Popularity and the politics of information, in P. Dahlgren and C. Sparks (eds) *Journalism and Popular Culture*. Newbury Park: Sage.

Glynn, K. (1990) Tabloid television's transgressive aesthetic: *a Current Affair* and the 'shows that taste forgot' *Wide Angle* 12(2): 22–44.

Grindstaff, L. (1997) Producing trash, class, and the money shot: a behind-the-scenes account of daytime TV talk shows, in J. Lull and S. Hinerman (eds) *Media Scandals: Morality and Desire in the Popular Culture Marketplace*. Cambridge: Polity Press.

Hallin, D.C. (1992) The passing of the 'high modernism' in American journalism, *Journal of Communication* 42(3): 14–24.

Hallin, D.C. and Gitlin, T. (1994) The Gulf War as popular culture and television drama, in W.L. Bennett and D.L. Paletz (eds) *Taken by Storm: The Media, Public Opinion, and U.S. Foreign Policy in the Gulf War*. Chicago: University of Chicago Press.

Haskins, J.B. (1984) Morbid curiosity and the mass media: a synergistic relationship, in J. Crook, J. Haskins and P. Ashdown (eds) *Proceedings of the Conference on Morbid Curiosity and the Mass Media*. Knoxville, TN: University of Tennessee Press.

Hays, C.L. (1998) Tapping into beer drinkers desires, *St. Petersburg Times*, 3 May, 1H, 10H.

Heider, D. (1998) Elephants and green beans: propping up local TV news, *Chronicle of Higher Education*, XLIV, 37, 22 May, B8.

Lull, J. and Hinerman, S. (1997) *Media Scandals: Morality and Desire in the Popular Culture Marketplace*. Cambridge: Polity Press.

Jensen, K.B. (1990) The politics of polysemy: television news. Everyday consciousness, and political action. *Media, Culture, and Society*, 12(1): 57–77.

Jhally, S. (1987) *The Codes of Advertising: Fetishism and the Political Economy of Meaning in the Consumer Society*. New York: St. Martin's Press.

Krajicek, D.J. (1998) *Scooped: Media Miss Real Story on Crime While Chasing Sex, Sleaze, and Celebrities*, New York: Columbia University Press.

Langer, J. (1992) Truly awful news on television in P. Dahlgren and C. Sparks (eds) *Journalism and Popular Culture*. Newbury Park: Sage.

Morley, D. (1980) *The Nationwide Audience*. London: BFI.

Newport, F. (1996) Younger adults up on popular culture and sports personalities, but weak on political figures. Gallup Poll Archives, 6:11. The Gallup Organization, Princeton. Available on-line at http://www.gallup.com/poll_archives

Parker, K. and Deane, C. (1997) Ten years of the Pew News Interest Index: Report of Presentation at the 1997 meeting of the American Association for Public Opinion Research. Available on-line at http://www.people-press.org/index.htm.

Pauly, J. (1988) Rupert Murdoch and the demonology of professional journalism, in J.W. Carey (ed.) *Media, Myths, and Narratives*. Newbury Park: Sage.

Pew Research Center for the People and the Press (1996) TV News Viewership Declines: Fall Off Greater for Young Adults and Computer Users. Available on-line at http://www.people-press.org/index.htm

Pew Research Center for the People and the Press (1997) The Times Mirror News Interest Index: 1989–95. Available on-line at http://www.people-press.org/index.htm.

Pew Research Center for the People and the Press (1998) Top 10 Stories of the Year: High Personal Contentment. Low News Interest Report. Available on-line at http://www.people-press.org/index.htm.

Price, V. and Czilli, E.J. (1996) Modelling patterns of news recognition and recall, *Journal of Communication*, 46 (2): 55–78.

Sparks, C. (1992) Popular journalism: theories and practice, in P. Dahlgren and C. Sparks (eds) *Journalism and Popular Culture*. London: Sage.

Stephens, M. (1988) *A History of News: From the Drum to the Satellite*. New York: Viking.

Tomlinson, J. (1997) And besides, the wench is dead: media scandals and the globalisation of communication, in J. Lull and S. Hinerman (eds), *Media Scandals: Morality and Desire in the Popular Culture Marketplace*. London: Polity Press.

Zuckerman, M. (1984) Is curiosity about morbid events an expression of sensation seeking? in J. Crook, J. Haskins and P. Ashdown (eds), *Proceedings of the Conference on Morbid Curiosity and the Mass Media*. Knoxville, TN: University of Tennessee Press.

THE OPINION POLLS:
STILL BIASED TO LABOUR

Ivor Crewe

THE significance of opinion polls for an election, and their prominence in campaigns, have ebbed and flowed over the years. In the 1950s and 1960s they were minor commentators on the electoral game, with little impact on how it was played. From the 1970s they moved onto the pitch influencing the election timing, campaign strategies, media coverage and, arguably, outcome. Campaign poll results came to dominate newspaper frontpages and party press conferences. Arcane aspects of polling methods became issues in their own right. Pollsters and polling commentators became minor media celebrities.

Yet in 1997 the opinion polls departed centre stage; and in 2001 they withdrew further into the wings. There were fewer of them, they figured less conspicuously in the media and they appeared to exert less influence on the campaign. Despite their lower profile, however, they made a significant contribution to the ambience of the election. An unchanging backdrop to the contest, the campaign polls influenced the assumptions of politicians and public alike; but the backdrop was deceptive, and had the polls been more accurate the character and consequences of the election might have been a little different.

From catastrophe to complacency: 1992, 1997 and 2001

The influence of opinion polls depends on their credibility. Until 1992 their forecasting record on election eve had been impressive, with an average

Ivor Crewe (2001) The opinion polls: still biased to Blair, *Parliamentary Affairs*, 54(4): 650–65. Reprinted by kind permission of Oxford University Press.

error of only 1.3% per party and of 3.1% on the winning party's majority. Only once before 1992 had they called a clear result wrongly, in 1970, when the Conservatives under Edward Heath won by 3% and 30 seats, even though three of the four final polls forecast a clear labour victory. But in that election the polls completed their interviewing three days before polling day and thus failed to detect a late swing to the Conservatives. After 1970 the polling organisations closed off this source of error by interviewing up to the day before the election for their final forecast poll.

In 1992 the polls met their Waterloo. Throughout the campaign they showed the Conservative and Labour parties level-pegging. The four final polls produced an average gap, in Labour's favour, of a mere 0.9%. Everything pointed to a hung parliament and a coalition government. In the event, the Conservatives won with an overall majority of 21 seats, 7.6% ahead of Labour in the popular vote. In their forecast of the lead, the polls were out by over eight points, having underestimated Conservative support and overestimated Labour support each by four percentage points.

The post-mortem conducted by the Market Research Society attributed the debacle to three causes: a small, late swing to the Conservatives on the eve and day of election; a 'spiral of silence' in which closet Conservatives, sensing a hostile climate of opinion, hid their true voting intentions; and faulty sample design, specifically unsuitable and misdefined 'quotas' by which interviewers selected respondents.[1] After 1992 the four main polling organisations experimented with various techniques and refinements to overcome these errors. By 1997 all had changed their methods, although each in slightly different ways. All interviewed until as late as possible on the eve of polling, although some relied on last-minute telephone call-backs to a sample of respondents interviewed earlier in the week. They tried to address the problem of 'shy Tories' by allocating non-disclosers (the 'don't knows', 'won't votes' and 'won't says') according to telltale signs of their real intentions, such as their preferred party leader, the party they identified with, the party they recalled supporting in 1992, or the party they thought the more competent at running the economy. They dealt with biased samples by drawing up more elaborate quotas, incorporating characteristics that were politically more sensitive (e.g. housing tenure and car ownership), and updating and cross-checking their estimates of the proportion of the electorate falling into each quota. More controversially, three of them (MORI being the exception) weighted the answer to their vote intention question so that recalled vote in 1992 came into line with the actual result in 1992, although they differed in their application of the weighting.[2]

In 1997 the opinion polls avoided the disaster of 1992. In their relief the pollsters swanked:

...through this election campaign, the publication of nearly every poll was accompanied by carping that the polls could not possibly be right, that they had again under estimated the Conservative share, and it was 'inconceivable' that Labour could win by the margins indicated.

Not in the 1997 general election.

Yesterday the five polling organisations got the average share of the vote for each party within the usually accepted plus or minus 3% sampling tolerance.[3]

The media largely accepted this claim, not least because all the polls had forecast the substantial victory that Labour achieved. In reality, however, their performance in 1997 was mediocre. Their mean error in forecasting the parties' vote shares was the third largest since the war. Five of the seven final polls and both exit polls underestimated the Conservative vote, albeit by smaller margins and within accepted sampling error. Contrary to their boast, they had not finally cracked the problem of 'closet Conservatives'. More significantly, eight of the nine final/exit polls overestimated the Labour vote, in four cases by more than the accepted 3% sampling error, and in three further cases by close to it. The probability that sampling error was responsible for overestimates of such consistency and magnitude was extremely remote. Evidently the polling organisations had not licked the other half of the problem in 1992 – the 'lost Labour voters'. They exaggerated Labour's lead by an average of 4%; seven of Britain's sixteen postwar elections have been won by smaller margins. What should have given the polling organisations most pause for thought was the difficulty of identifying which of the refinements they had adopted since 1992 had made a clear contribution to greater accuracy.

Satisfied with their patchy performance in 1997, the polling organisations engaged in much less self-analysis and development than they had after 1992. There was no self-consciousness about the fact that for the third election in succession they had exaggerated the Labour vote and understated the Conservative vote.[4] Yet there were warning signs after 1997 that at least some of the polling organisations were consistently inaccurate and, in particular, that most were continuing to inflate Labour's true support to a marked degree. Three of the main polling organisations conducted monthly polls for newspapers: Gallup for the *Daily Telegraph*, ICM for the *Guardian* and MORI for *The Times*. Throughout the 1997–2001 Parliament, except for the two months of the petrol tax protest and its aftermath in September/October 2000, the polls continuously reported double-digit leads for Labour. But ICM consistently reported a smaller Labour lead, by

6 percentage points, than Gallup or MORI did (see Table 6.1). Compared with Gallup and MORI, whose figures were very similar, ICM attributed four points less support to Labour, and two points more support to both the Conservative and Liberal Democrat Parties. The explanation was that ICM adjusted its results so as to bring the recalled 1997 vote of its respondents in line with the actual 1997 result, whereas MORI and Gallup did not. In this way ICM could compensate for the possibility raised in the 1992 and 1997 elections that opinion poll samples were for various reasons systematically biased in favour of Labour supporters.

Table 6.1 Monthly polls by gallup, MORI and ICM, May 1997–April 2001

Polling organisation	Number of polls	Labour lead	Cons	Labour	LibDem	Other
Gallup	48	23.7	28.4	52.1	13.7	5.6
MORI	47	24.0	28.2	52.2	14.3	5.3
ICM	47	17.5	30.6	48.0	16.0	5.5

Source: Author's database of opinion polls.

The discrepancy between ICM, and the Gallup and MORI polls during 1997–2001 did not, of course, prove that one or other was the more accurate; the ICM and Gallup final forecast polls had shared the honours in 1997 (ICM for the parties' vote shares, Gallup for the percentage majority). But the consistency of the divergence over four years did suggest that either ICM or MORI and Gallup were applying faulty methods.

Warning lights that the true Labour lead was closer to ICM's estimates than those of MORI and Gallup were indicated by the failure of the polls in the Scottish Parliamentary election of May 1999, the Euro-election of June 1999, and the London mayoral election of 2000. For example, a MORI/ *Sunday Herald* poll, completed a week before the election to the Scottish Parliament (and thus not a forecast poll) reported Labour's level of support at 48% in the constituency ballot and at 44% in the party list ballot; in the election the actual figures were 39 and 34% respectively. Conservative support was understated by 8 and 6 percentage points in the two ballots.[5] A Gallup/*Daily Telegraph* poll, whose fieldwork was completed a week before the European elections, reported that 33% would 'definitely' vote and that among those intending to vote, Labour enjoyed a 48% to 26% lead over the Conservatives. In the event only 23% turned out to vote and Labour trailed 28% to the Conservatives' 35% – a huge 29 percentage point discrepancy.[6] This was not a forecast poll: a late swing to the Conservatives and, more likely, the exceptionally low turnout, can explain part of the discrepancy, but its size should have alerted the polling community to the possibility that poll samples were biased in favour of Labour voters.

In the May 2000 elections for London's mayor and Assembly, MORI's final forecast poll for Carlton TV proved seriously inaccurate, again in Labour's favour. It reported a 44–29 Labour-to-Conservative lead in the first (constituency) ballot for the Assembly, when the actual result was a narrow Conservative lead of 33–32: the forecast of the gap was 16 percentage points awry. In its forecast of the second (party list) ballot, the MORI poll was 15 points awry. In both cases it seriously underestimated support for the Greens. In the mayoral election MORI forecast a 46% to 23% margin for Ken Livingstone over Steve Norris; in reality the margin was 39% to 27%. The low turnout (a mere 31%) explains part of the inaccuracy, but only part. The forecast for the mayoral election was based only on respondents claiming they were 'certain to vote'.[7] Although low turnout does make the polling organisations' task more difficult, it cannot always be cited as the explanation for inaccuracy. Turnout in the Scottish parliamentary elections, for example, was a respectable 58%. Moreover, the polling organisations had coped with low turnout in the past, notably the Euro-elections of 1994, when turnout was 37%, and 'super-adjusted' polls by Gallup and MORI came very close to the result.[8] A dispassionate analyst of the pollsters' record during the 1997–2001 Parliament would conclude that some of the polling organisations were systematically over-estimating the Labour vote and underestimating the Conservative vote, even allowing for the distorting effects of turnout, and that an exploration of techniques to address the problem might be wise; but it did not transpire.

Opinion polls in the 2001 campaign

Five polling organisations conducted regular national polls in the 2001 campaign: Gallup for the *Daily Telegraph*, ICM for the *Guardian* and the *Observer*, MORI for *The Times, Sunday Telegraph* and the *Economist*, NOP for the *Sunday Times* and Rasmussen Research, an American company new to political polling in the UK, for the *Independent*.[9] Each adopted slightly different approaches, in particular to the potential problems of pro-Labour samples and low turnout, and one changed its methods in mid-campaign.

Rasmussen Research adopted the most radical approach, a computer-based telephone poll. It replaced human interviewers with a computer that randomly dialled telephone owners and used an embedded voice recording to ask questions. Respondents answered by pressing the number corresponding to their answer on their telephone keypad. Weighting was applied to bring the social profile of respondents in line with that of the electorate. To general scepticism in the polling community Rasmussen claimed that the disembodied anonymity of the process would encourage respondents conscious of their minority views, such as 'shy Tories', to cooperate, and would discourage their giving politically 'correct' answers.[10]

ICM, NOP and Gallup conducted telephone surveys of the conventional kind and only MORI stuck to traditional face-to-face interviewing for *The Times*.[11] ICM continued with the methods that made it the most accurate of the pollsters in 1997. To overcome the problem of a pro-Labour bias in its samples (whether arising from Conservatives refusing to cooperate or from Labour supporters being more accessible by telephone) it weighted its sample according to respondents' recall of their 1997 vote, bringing it into line with the actual 1997 result. In addition, ICM included the main party names in its vote intention question. The combined effect was to report higher support than other polls for the Conservatives and, more noticeably, the Liberal Democrats, at the expense of Labour. NOP did not prompt by party but during the campaign did weight by recalled 1997 vote.

Gallup changed its methods specifically for the election. Conscious that turnout was likely to fall, it adopted the tried and tested 'likelihood-to-vote' model of its sister organisation in the United States, where low turnout has always been a challenge to accurate polling. Based on a battery of questions about past voting, party identification, interest in politics and so forth, the model estimates and rank orders the probability of a respondent turning out to vote. Gallup reported the vote intentions only of those respondents identified as likely to vote for the level of turnout that Gallup predicted (by means not revealed) would occur. It also used the party prompt in its vote intention question, to catch tactical voters.[12] Finally, it allocated non-disclosers to a party if they gave a consistently partisan answer to the questions of which party leader they would prefer as prime minister and which party would manage the economy more competently.

MORI made the most startling change of approach, at least in terms of outcome. Among all the polling organisations, MORI has been the least inclined to adopt what it regards as the unproven techniques of its competitors, such as weighting by recalled vote, the allocation of non-disclosers, and adjustments for turnout. In its penultimate poll for *The Times*, however, MORI incorporated the names of parties and constituency candidates in the vote intention question. The result was dramatic: the reported Labour lead of 25% the previous week fell to 18%. This was because, while Conservative support was unchanged, at 30%, Labour support fell from 55% to 48% (and Liberal Democrat support increased from 11% to

16%).[13] MORI claimed that it was merely repeating what it had done in 1997, providing the names of candidates once nominations of candidates had closed. But in 1997 it made the change for its final forecast poll only (and the change made almost no difference). The probable explanation is that MORI became concerned that it was reporting much larger Labour leads – always above 20% – than its competitors were, and had a failure of nerve.[14] It was, wrote one commentator, 'as though the scoreboard at a football match shows one side three-nil up until the 89th minute when the referee suddenly announces that he has made a mistake and it is only two-nil'.[15] Whether failure of nerve or wise judgment, it saved MORI and *The Times* from being embarrassingly adrift on election day.

Opinion polls, the media and the 2001 campaign

Opinion polls retreated from the spotlight in 2001. The overall amount of polling, which had slowly grown from 1959 to 1979, and then accelerated from 1983 to 1992, fell back in 1997 and again in 2001 (see Table 6.2).

Table 6.2 Growth and decline of national opinion polls in general election campaigns, 1945–2001

Year	Number of national polls in campaign	Number of different agencies conducting polls	Number of different newspaper/TV programmes commissioning polls
1945	1	1	1
1950	11	2	2
1951	n/a	3	3
1955	n/a	2	2
1959	20	2	4
1964	23	4	4
1966	26	4	8
1970	25	5	6
Feb 74	25	6	9
Oct 74	27	6	11
1979	26	5	8
1983	46	6	14
1987	54	7	15
1992	57	7	18
1997	44	5	13
2001	32	5	11

Note: The number of polls excludes election-day surveys and private polling by the parties, as well as regional and local surveys.

Fewer agencies conducted polls and fewer newspapers or television pro-grammes commissioned them; as a result the total number of national polls conducted and published during the campaign shrunk to its lowest level since 1979.[16] The four main daily broadsheets published weekly polls, but only two of the Sunday broadsheets (*Sunday Times* and *Observer*) did so. The tabloids largely confined themselves to two-sentence summary reports of the broadsheets' polls; and some of the middlebrow tabloids reported the views of 'focus groups', typically in marginal constituencies, a cheap and reader-friendly way of describing public opinion, but in no sense an opinion poll. Most broadsheets also featured similar focus groups. As in 1997, television steered away from commissioning polls, with the exception of Channel 4 for which NOP polled weekly but did not publish vote intention figures. Notably rare were special polls of regions, marginal seats, single constituencies, or special groups such as ethnic minorities, first-time voters or particular occupations, which had been such a feature of the 'saturation polling' in 1983, 1987 and 1992. Instead the media resorted to unstruc-tured interviews with small panels of students, first-time voters and people living in marginal seats.

Media attention to the polls also declined. Television news never led on a poll and limited itself to brief factual reports well down the bulletin running order. The BBC and ITN did a weekly wrap-up of the polls, with Peter Snow for the BBC doing his best to breathe life into them through ingenious graphics. Newspapers rarely devoted their lead story to a poll, even when reporting their own; more often the frontpage carried a capsule summary while the main report was confined to an inside page. About a fifth of all frontpage lead stories in the national press were devoted to the polls in 1987 (20%) and 1992 (18%); in 1997 the proportion dropped to 4% and in 2001 to 3%.

The decline in the media's demand for polls is all the more striking in the light of Deacon et al.'s content analysis of the media for this volume, which shows that stories about the election process absorbed almost half the campaign coverage by television and the press. The paucity of poll stories reflected commercial realities and media values. The polls had pointed to Labour's comfortable re-election throughout the 1997–2001 Parliament. The only exception was the six-week period in September/October 2001, after the petrol tax protest, when the Conservatives briefly captured the lead. Immediately a flurry of additional polls appeared: instead of the usual four there were fifteen. But editors noticed how quickly Labour recovered. By January 2001, Labour had restored its percentage lead to 16 points and by February to 19 points. Thereon the chartlines for party support were unremittingly flat. In these circumstances it was hardly surprising that

Table 6.3 Opinion polls and the 2001 election

Date of field work	Number of polls	Polling organisation/outlet	Lab maj. (%)	Con (%)	Lab (%)	LibDem (%)	Other (%)
Pre-campaign polls							
Jan 2001	7		−16.3	32.3	48.6	13.7	5.4
Feb 2001	6		−19.3	30.5	49.8	14.2	5.6
March 2001	7		−18.1	31.7	49.9	13.6	4.9
April 2001	6		−20.7	30.0	50.7	13.3	6.0
Campaign polls							
30 Apr–13 May	11		−18.4	31.2	49.6	13.5	5.8
14–20 May	5		−17.0	31.0	48.0	14.4	7.0
21–27 May	5		−18.2	30.4	48.6	14.8	6.2
28 May–3 June	7		−16.4	30.4	46.9	16.7	6.0
Final forecast polls							
June 1–3		NOP/*Sunday Times*	−17	30	47	16	7
June 2–3		Rasmussen/*Independent*	−11	33	44	16	7
June 2–4		ICM/*Guardian*	−11	32	43	19	6
June 5–6		MORI/*The Times*	−15	30	45	18	7
June 6		Gallup/*Daily Telegraph*	−16	30	47	18	5
Exit polls		NOP/BBC	−12	32	44	17	7
Exit polls		MORI/ITN	−13	31	44	19	7
Final poll mean	5		−14.0	31.0	45.2	17.4	6.4
Forecast poll mean	3		−14.0	30.7	45.0	18.3	6.0
Exit poll mean	2		−12.5	31.5	44.0	18.0	7.0
Actual result (GB)			−9.3	32.7	42.0	18.8	6.5

Note: Excludes the YouGov Internet poll for *Sunday Business*.

Table 6.4 Comparison of vote intention figures between different polling organisations

Polling organisation	Number of polls	Labour lead	Con (%)	Lab (%)	LibDem (%)	Other (%)
MORI	7	−22.7	28.7	51.4	14.4	5.4
NOP	5	−18.4	30.6	49.0	14.0	6.4
Gallup	5	−16.2	31.4	47.8	15.0	5.8
ICM	9	−14.6	31.3	45.9	16.7	6.2
Rasmussen	4	−12.0	32.5	44.5	15.5	7.8
Actual result (GB)		−9.3	32.7	42.0	18.8	6.5

Note: All national polls published by these companies during the campaign (1 May–6 June 2001).

editors were reluctant to go to the considerable expense of commissioning additional polls: they were unlikely to make a splash.

In the campaign the polls pointed with tedious persistence to another runaway Labour win ... Apart from the small increase of about one percentage point a week in the Liberal Democrats' support, at Labour's expense, change from week to week was glacial, as Table 6.4 shows: the Labour lead drifted down from (apparently) 18% to 16%. Conservative support appeared to be firmly stuck at about 30%, presumably its core: 26 of the 32 campaign polls placed the Conservatives in the 28%–32% range and 30 out of 32 in the 27% to 33% range. Labour support varied more, but the variation was between different polling companies, reflecting their fieldwork methods, rather than within the same polling organisation, reflecting real changes during the campaign. As Table 6.4 shows, Rasmussen for the *Independent* typically put Labour ahead of the Conservatives by 44.5% to 32.5% whereas NOP for the *Sunday Times* typically put Labour ahead by the much wider margin of 49% to 31%. But in the four Rasmussen polls Conservative support fluctuated between 32 ad 33% and Labour support between 44 and 46%. In the four NOP polls for the *Sunday Times* the variation was almost as narrow: Conservative support varied between 30 and 32% and Labour support between 47 and 49%.[17]

Had the gap between the two major parties been in single figures, sampling error and rogue polls might have occasionally suggested a hung parliament, or narrow Conservative victory, or at the very least some momentum in the Conservatives' favour. As it turned out, the only rogue polls pointed to a Labour avalanche rather than landslide: MORI, which was consistently reporting larger Labour leads than the other polling organisations, put Labour 28% ahead in a poll for the *Economist* in mid-May and 26% and 25% ahead in consecutive polls for *The Times* in the second and third weeks of May. Unlike 1997 (and in 1987 when party fortunes were reversed) not a single poll fell foul of sampling error in the other direction to suggest that the losing party was catching up. Moreover, Labour's perpetually big leads were reinforced by superiority on almost every other measure of party support. Blair's advantage over Hague as a prospective prime minister was even larger than his party's lead over the Conservatives. Labour was the preferred party, typically by double-figure margins, on almost all issues, the main exception being asylum seekers on which the Conservatives were narrowly ahead. Polls in London and Scotland confirmed the picture. From the very beginning of the campaign, therefore, the media could do little more than report the near certainty of a comfortable Labour victory and the possibility of similar or even greater humiliation for the Conservatives than in 1997.

The following headlines to poll stories in the press, listed in chronological order, convey the unremitting message that a large Labour win was a foregone conclusion:

'BLAIR BY 250' (frontpage, *Daily Express*, 9.5.01)

'HAGUE HASN'T GOT A PRAYER' (frontpage, *Sun*, 9.5.01)

'LABOUR LEAD HOLDS AS HAGUE FAILS TO LIFT OFF' (*Sunday Telegraph*, 13.5.01)

'LABOUR TO HOLD ALL 56 SCOTS SEATS' (frontpage, *Scotsman*, 15.5.01)

'RECORD LEAD FOR LABOUR: MORI POLL POINTS TO HUGE VICTORY' (frontpage, *The Times*, 24.5.01)

'TORIES FACE EXTINCTION: POLL PREDICTS A LABOUR MAJORITY OF 355' (*Sun*, 23.5.01)

'TORIES FACE POLL MELTDOWN' (frontpage, *Guardian*, 30.5.01)

'LANDSLIDE: POLL SHOWS BLAIR WILL WIN BY 197 SEATS' (*News of the World*, 3.6.01)

'VOTERS SIGNAL A POLITICAL EARTHQUAKE' (*Observer*, 3.6.01)

'TORIES: WE KNOW WE'RE BEATEN' (frontpage, *Sunday Times*, 3.6.01)

'BLAIR HEADS FOR SECOND LANDSLIDE' (frontpage, *The Times*, 7.6.01)

'BLAIR STILL ON FOR A LANDSLIDE, SAY POLLS' (frontpage, *Daily Mail*, 7.6.01)

Barely a single poll story gave readers any reason to believe that the Conservatives were closing the gap, let alone within striking distance of victory.

A cruelly headlined story in the *Independent* (29.5.01) 'AT LAST A POLL THAT BRINGS SOME CHEER TO HAGUE', referred to a finding that William Hague was not quite as unpopular as Michael Foot in 1983. A few stories towards the end of the campaign underlined the gradual growth in support for the Liberal Democrats which may have boosted morale among the party's workers and encouraged its more hesitant supporters.

The polls signalled a Labour landslide. They also forecast a decline in turnout, which fed the themes of public apathy and alienation that threaded together a wide variety of stories in the broadsheets. The main polls reported that the proportion of respondents claiming to be 'definite' or '(very) certain' voters had fallen since the 1997 campaign, typically by 5 to 9 percentage points, and was well below 1997's actual turnout of 71%.[18] The evidence about the impact of a lower turnout on party fortunes was mixed but generally pointed to a slight disadvantage to Labour. Assuming that the 'definite'/'certain to' voters would indeed cast a ballot, the consensus among the poll commentators was that the percentage turnout would fall to the mid-60s. In the event it plummeted much further than expected, to 59%, and may have contributed to the polls' overestimate of the Labour vote.

The performance of the polls

Measuring the performance of the polls is more difficult in 2001 than in previous elections. The standard test is to compare the final forecast polls of the main polling organisations with the four parties' percentage shares of the actual vote. Typically the commissioning media publish their final poll on the day of the election, based on interviews conducted, in the main, on the Tuesday and Wednesday before election day. In 1997 six polls fell into this category but in 2001 only two did, MORI for *The Times* and Gallup for the *Daily Telegraph*. The ICM poll for the *Guardian* was published on the Wednesday and based on interviews conducted over the weekend and Monday. The Rasmussen poll for the *Independent* was published on the Tuesday and based on fieldwork conducted over the weekend. The NOP poll for the *Sunday Times* was published on the Sunday and based on fieldwork conducted the previous week. These were the final polls of the five main polling organisations but the latter two, in particular, were not *forecast* polls by the conventional understanding of the term because fieldwork ended at least four days before the election.[19] This, after all, was the source of the polls' failure in 1970. The fact that in 2001 they did not interview right up to the wire was a sign of the media's and polling organisations' confidence that they had the result reasonably right.

In this election, as in 1997, there was no repeat of the debacle of 1992. The five final polls all indicated a substantial Labour victory and in that crude sense got the result right. But, again as in 1997, the Labour lead they reported varied from ICM/*Guardian*'s and Rasmussen/*Independent*'s 11-point lead to the 17-point leads of NOP/*Sunday Times* and Gallup/*Daily Telegraph* (see Table 6.3.) The forecasts of the two exit polls, NOP for the BBC and MORI for ITN, were at the lower end of the range, at 12 and 13 percentage points respectively.

The true test of a poll's accuracy is the mean of the difference between each party's percentage share of the vote (counting 'other' parties as a single party) and the poll's forecast of that share. By that yardstick, the ICM/*Guardian* poll was the runaway winner for the second successive election, with a mean score of 0.75, followed by the Rasmussen/*Independent* poll with a mean score of 1.25, MORI/*The Times* (1.75) and Gallup/*Daily Telegraph* and NOP/*Sunday Times* taking up the rear with 2.75 each. MORI and NOP could at least comfort themselves that their exit polls were well within sampling error with scores of 1.25 and 1.0 respectively, although of course much greater accuracy should be expected of exit polls than conventional polls, because the former do not have to address the problem of turnout.[20]

According to APOPO the performance of the polls was a triumph. The day after the election it bragged:

> The opinion polls conducted in the last week of the campaign proved the most accurate since 1987 ... this level of accuracy in the polls was achieved despite the record low level of turnout, which made fore-casting far more difficult.[21]

This self-promotion was predictable but disingenuous, being based on a partial selection of polls.[22] In reality, the performance of the polls was disappointing, both by historical and statistical standards, in a number of ways:

1 As Table 6.5 shows, the mean error in the five final polls (and the three 'forecast' polls) was 1.8, the fifth largest out of the sixteen elections since 1945, although slightly lower than in 1997. By historical standards, 2001 was a small improvement on 1997, but still a relatively poor year.

2 All five final polls, and the two exit polls, overestimated the Labour vote. The phenomenon cannot be attributed plausibly to a very late swing to the Conservatives, since no such trend was reported from the Wednesday polling and the two polls whose interviewers stayed in the

Table 6.5 Accuracy of the final forecast polls in general elections, 1945–2001

Year	Outgoing government	Number of forecast polls	Deviation of mean from share of the vote				Mean error per party	Mean error on gap between first and second party
			Con	Lab	LibDem	Others		
1945	Coalition	1	2	−2	1	−1	1.5	−4
1950	Labour	2	1	−2	2	0	1.3	−3
1951	Labour	3	2	−4	1	1	2.3	−6
1955	Conservative	2	1	1	−1	−1	1.0	0
1959	Conservative	3	0	−1	0	0	0.3	1
1964	Conservative	4	1	1	−1	0	1.0	0
1966	Labour	3	−1	3	−1	0	1.3	4
1970	Labour	5	−2	4	−1	−1	2.0	−6
Feb 74	Conservative	6	0	−2	2	0	1.0	2
Oct 74	Labour	5	−2	3	0	−1	1.5	5
1979	Labour	5	0	1	0	0	0.3	−1
1983	Conservative	7	3	−2	0	−1	1.5	5
1987	Conservative	7	−1	2	−2	0	1.3	−3
1992	Conservative	4	−4	4	1	−1	3.0	−9
1997	Conservative	6	−1	3	−1	−1	2.0	4
2001(a)	Labour	5	−2	3	−2	0	1.8	5
2001(b)	Labour	3	−2	3	−1	−1	1.8	5

Note: A 'final forecast' poll is defined for 1959–97 as any published on polling day and for earlier elections as any described as such. From February 1974 onwards interviews were generally conducted on the Tuesday and Wednesday immediately before election day. The definition for 2001 distinguishing between (a) final polls and (b) forecast polls is explained in the text.

field longest (MORI/*The Times* and Gallup/*Daily Telegraph*) showed no signs of Conservative recovery (if anything, the reverse). Nor can it be attributed to last minute tactical switching from Labour to Liberal Democrat: the MORI and Gallup estimates of Liberal Democrat support were accurate. Moreover, both exit polls, which are immune to late swing, also overestimated the Labour vote, albeit by a smaller margin.

3   Indeed every single poll during the campaign estimated Labour support at more than the 42.0% of the vote it actually received. This universal exaggeration of Labour support suggests that sample bias, not random sampling error or late swing, is the key explanation. The polls did not

crack the problem that caused them so much grief in the much closer election of 1992 and that persisted, if less conspicuously, in 1997.

4 Four of the five final polls underestimated the Conservative vote (Rasmussen for The Independent being the honourable exception), as did both exit polls. Of the 32 campaign polls only four put support for the Conservatives at or above the 33% vote they actually obtained. The near-universality with which the polls understated Conservative support, as they did in both 1997 and 1992, reinforces the conclusion that the main polling organisations systematically obtained samples with a pro-Labour and anti-Conservative bias and, except for ICM, failed to address it.

5 By consistently overestimating the Labour vote and underestimating the Conservative vote, the five final polls (and the two exit polls) all exaggerated Labour's lead. Labour's actual margin of victory was 9.3%, but the average lead attributed to Labour in the 32 campaign polls was almost double – 17.1% – and not a single poll throughout the campaign gave Labour a lead of under 10%. The mean difference between the forecast and actual gap was 5 percentage points, the (equal) fourth worst performance of the polls by that criterion since the war. Seven of the sixteen postwar elections have been won by smaller margins.

Credibility confirmed or complacency continued?

In a parallel analysis of the opinion polls in 1997, I concluded:

> The widespread overestimate of the Labour vote, repeating a pattern found in 1992 and 1987, pinpoints a problem for the polling organisations to address with as much energy as they addressed the issue of 'closet Conservatives'. Lost Labour voters may matter more next time, if the contest is closer...[23]

Buoyed by their restored credibility in 1997, the polling organisations chose to ignore or deny the problem, despite strong evidence from the Scottish Parliamentary, European and London elections that they were constantly exaggerating Labour's support. This systematic defect in the opinion polls was masked by the size of the Blair victory. In a landslide they are bound to pick the winner.[24]

It is now evident that most of the established pollsters have been inflating Labour support (with ICM again the exception) and that this is a systematic feature of their sampling design. Roger Mortimore has recently argued that the overestimate of Labour support in 2001 was a function of the exceptionally low turnout.[25] But this claim fails to account for the even greater exaggeration of Labour support in 1992, when turnout, at 78%, was unusually high; or for the more accurate estimates of Labour support by Rasmussen and ICM, neither of which sought to adjust for turnout; or for the fact that in 2001 turnout fell almost as sharply in the Conservative heartlands (by 11.6 percentage points) as in Labour's (by 13.1 percentage points). To establish low turnout as the explanation, one needs to show that Labour-supporting respondents abstained in significantly greater numbers than their Conservative counterparts. Whether or not they did awaits careful reanalysis of the polling data. So far it has not been demonstrated that they did.

What is much easier to establish is that, judging by respondents' recall of their vote at the previous election, most opinion poll samples contained too many Labour voters. One element of this is false recall: some respondents, such as anti-Conservative tactical voters for the Liberal Democrats, will mis-recall voting Labour. But a substantial part must be due to opinion polls disproportionately selecting Labour voters either because they are less reluctant than Conservatives to cooperate, or because they are more immediately accessible. The possible explanations for this phenomenon are numerous and need serious exploration. In this context the polling organisations should acknowledge that interviews of samples of 1,000 or more conducted over a one or two-day period are subject to low response rates because the polling company does not have the time for multiple follow-ups of refusers. Low and progressively declining response rates (which are never divulged, and sometimes not recorded) inevitably introduce bias into the sample. In reality opinion poll samples are representative not of the whole electorate but of that minority within it willing to answer political questions at short notice. Polling organisations should also acknowledge that weighting by the standard demographic characteristics of age, sex and social class is increasingly irrelevant for polls because nowadays each of these characteristics is only weakly associated with party preference.[26]

How much does it really matter if the opinion polls inflate Labour's support and understate the Conservatives' by a few percentage points? Is it not carping to criticise? The answer can be given by imagining what the 2001 campaign and its aftermath might have been like if the opinion polls had been consistently accurate. Assuming that the true Labour lead over the Conservatives was about 10 percentage points throughout the campaign, well-designed polls based on random samples of about 1,000 respondents would have reported Labour leads of between 7 and 13%; a probable Labour victory, but not an inevitable one; a clear Labour majority, but not a landslide; an election to play for, not a foregone conclusion. Labour supporters would have been less complacent, Conservatives less despondent. Conservative Party morale would have been higher and the desperate gamble of staking all on the issue of the Euro might have seemed less attractive. And, after the election, the grotesque disproportionality of a 165-seat overall majority based on a 9-percentage point majority would be more obvious. Turnout and other forms of participation would almost certainly have been higher and the sense that the government won a landslide, but not a mandate, less prevalent. Accuracy in polls matters even when the outcome is clear-cut and inevitable. In 2005/6 when the outcome might be less certain, accuracy in polls will matter even more but, given the prevalent mood of complacency in the polling industry, may be no nearer achievement.

Notes

1   See Market Research Society, *The Opinion Polls and the 1992 General Election*, July 1994.

2   See I. Crewe, 'The Opinion Polls: Confidence Restored?', *Parliamentary Affairs*, 50, October 1997, p. 572.

3   APOPO (Association of Professional Opinion Polling Organisations) 'General Election '97 Result', press release, 2.5.97.

4   In 1987 the seven forecast polls averaged at 1% under for the Conservatives and 2% over for Labour. See I. Crewe, ibid., p. 581.

5   See *Sunday Herald* (Scotland), 2.5.99 and the MORI website: http://www.mori.com/polls/1999/sh990409.shtml.

6   See The Gallup Organisation, *Gallup Political Index*, Report No. 466, June 1999, p. 8.

7   See Market & Opinion Research International, *British Public Opinion*, Vol. XXIII, No. 4, May 2000, p. 7.

8   See I. Crewe, ibid., p. 573. Gallup forecast: Con 28, Lab 44, LD 19.5 and MORI forecast Con 27, Lab 47, LD 20. The result was: Con 28, Lab 44, LD 16.5. Both Gallup and MORI re-allocated their non-disclosers and in addition Gallup weighted their data by recall of vote in 1992. In 1999 neither organisation made adjustments of this kind.

9   Gallup also conducted a cumulative daily 'rolling rhunder' survey for the British Election Study at the University of Essex, the full results of which were available on the BES website. It indicated very large Labour leads, often exceeding 30%, but it was not claimed to be a predictive poll: no weighting or any other adjustments were made to the raw data. NOP also conducted regular online polls for Channel 4 but the voting figures from these were not published. YouGov, the online partner of the British Election Study, organised an Internet

poll based on 7,885 web-users for the *Sunday Business* of 3 June (see p. 1). It reported the parties' standing as Lab 45%, Con 34%, LibDem 14%.

10 'A new kind of polling', *Independent*, 25.5.01, p. 6.

11 It interviewed by telephone for the *Sunday Telegraph* and the *Economist* and telephoned a subsample on the Wednesday before polling day, to check for last-minute swing, for its forecast poll in *The Times*.

12 'Experience suggests that if people are asked in a general way how they intend to vote, they respond in terms of which party they want to win the election, rather than in terms of how they themselves will actually vote in their own constituency.' See 'How our campaign Gallups work', *Daily Telegraph*, 17.5.01, p. 8.

13 Not all of the change can necessarily be attributed to the change in question wording. MORI probably happened to select a less pro-Labour sample for this poll. See John Curtice, 'LibDems climb the wobbly poll', *Scotsman*, 1.6.01, p. 10.

14 The Labour lead reported by MORI in its polls before the change of question wording was 24% in *The Times* of 8 May, 20% in the *Sunday Telegraph* of 13 May, 26% in *The Times* of 17 May, 28% in the *Economist* of 18 May and 25% in *The Times* of 24 May.

15 Alan Travis, *Guardian*, 1.6.01, p. 18.

16 However, if the length of the campaign is taken into account the number in 2001 (1.0 per campaign day) was identical to the number in 1997 (also 1.0).

17 NOP also conducted a poll for the *Daily Express*, early in the campaign, putting parties' standing at Con 31%, Lab 51%, LibDem 13%.

18 See, for example, 'Voters plan boycott', *Daily Mail*, 12 May; Anthony King, 'Lowest turnout since 1874 forecast', *Daily Telegraph*, 17 May. One commentator who noticed that the proportion of 'certain/very likely' voters was running at 11 to 12 percentage points below the level of four years previously and thus pointed to the possibility of turnout falling to 60% or worse was Dr Roger Mortimore of MORI. See his 'Turnout: how low might it go?', *MORI Poll Digest*, 27.4.01, MORI website: http://www.mori.com/digest.

19 NOP's unpublished poll for Channel 4 based on interviews conducted over the weekend before the election gave Labour a 27 point lead over the Conservatives (52% to 27%). If broadcast, the public record of the final forecast polls would have appeared considerably worse. ICM also conducted a poll for the *Evening Standard* on Monday 4 June, based on weekend interviews, which gave Labour a 47% to 30% lead and MORI conducted a poll for the *Economist*, based on interviews on the Monday and Tuesday, which gave Labour a 43% to 31% lead. The latter is described as published on election day but it would be more realistic to give Friday 8 June as the date, this being the publication date of the *Economist* both in hardcopy and on the web. These two polls are excluded from the list both of final and forecast polls because the polling organisations concerned published other polls based on later fieldwork dates.

20 Strictly speaking even exit polls have to adjust for the impact of postal voting,

which increased under more lenient regulations in 2001; but they do not have to estimate which respondents will turn up at the polling stations. The sources of error in exit polls are biases in the sample of polling stations, or in the sample of voters exiting them, and the partisan unrepresentativeness of respondents who refused to say how they voted.

21 Association of Professional Opinion Polling Organisations, 'Polls confound sceptics', 8.6.01.

22 The estimate included two ICM polls and two MORI polls, including the MORI poll for the *Economist* which was effectively not published until the day after the election. Moreover, it is unusual for APOPO to base its claims on all polls conducted in the final week since in the past it has argued that polls completing their fieldwork by or before the weekend should not be judged against the election result.

23 Ivor Crewe, op. cit., pp. 569–85 (p. 583).

24 As discussed by Curtice, in this volume, Labour also benefited slightly, as they did in 1997, from the pattern of constituency swings.

25 'What shy Tories?', *MORI Poll Digest*, 6.7.01, MORI website:www.mori.com/digest.

26 Weighting by a characteristic more strongly associated with party preferences, such as newspaper readership, would be a more effective way of reducing biases in the sample.

AUDIENCE COMMUNITIES, SEGMENTS AND COMMODITIES

The 'cultural turn' in audience research made it possible to imagine an approach to audience research that might counteract the dominant discourses of mass communication and question the consumerist agenda of market research and syndicated ratings services. Where the marketing approach erases the differences between audience members by registering only the most abstract dimension of their media use, cultural research makes it possible to engage with the things people say about media texts, the reasons they give for the opinions they hold about them, the discourses the texts generate and the rationales they develop to explain the importance (or not) of particular media materials in their lives. In other words, the 'cultural turn' opened the lid on a box of research methods that could now be used to investigate textual engagement. The 'ethnographic' heritage of the cultural methods meant they were ideal for use with small groups of participants, and with people who were traditionally marginalized by the dominant culture.

Perhaps the most pervasive research method used in audience research today is the focus group. Morrison (Chapter 7) reminds us that this method was pioneered by Robert Merton, and used extensively in the early functionalist research. In this article, Morrison outlines the basics of good and bad focus group practice and points to the careful preparation this method requires, especially as regards the nature of group moderation and the people skills required to manage group interaction effectively. The aim is to make it possible for all members of the group to contribute to the discussion. Focus groups are also routinely used in commercial audience research, but generally their use is confined to the exploration of audience attitudes.

The 'cultural turn' encouraged a more experimental use of the focus group, in ways that allow the participants more freedom to present their ideas, and the researcher to take a more interpretative role in the analysis of the group interaction. Such audience research questions the assumptions of cultural uniformity adopted by mass media like television and radio, which are built into much contemporary social science method. Instead it documents the media practices, activities and passions of people who make up only small sections of the mass audience and whose interests are overlooked in the search for commercially viable audience segments and niches.

There has been a tendency for researchers to overlook the media interests of certain niche audiences, who are part of the dominant audience but have special needs that are seldom represented. Karen Ross (Chapter 8) took on the challenge of investigating radio listeners with disabilities and discusses their views on the ways in which disability (people and themes) is represented on radio. Ross suggests, unsurprisingly, that listeners have quite different responses to the same material, although there were some clear areas of shared concern. These areas included the invisibility of 'less attractive' disabilities, and the apparent aversion to risk-taking that meant that too few radio producers were willing to integrate the disability themes seriously in radio programming.

A quite different approach to diversity within the mass audience is taken by Marie Gillespie (Chapter 9). Her contribution looks at young people in one of Britain's ethnic communities – young British Asian people living in South London. Gillespie uses ethnographic methods of observation and interviewing to explore the media interests and experiences of these young people. Her analysis of the role of transnational media in their lives is of considerable interest, in that she documents how they position themselves in relation to global, local and ethnic media discourses in the process of framing their 'British Asian' identity. Specifically, Gillespie shows that these young people often read 'traditional' narratives against the grain, and develop strategies that allow them to make sense of the differences between the 'here' and the 'there'. They are culturally situated simultaneously in Britain and in India.

Children make up a very large and diverse category within the mass audience. But even children struggle to have the media recognize their special needs. The general public concern about their viewing activities is not matched by a commitment to provide good quality programming for children. And the prevalence of poor quality programming for children ensures continuing demands for control of children's viewing rather than for better programming. David Buckingham (Chapter 10) provides an extensive and critical overview of the voluminous studies on the topic of children and the media, briefly documenting the never-ending search for negative effects of the media on children; the intense desire of adults to control and censor children's viewing, and the questions about the ages at which children are able to tell the difference between advertisements and programmes, or between reality and fiction. Research about children and the media is often motivated by awareness that children are unlikely to possess the cultural power to demand the type of media materials they want or to ensure the continued production of media materials that address their interests. Also, the child audience sometimes attracts researchers who purport to speak for children and to support their interests when motivated by quite other concerns – perhaps of a religious, moral or political nature. Buckingham deftly sorts through these complex motives and organizes the material in an intelligent way in order to render the various contradictions and similarities comprehensible and meaningful.

These three readings demonstrate the ways that the mass audience includes audience formations that fall outside the demographic categories that make a difference for ratings or programming purposes. When such groups attempt to make their particular media interests known, they are usually dismissed as too small to warrant special consideration by media industries. Sometimes such groups are also ethnic communities, whose shared traditions and common histories of migration lead them to develop specific strategies for interpreting media materials so that they become more interesting. Sometimes such formations may take the form of age cohorts, as for children's viewing. Other audience formations form around issues like disability, or support for victims of crime, or cancer sufferers. Yet the structural characteristics of the media and the financial constraints within which they operate mean that such groups are forced to take an activist stance in terms of production.

The work of Webster, Phalen and Lichty (Chapter 11) provides a marked contrast with the special interest focus of the other readings in this section. The mass audience is so large that it meets the needs of everyone in a general way and of no one in particular. Meehan (Chapter 12) suggests that it is the consumerist class only that is addressed by mass media. In the article included here, Webster, Phalen and Lichty provide one of the few models of 'audience exposure' to be developed outside the arena of marketing. While this work embraces a consumerist approach to researching audiences, it also provides access to a better understanding of the meaning that audiences, because of the attachments they develop to particular media programmes, have for media professionals. Webster, Phalen and Lichty frankly admit that audiences are commodities, the goods traded between media companies and advertisers. They pay little attention to the ways that the commodification of audiences privileges members of the audience who are most able to participate in the consumerist lifestyle promoted through advertising. This is the issue taken up by Eileen Meehan.

Meehan's contribution has been selected because it provides a critique of ratings and their consumerist assumptions in an article that has not been as widely read and discussed as it deserves. She introduces the notion of the consumerist caste, to denote the members of the general public targeted by advertising, and notes how they are likely to be better served in terms of the programming developed for the media. In particular she points out that the consumerist caste is not the same as the general public – although it may encompass a sizeable component of the general public. This means that particular interests that people have as 'the general public' (whether they are also members of the consumerist caste) are routinely neglected because the interests of the general public and those of a consumerist caste are understood quite differently, and suggest very different responsibilities for media industries.

Overall, Part II includes studies of audiences that look at the types of research carried out to investigate special interest groups, communities and age cohorts within the mass audience. The mass audience is not a uniform whole, and one size (in programming) does not fit all. The readings in this section draw attention to the extreme diversity that can be found within the mass audiences. The study of such audiences reveals the diversity of the approaches they take to shaping themselves and their identities in the context of media that seldom recognize their significance and provide little in the way of imaginative stimulation to encourage experimentation. This part also demonstrates the polar opposites in audience research method that are used in audience research.

GOOD AND BAD PRACTICE IN FOCUS GROUP RESEARCH

David E. Morrison

There is no set way to conduct focus groups. Mary Brotherson states: 'Design in qualitative research is a recursive process whereby each component of the process informs the next and is therefore continuously emergent and flexible. (Patton 1990; Tesch 1990) Thus, there is no set process for conducting focus group interviewing research'. (Brotherson 1994:106) Edward Fern, in fact, casts doubt on some of the assumptions that both academics and market researchers hold in conducting focus groups. Fern was keen to see if the assumptions held by focus group practitioners stood up to empirical investigation. He examined four basic assumptions:

1   that focus groups provide more information that is qualitatively better than individual interviews;
2   that the ideal size is between eight to twelve members;
3   that the moderator plays a crucial role;
4   within a group, homogeneity of members should be maintained.

Fern argues that the empirical evidence 'casts doubt on the validity of some of these assumptions. Yet other evidence seems to support these assumptions.' (Fern 1983:124) The problem with Fern's empirical evidence, however, is that most of the findings were not taken from focus group

David E. Morrison (1998) Good and bad practice in focus group research, *The Search for a Method: Focus Groups and the Development of Mass Communication Research*. Luton: University of Luton Press, pp. 207–23. Reprinted by kind permission of University of Luton Enterprises Ltd.

studies as such, but from fields such as psychotherapy, the findings of which may not be capable of being carried across to focus group research. Fern recognises this himself: 'In most cases the studies were done in situations quite different from typical focus group interviews. Focus groups are not normally recruited from a population of chronic schizophrenics. And personality is not usually a variable upon which within group homogeneity is sought'. (Fern 1983: 125). Fern is right to search for empirical evidence that the assumptions brought to the conducting of focus groups are sustainable, but any firm conclusion cannot be made from Fern's attempt to do so. However, Morgan and Spanish, writing in *Qualitative Sociology*, provide a thoughtful review of another study by Fern (1982) that addresses the question of empirical evidence for the assumptions upon which much focus group research proceeds:

> Fern compared focus groups of different sizes, moderated vs unmoderated focus groups, and groups composed of strangers vs acquaintances. The current 'tricks of the trade' in market research would call for a group of at least eight, with a professionally trained moderator, and a set of participants who were all strangers to one another. With regard to group size, Fern found that the number of ideas generated did not double as group size increased from four to eight, and that the ideas produced in groups were not necessarily superior in quality to those produced in individual interviews. He also found that moderated focus groups may have some advantages to unmoderated focus groups and that groups of strangers may be preferable to groups of acquaintances, but in neither case were the differences large. ... The important conclusion that we draw from Fern's work is that there is nothing sacred (or even necessarily correct) about the current ways that focus groups are conducted in market research. Overall, we see Fern's results as pointing toward a set of dimensions that the researcher can use to decide which form of focus group is best suited to his or her research questions. This flexibility was one of the things that originally attracted us to focus groups. (Morgan and Spanish 1984:255)

The idea of measuring success as advanced by Fern, counting the number of ideas and then questioning the assumptions made about group size because doubling the number of participants did not double the number of ideas, would seem to be a sterile exercise in arithmetic. Even though one might admit that the use of focus groups for brainstorming – the generation of ideas – might make sense, this is not the purpose to which most focus group research is put, nor would one have thought it possible in the arithmetic way suggested to measure the quality of the ideas generated. Of course one might have a panel judging the quality of ideas in the same way that for the construction of some measurement scales one has a panel to adjudicate on the value of the items to be used in the scale, but the judge of the quality of the responses in most focus group research is the researcher herself or himself.

Focus groups are a reflexive operation, and one knows in the course of the discussions if the focus group is moving in directions that are helpful to the research. That is what quality means, whether the data gathered is helpful or not; only the researcher who is in possession of the overall purpose and design of the project is capable of judging the quality of the data achieved. It is not uncommon after conducting a focus group to find researchers saying to one another, 'this is not working', and then examine why it is not working and come up with solutions to make it work. That, as Morgan and Spanish confess, is the type of flexibility inherent in the method that led them into the use of focus group research. Most quantification research does not have that flexibility. Once the survey questionnaire is in the field the researchers lose all control over its effectiveness as a research instrument. With focus group research knowledge on the part of the researcher is built as the research proceeds. As the learning increases that knowledge might be transferred to new questions for subsequent groups, or the original groups reconvened to gather their views on the researcher's new approach to the issues at hand. It is, in short, a method constantly being constituted, but that does not mean that the researcher need have no set of procedures for exploiting the full dynamic of the process, or that success will be achieved without having formulated a set of procedures on how to conduct the focus group. Preparation is as important for success in focus group research as in any other research, and one of the key factors is preparation of questions, and, unless the groups are being conducted for the purpose of exposing oneself to new territory, knowledge of the area under examination. That is why Merton was keen that a content analysis should be undertaken before subjects registered their responses to programmes using the Lazarsfeld-Stanton programme analyser.

It is the understanding of the area, even if only at a general level, that allows the researcher to place comments made in a wider system of understanding. This familiarity with the area, furthermore, allows the registering of the significance of an 'odd' comment which to the uninitiated might get overlooked but which in fact ought to be followed up. Thus, it is not a good idea for an academic project, even if affordable, to employ a professional moderator to run the groups. Unless the market research company is very specialised indeed, an academic communications researcher ought to have a greater understanding of media processes than a market researcher, and further, the academic is likely to proceed from a body of literature unknown to market research, and it is that literature, as likely as not, that has assisted the shaping of the research question.

Much academic work is an internal discourse, and thus it is very difficult to brief the outsider on its intricacies. Given that the knowledge gained in the course of focus group research is a developing reflexive knowledge, what the professional moderator considers an important avenue to follow the academic may not. In fact, this problem of differences in approach and differences in reception to information received afflicts academic focus group research if conducted by a team of researchers.

Despite Fern's challenge to the importance of the moderator, the success of focus group research is very much dependent on the skills and ability of the moderator. Different researchers will, at the level of performance, approach groups differently to other researchers, based on differences in personality and other factors, but that aside, intellectual differences between researchers in terms of their thinking on a topic will manifest itself in the material gathered. This is not an insurmountable problem, but it does mean that if a team of researchers are conducting the focus group project, close association and sharing of ideas is absolutely essential. Otherwise, quite disparate material is returned which may reflect the individual's interests and thinking, but which does not fit with the material gathered by others in advancing the centrally defined purpose of the study. Indeed, a problem of focus group research is the reliability of the data gathered; hence my argument, following Merton, that focus groups are not very satisfactory research tools when used alone.[1]

Importance of the moderator

Strange as it may seem the moderator is much more in control of the interview situation in focus group research than the interviewer is in the single in-depth interview. Both situations require the interviewer to have a schedule of some sort, a check list of areas that he or she wishes the interview to address. While it may seem that directing the flow of conversation of eight to ten people to stop it meandering is more difficult than focusing a single individual on the topic of interest, it is not. To begin with, usually in focus group research one has some stimuli material to help focus the discussion; secondly, it is easier to interrupt the individual in a group context without appearing brutish, by asking for comments from others in the group, and thus steer the discussion back to the central ground than it is to interrupt the conversation of a single interview if it strays. Should the single interview falter because the interviewee becomes irritated at not being allowed to say what they want, it is difficult to restart the interviewer and rebuild the familiarity necessary for a good interview, and an absolute disaster if such 'breaks' become frequent. In the single interview there is no one to play the interviewee off against, and any interruption by the interviewer is obviously directed at the interviewee in a most pointed fashion; whereas in the group situation it can be made to appear that the point the participant has made is so interesting that the moderator is only interrupting to collect the thoughts of others on the point. The moderator then only needs to allow the briefest of comments from a person who is not the holder of the original point, and thus does not feel emotionally possessive about it when the moderator shuts down the conversation by asking the opinion of someone else on a point more relevant to the research.

There is no question that the personality of the moderator in the focus group situation, and their skills in social manipulation, is an essential part of the success of the enterprise. In the single interview, especially if conducted with very confident elite figures, it is the interviewer who faces the full force of the successful personality and is the subject of manipulation rather than the interviewee. Within the media, and television in particular, the projection of the personality and the imposition of the ego on others is not only the mark of the successful person, but a characteristic making for success. A strong belief in the self is common to practically all who hold senior positions in the industry, and such people, though courteous and charming – their social skills have been cultivated as essentials for the manipulation of people – do tend to consider that what they have to say is important. Thus to attempt to direct the conversation away from the topic the interviewee is addressing to other topics that the interviewer considers more important can meet with resistance. Charm can easily be dropped when it fails to serve its purpose, to be replaced by a forceful insistence that one takes note of what the speaker is saying, or that the question put is not 'relevant' to the subject at hand. Interviews with elite people tend not to give the researcher more than the interviewee wishes to give. Success in conducting such interviews rests on the interviewer's ability to extract to the limit that which the interviewee is prepared to expose about themselves or the organisation they work for. The negotiation of 'space' is, especially for senior people in the media, a well-honed skill. The situation is not easy to control, especially if the time limit rests with the interviewee, as it almost always does.

The role of personality and the skill of performance should never be underplayed in the conducting of any interview, and no more so than in conducting a group discussion. This is not to say, however, that the moderator ought to impose themselves on the group, but that the moderator must be in control of the proceedings. If control is lost a focus group can become a shambles. Thus, any especially offensive person, someone who repeatedly turns on other members of the group, must be asked to leave. In any experience such offensiveness is usually associated with drink, and sometimes, but not often, with drugs. The best approach is to first try and isolate such people and only as a last resort eject them. If it is necessary to eject someone the group can always be brought back together by some light-hearted banter relating to the ejected participant, and restarted once the tension has been released.

There are some people who just are unpleasant. They must be removed if they become intimidating to other members of the group. A suggestion once in a Northern male working-class group by one participant that some facilities in the town that had previously been a social club for a local football team and had now been turned into a ballet centre subsidised by council funds was a good use of rate payers' money brought a vicious enquiry from another participant of whether or not the speaker was 'queer'. Despite the fact that the focus group had nothing to do with sexuality, the question of 'manliness', accompanied by dark looks towards the individual who had defended the ballet school, entered at a surprising number of points with an inventiveness that was creative in its ingenuity. It was not a successful focus group. In such a situation there is nothing to do but abandon the whole exercise. That is, to bring the focus group to completion as quickly as possible.

By and large focus groups are pleasant experiences for all concerned, and always work best when that is the case. This is not difficult in the area of media research, since people generally like to discuss communication issues. It is in such situations that what might be termed the 'normal' functioning of the moderator comes into play.

As we have seen, Paul Lazarsfeld and his colleague, Robert Merton, attempted to develop a graduate training school for the social sciences at Columbia University in the 1950s. Together they developed a long and carefully thought out document (*Proposal to Establish an Institute for Training in Social Research*, BASR Library 1950) in which they laid out how they considered such training could be given, and what its functions and purposes were. As part of the exercise they addressed themselves to the problem of how one could train researchers for areas of research that depended very much on individualistic 'talent' rather than the performance of set technical skills. It is interesting, therefore, that the article written by Merton and Kendall in 1946 on the focused interview anticipates ideas on qualitative training that surfaced in the 1950 proposal. Indeed, focus group research is an area where it is difficult to say how, in any absolutely precise way, one ought to operate and what skills are required on the part of the moderator for the successful completion of such groups. In fact, it is quite difficult to measure success. At least with survey research one can quickly tell if the sample is wrong, or if the question construction was poor as evidenced by the high number of missing values or contradictory answers to questions, all of which would suggest that respondents had difficulty either following the question routing or in understanding the questions.

Lazarsfeld himself was a keen educator. Educational change and educational instruction formed, along with his fascination with methods, his central intellectual interests. It is reasonable to presume that Merton's exposure to focus group research and the difficulties faced in instructing on their operational principles and practice, found their way into his daily conversations with Lazarsfeld. The partnership of Merton and Lazarsfeld was as intense as it was productive. It is highly likely, therefore, that Merton's involvement in focus group research added substantially to the thinking about research training in the area of qualitative research that went into the 1950 proposal to establish a school of research training. Certainly the following passage from Merton and Kendall's article of 1946 reads as if it been lifted straight out of the Proposal:

> A successful interview is not the automatic product of conforming to a fixed routine or mechanically applicable techniques. Nor is interviewing an elusive, private, and incommunicable art. ... There are recurrent situations and problems in the focused interview which can be met successfully by communicable and teachable procedures. We have found that the proficiency of all interviews, even the less skilful, can be considerably heightened by training them to recognise type situations and to draw upon an array of flexible, though standardised, procedures for dealing with these procedures. (Merton and Kendall 1946: 544,545)

Both Lazarsfeld and Merton were enthused with the idea of building up cases for use in student instruction, and their procedures were modelled on medical instruction. In the writings of both one finds frequent medical references, and in the case of the proposed training school students are at times referred to as 'interns'. It is the building up of cases that Merton and Kendall recommend in overcoming the mysteries of transmitting qualitative skills. They remark: 'In his search for 'significant data', moreover, the interviewer must develop a capacity for continuously evaluating the interview as it is in process', and they lay out how this capacity can be instructed. A central instructional technique of Lazarsfeld and Merton was the case; that is, building up a body of work that conforms to good practice, or from which good practice can be deduced:

> By drawing upon a large number of interview transcripts, in which the interviewer's comments as well as the subjects' responses have been recorded, we have found it possible to establish a set of provisional criteria by which productive and unproductive interview material can be distinguished. (Merton and Kendall 1946:545)

This procedure led Merton and Kendall to outline four areas of practice:

1 Non-direction: In the interview, guidance and direction by the interviewer should be at a minimum.
2 Specificity: Subjects' definitions of the situation should find full and specific expression.
3 Range: The interview should maximise the range of evocative stimuli and responses reported by the subject.
4 Depth and personal context: The interviewer should bring out the affective and value- laden implications of the subjects' responses, to determine whether the experiences had central or peripheral significance. It should elicit the relevant personal context, the idiosyncratic associations, beliefs, and ideas.

True to their precise thinking and regard for the process of verification, Merton and Kendal comment that 'since these procedures have been derived from clinical analysis of interview material rather than through experimental test, they must be considered entirely provisional'. (Merton and Kendall 1946:545) As they rightly point out the above criteria although listed out are in fact interrelated, 'merely different dimensions of the same concrete body of interview materials'. However, it is the criteria of non-direction that are worthwhile to examine in more detail, since it is that area, the interaction of the 'observer' with the 'participants', that creates the greatest difficulty in conducting focus group research, and the one where the values, beliefs, and thinking of the researcher infuse the discussion to a degree where it is impossible to decipher what voices are in what discourse. Furthermore, as Merton and Kendal comment in their examination of procedures: 'The interrelations of our criteria at once become evident when we observe that non-direction simultaneously serves to elicit depth, range and specificity of responses. For this reason the tactics of non-direction require special consideration'. (Merton and Kendall 1946:546)

Guiding the discussion

In discussing the nature of unstructured questions Merton and Kendall note that there are various degrees of structuring, the most unstructured being one that 'does not fix attention on any specific aspect of the stimulus situation or of the response; it is, so to speak, a blank page to be filled in by the subject.' They go on to say that the fully unstructured question is particularly appropriate at the beginning of the interview session, but that it might be fruitfully applied at various points in the overall interview. They consider that at some points it may be necessary for the moderator 'to assume more control' particularly in later stages of the interview, 'if the other criteria – specificity, range, and depth – are to be satisfied'. However, even in such cases where more control is required, they warn that 'moderate rather than full direction is fruitful; questions should be partial rather than fully structured'.

For Merton and Kendall, the focused interview is a vehicle for discovering what participants think and feel, not a hobby horse for allowing participants to discover what the moderator thinks. Under the title, 'Imposing the interviewer's frame of reference', Merton and Kendall, while sympathetic to the strains of the interview situation, offer instruction on curbing the appetite of the moderator to interfere:

> At some points in almost every protracted interview, the interviewer is tempted to take the role of educator or propagandist rather than that of sympathetic listener. He may either interject his personal sentiments or voice his views in answer to questions put to him by subjects. Should be yield to either temptation, the interview is then no longer an informal listening-post or 'clinic' or 'laboratory' in which subjects spontaneously talk about a set of experiences, but it becomes, instead, a debating society or an authoritarian arena in which the interviewer defines the situation.

The consequences of doing so are:

> By expressing his own sentiments the interviewer generally invites spurious comments or defensive remarks, or else inhibits certain discussions altogether. Any such behaviour by the interviewer introduces a 'leader effect', modifying the informant's own expression of feelings. Or should the interviewer implicitly challenge a comment, the informant will often react by defensively reiterating his original statement. The spontaneous flow of the interview halts while the subject seeks to maintain his ego-level intact by reaffirming his violated sentiments. (Merton and Kendall 1946:547)

The 'leader effect' referred to here is not the same phenomenon as 'moderator demand', although it does have similarities in that both call forth responses that would not have occurred 'naturally'. Moderator demand refers to the situation where the nature of the questions given by the moderator results in an attempt by the participant to feed information that they think would be useful to the researcher, or modify their position in line with the perceived value position of the moderator. 'Leader effect' refers to an interference in the discussion by the moderator that alters the 'quality' of the responses by forcing the participants to recognise the ideas that the moderator holds.

Merton and Kendall are against the interviewer becoming involved in any confrontation with participants through the expression of their own beliefs or opinions, even when the participants might deliberately seek out such information. Without doubt it is best for the moderator not to give an opinion on a topic under discussion, even if asked. Such queries are not difficult to fend off. Comments such as, 'I am not sure what I think, that's why I was interested in what you were saying', are usually sufficient to avoid the moment of 'exposure', especially given that the questioner is surrounded by other people so that the question put to the moderator can be turned straight back to some one else in the group – 'I'm not sure, I wonder what X thinks'. This is not a strategy available to the interviewer in the single elite interview. But then in such interviews it does not matter if one is asked for an opinion no more than can a response be avoided in what is a very directed intellectual exchange. Indeed, such interrogation can act as a stimulus for exploration of the other person's thinking as challenge and counter-challenge takes place, always of course in a probing and not combative way. The major difference, however, between the group situation and the single interview is that the exchange in the latter is private, not public. Thus the interviewee in the single interview has no need to guard their ego or feel that they have been 'exposed', or at least not to the same extent as in the setting of a focus group.

While agreeing that one should not expose one's own position on some topic in the situation of the focus group, matters are somewhat different when it comes to challenging the points made by discussants. As ever, much depends on individual judgement. Focus groups, in the main, are fluid encounters, in which familiarity must be established quickly. The 'friendship' is a very brief affair, lasting only for an hour or two. The skill of the moderator is in her or his ability to quickly make the participants relax so that a minimum of trust is established sufficient for them to feel comfortable in exposing feelings and giving opinion. The moderator, however, does not work alone, but with the people who have agreed to participate in the groups. The atmosphere, therefore, also depends on the personalities of those interviewed. Some groups, for that reason, just work better than other groups. The young, 16 to 18 year olds, are invariably hard-going, having often little to say, or if they do, often affecting a bored look, especially so in the case of male youths.

The struggle for the establishment of self-identity, a mark of that age group, offers a picture of self-centredness that fails to include attention to the world outside their immediate self. Thus, although not always, it is difficult to promote a flowing discussion of broad-based issues. The embarrassed silences often prompt one or two participants to speak in situations where one feels that they would rather not, and thus one is never quite sure if the opinions expressed are genuinely held or the forced classroom response where to say something is better than to say nothing. With such age groups it is essential to have stimuli that will promote engagement and discussion, and not have the proceedings depend simply on the stimuli of verbal prompts. In such a situation one would never challenge the veracity of the statements made by the participants; the whole situation is too fragile to risk disturbance through challenge.

In other groups of older, more confident individuals, especially where the atmosphere is relaxed, usually achieved by the presence of one or two 'characters' who open up the meeting by the sheer warmth of their per-sonalities, challenge to opinion can take place. Even so, such challenge is best reserved until one 'knows' the group and can judge if such interroga-tion is called for. It all depends on the rapport that has been established, and each group differs in this respect. Moderating is an individual act, in the same way that giving a lecture is an individual act – sometimes one feels good and the performance matches the feeling, other times the reverse is the case. At times, therefore, one may not feel confident or relaxed enough with one's own performance to engage in the delicate judgement of risking challenge. Yet, if the situation is felt to be right, to question the statement of some-one can be very productive. Saying, 'do you really believe that' accompanied by some incredulity in the voice, or presenting a gentle argument against the point made, without giving away one's own position, is powerful tool for examining thought. Disputation, as a method, is always good for establishing truth, but it must not be undertaken in a manner that prevents further reflection and engagement on the discussant's part.

The actual beliefs that people hold are often to be discovered in the qualifying statements that follow the original point that they make. It is often only through challenge to the original point that the qualifying statement is offered. The constant, 'why do you believe that?' or 'why did you say that?' is not always sufficient to excavate meaning.

The moderator's skill in offering challenge to statements is in knowing how far to press the challenge. As a general rule one stops the challenge once one feels that the 'interrogation' has gone far enough to allow the participant the opportunity of revealing what they mean by their answers. This exchange, however, must be done in a manner pleasurable to the participant. By doing so, the discussant feels that the moderator has genuinely listened to what they have said, and has taken their contribution seriously. The worst crime is to be dismissive of the discussant, either through verbal expression, or displaying lack of interest in what she or he has to say.

The strain of conducting focus groups is high, especially if several are conducted in the same day, which for the sake of economy often happens. The success of the exercise does depend, to a large extent, on the individual performance of the moderator. Yet this does not mean that the value of focus group research should be all down to the whim of the moderator on the day. A well-prepared interview schedule designed to foster discussion geared to the central interests of the study is one way to ensure success, and a second method is to provide visual or other stimulatory material that will trigger and focus discussion independent almost of the moderator's performance. It ought not to be the case that no other moderator would have received responses that proximate to those recorded. If so, then suspicion must enter that the material had been 'conjured' by the moderator. The skill of the moderator is as a facilitator of discussion, not as the scripter of it, otherwise the data is idiosyncratic and of little social scientific value.

Because of the pressures of the performance, the sheer strain of holding bits of information and mentally noting who has said what means that it is often helpful to have two moderators, one taking the lead and the other acting as a support who can log particularly significant comments for exploration at later points. The support moderator can also relieve the primary moderator by occasionally entering the discussion so that the primary moderator can take quick mental stock of how the discussion is proceeding and re-focus the discussion should be or she consider that 'drift' from the main theme has occurred. The presence of a second moderator is also useful in that following completion of a group each can check notes and generally de-brief each other as to what were the significant trains of thought that might have emerged which had not been expected, but which could usefully be carried over to the next group discussion for further exploration. A word of warning is necessary, however. Focus groups, as they progress, allow the researcher to build up a picture of feelings and responses to the subject matter under enquiry, but the picture is a 'developing one' and may not be clear, or in full focus, at any one point in time. Thus the findings from any one particular focus group, certainly after its immediate completion, can often be deceptive as to their full value or meaning. It is often the case that a group that one thought did not go particularly well, on examination of the transcript in the calm of the office at a much later date turns out to provide more insights than some other focus group that the moderator had judged to have gone very well simply because the discussion in that group flowed. It must also be remembered that although a single focus group can give insight into the question under examination, it is not just individual insights that one is collecting, but the pattern of responses that show that the comments made are related to collective experiences that have, at least for the sociologist, a sociological presence. Here we return to the earlier observation that focus groups are better seen as a beginning and not an end. That is, if one is after a sociological presence, and mostly one is, even the market researcher, having found such a presence, further work using different methods becomes a requirement of the research.

Of course one might simply be interested in using focus groups for concept development, hypothesis construction, to alert the researcher to ways of thinking, for the exploration of language usage, or the possibilities that they offer for the development of theoretical formulation of issues, in which case the pattern of the responses may not be of overriding importance, although they still ought to be of some interest. If this is the case, that they are mere explorations for developmental purposes, the findings of the focus groups should not be published as if they were complete studies. Indeed, it is not surprising, referring back to the comments by Morgan, that the focus group method is not given due publicity by scholars when used as part of a collected set of methods, for the simple reason that they do not deserve great prominence. They are not given prominence because they have served their job as developmental tools, or as illustrations to support more 'powerfully' grounded findings. In other words, in research that uses a variety of methods the results of focus groups are handled with the respect owed the method, and not as stand-alone findings of a generalisable nature. It is only because they have come to be used as a stand-alone method, and thus form the basis of a whole study, that they have assumed the importance they have. But if the habit has developed of having the method form the basis of one's study, it is not surprising that researchers who do so should wish it to be given as much prominence as possible.

For studies that use focus groups as one component in a larger package of procedures, it is not surprising that they will only be accorded the role that they have played in the overall scheme of things. Even then, as important as they may have been in an intellectual creative sense, they often come to be overshadowed in the report stage of the presentation of findings by other methods. The researcher who uses focus groups as part of a package of procedures has no need to 'talk the method up' since the overall methodological strength of the study will speak for itself, perhaps one reason why Merton did not need to signal his use of focus groups in the *The Student Physician* (Merton 1957).

Building understanding

In media research, there is a temptation to use the findings as a pattern of responses illustrative of a wider tapestry. But the pattern of responses found in one focus group does not necessarily infer that such a pattern will be found overall when the totality of responses are examined. A simple illustration of this can be given from the quantification approach to knowledge of survey research. Data are often entered into the computer as and when they arrive, and a large sample may take some time before all the returns are in. For various reasons one sometimes makes the first run of the data on the small numbers gathered by the first post-back of responses. It is exciting to read the print out of this first haul. Yet time and again those responses drawn from the incomplete sample, and which on reading one often concludes a pattern, turns out to be wrong when the full data set is received. This underscores the point that it is dangerous to draw general conclusions from the small numbers involved in focus group research, especially given that the form of questioning generally speaking is not designed for quantification. It also warns against making general assumptions about the pattern of responses within focus group research that is itself based on incomplete returns, that is, from groups conducted at an early stage.

Focus group research is a built procedure, this is one of its absolute strengths, but the building only becomes secure as more bricks, in the form of additional groups, are added. But as we have seen, at some point, and usually before too long, the shape of the building can be seen, and unless one wishes to add the fine points of architectural design the conducting of further groups becomes unnecessary. This does not mean that the story is complete once the first storey, to stick with the building metaphor, is constructed. Indeed, to come to conclusions early on in the research about the eventual shape of the building is to construct the building on shaky foundations. That is, the questioning in subsequent groups is framed by the conclusions already made from the initial groups, which entails the danger that the eventually building looks remarkably like the one originally imagined. There is no easy way to overcome this, and this is why focus group research does require checks on findings drawn from additional methodology.

Although the conducting of focus group research is a discursive activity, it is essential that each group covers the same ground, or does so to the extent that the information gained from the groups is comparable. This does not mean that exactly the same questions, put in the very same way, have to be asked of each group. Simply that the same interview guide is followed for each group. One of the great benefits of focus group research is its flexibility. As the researcher's knowledge increases so new elements gained in the course of the groups can be fed in, but these new elements should be variations of the basic elements that formed the foundation of the original interview guide or schedule. Even so one needs to guard against rigidity in the application of the guide; the guide is to ensure that the researcher covers the intended topics with the group. It is not a questionnaire. Merton and Kendall warn:

> The interview guide does, however, lend itself to misuse. Even when the interviewer recognises that it is only suggestive, he may come to use it as a fixed questionnaire, as a kind of interviewing strait jacket ... Though it is convenient for the interviewer not to have to improvise all questions in the course of the interview, predetermined questions may easily become a liability; for, if the interviewer recognises in the respondent's comment an allusion to an area of enquiry previously defined in the guide, he is likely to introduce one of the type questions contained in the guide. This is all well and good *if* the question happens to be appropriate in the given case. But unproductive interviews are those cluttered with the corpses of fixed, irrelevant queries; for often the interviewer, equipped with fixed questions dealing with a given topic, does not listen closely or analytically to the subject's comments and thus fails to respond to the cues and implications of these comments, substituting, instead, one of the routine questions from the guide. If the interviewer is primarily orientated towards the guide, he may thus readily overlook the unanticipated implications of the subject's remark. (Merton and Kendall 1946:548)

Merton and Kendall's warning is necessary. There is something wrong if the moderator needs to constantly 'read off' from his or her interview guide, certainly after the first one or two groups have been conducted. Having written out the guide the moderator should commit the areas or topics to be covered to memory. This rehearsal of the guide thus frees the moderator in the actual interview to give full attention to what is being said, and respond accordingly with his or her own enquiry for explanations and further comment to points made, always holding in the background the general scheme for the interview.

The basic purpose of the focus group is to get people to talk about what you want them to talk about, but to do so in their own words. There is a great danger of over-complicating what really is a very simple process. Because it is simple, however, does not mean it is easy to do well. Kitzinger (1994) mentions the use of various exercises adopted by the Glasgow University Media Group in course of their focus group research:

> At the start of the session, for example, participants were asked to play 'the news game' which involved dividing into two small teams and writing their own news bulletin using a pre-selected set of photographs taken from actual TV news bulletins. Later they were presented with a pack of cards bearing statements about who might be 'at risk' from AIDS and asked, as a group, to sort the cards into different piles indicating the degree of 'risk' attached to each 'type of person' (Kitzinger 1994:106)

Such a technique would appear to be a very inventive way of having participants work among themselves with very little intervention from the moderator, and at the same time provide base line information which could be carried across for comparative analysis with other groups if it was so wished. It also, one presumes, forms a very good stimuli for conversation. But as Kitzinger herself points out in reference to games in general: 'Unfortunately some people, of course, do not like party games and at worst such games could make people feel uncomfortable and reminded some research participants of school lessons!' (Kitzinger 1994:107).

Some participant certainly do not like to engage in games or role playing exercises, but it must also be pointed out that neither do some researchers feel comfortable as 'party organisers'. One might believe in the benefit of some game type exercise, but if one feels embarrassed running them they will not work well, and are best left alone. Yet it is in market research that the development of exploratory techniques have been pushed the furthest. Projection techniques have proved particularly popular. The main ones are: personality association, situational association, forced relationships, collage creation, sentence completions, expressive drawings and anthromorphisation. Writing on these techniques Thomas Greenbaum comments:

> Projective techniques are a group of focus group moderating tools that generate information from participants by encouraging them to make associations with other stimuli as a way of expressing their feelings towards the specific conceptual idea, product, service or other entity with which they are being presented. Essentially, these techniques evoke reactions to a familiar stimulus in order to help people share

their feelings about a new one. They are not unlike the ink blot tests that psychologists use to get their patients to express their innermost feelings. How a psychologist interprets patients' comments is much more complicated than how a moderator interprets participants' comments, but the principle is the same: They both use a secondary stimulus to elicit the individual's feelings. (Greenbaum 1993:104)

Anyone wishing to follow up in detail these projective techniques ought to refer to Greenbaum directly. It is difficult to see their use in social scientific research. The problem with such techniques is that one really does not know what one is measuring, listening to or observing. Greenbaum, for example, gives the example of a forced relationship exercise using animals, something not uncommon in market research. A bear, so he says, is often associated with caring organisations, ones that are large and friendly. A lion is associated as the king of the jungle, a strong organisation that has great power. A turtle is associated with a very slow-moving or backward organisations. In researching the image that an organisation has in public consciousness one can well see how the technique might be brought into play. But even then, why not ask people how they see a bank, or an oil company, rather than what animal they associate with the organisation? Such techniques would seem only to introduce another variable, the meaning of which one cannot be sure of. Even Greenbaum admits: 'Some participants at first react to this type of exercise with a reasonably negative attitude, feeling that it is silly. (Greenbaum 1993:115)

There may be a temptation by academics to be overly influenced by the success that commercial researchers have had with focus groups and the claims that they make for them. David Morgan in his commentary on the history of focus groups recognises their origins in sociology, but also points to the special role that market research has played in their adoption and development: 'Returning the focus group technique to social science research will thus require considerable borrowing and considerable innovation.' He sensibly notes, however, as if to offer a warning of the danger of straightforward imitation, that the issues market researchers have addressed 'bear little resemblance to the questions that social scientists usually investigate'. (Morgan 1988:10) This is so only to a certain extent. The prefixing of the term market to research understandably conjures images of product research, corporate imagery research and so on, but a lot of research undertaken in the commercial domain, and for which focus groups are used, is social research that has close proximity to work undertaken in the academy. However, it is certainly true that in certain areas academic researchers have little or nothing to learn from their market research cousins.

The adoption of focus groups by market research companies, and the contribution they have made to company revenue, has meant an increased search for new areas of application. For example, one of the more recent additions in America has been their adoption by the legal profession 'as a vehicle to help litigators improve the overall quality of the cases they are preparing for trial.' (Greenbaum 1993:xiii) Market research as a seller of a service as well as a provider of knowledge is constantly on the look-out for new techniques as an aid to sell their services, and not necessarily as a way of improving the quality of the knowledge provided. This is not to say that market researchers are necessarily duplicitous, since they are wrapped up in occupational ideological practices that ferment a genuine belief that the provision of the former assist the creation of the latter, that new techniques will always create not just new knowledge, but better knowledge. Thus it is interesting that in surveying the field Greenbaum notes the many changes that have taken place in the use of focus groups by market research:

> Researchers have come to understand the need for more professional recruiting, better physical plants, and a more of a partnership between the moderator, the client, and the focus group facility. At the present time, the weakest link in the focus group chain is probably the facility.

The term 'better physical plant' is resonant with ideas of truly professionalising a method. The incorporation, furthermore, of a language drawn from engineering helps consolidate focus groups as a specialised activity to be undertaken only by those with access to the means of production. However, a room equipped with two-way mirrors is totally unnecessary for academic researchers, although this is beginning to change along with increasing video taping of groups, and indeed is not all that much used by market researchers in Britain. The two-way mirror, or to use Greenbaum's term, the better 'physical plant', is purely for the benefit of the client who may wish too watch the proceedings, and has nothing to do with the quality of the responses received from participants to the group. In American market research technocratising focus group research has even progressed to a state where the moderator might be equipped with an ear-piece to receive instruction from the client. One can understand this in terms of the moderator-client relationship in market research, but even so to have a client watch focus group in operation is damaging to the method. If one has moderator demand, one now has client demand. That is, 'tricks' are engaged in by the moderator and a performance staged that is for the benefit of the client, not for eliciting information. Indeed, the common practice by some market researchers of always recruiting ten participants, not nine, not eleven, has nothing to do with preferred numbers for facilitating group dynamics or interviewer control, but so that innumerate clients taking notes can easily put percentages on responses.

The requirements of the academic are, in general, different from that of the market researcher. To begin with, practically any location (physical plant) will suffice to conduct focus groups, but in my experience to achieve the most relaxed atmosphere it is better to conduct them in a private dwelling, rather than in a hotel, the upstairs room of a public house, community centre or other such public place. Wherever the focus group takes place the participants need to feel relaxed and be able to offer their contribution in a non-threatening climate. Indeed, focus group discussions can at times become quite heated. Participants can say things that in more calm moments they would not have said, and may later come to regret being so open. Focus group research does in fact throw up special ethical difficulties that require attention.

Note

1   It must be noted that Lunt and Livingstone in their paper 'Rethinking the Focus Group in Media and Communication Research' would consider this position to be too narrow and depart strongly from Merton's demand for reliability, considering that qualitative research should not be infected by evaluations of data that are used in quantitative studies. They put forward the case that 'qualitative methods compensate for the lack of reliability with greater validity'. Even so, they make a case for the reliability of the data gathered in focus groups by saying: 'Conducting focus groups produces a flood of ideas and information in the early groups, which is then reiterated y subsequent groups until (sometimes sooner than others) no new stories are told. Thus, although there is variation from one group to another, there is a point at which the new information gain drops with each new group. One could argue, then, that the exhaustion of the various things to be said on a given topic is part of the content validity of the method, offering a notion of reliability related not to the identity of two runs of the method, but to the rate of information gain.' (Lunt and Livingstone 1996:92) However, as I have pointed out previously the exhaustion of new information only means that one has collected the range of views in a population, it does not give one the distribution of the views.

References

Brotherson, M. (1994) Interactive focus group interviewing: a qualitative research method, *Early Intervention. Topics in Early Childhood Special Education*, 14(1).

Fern, E.F. (1982) The use of focus groups for idea generation: the effect of group size, acquaintanceship and moderators in response quality and quantity, *Journal of Marketing Research*, 19.

Fern, E.F. (1983) Focus groups: a review of some contradictory evidence, implications and suggestions for future research, *Advances in Consumer Research*, 10.

Greenbaum, T.L. (1993) *The Handbook for Focus Group Research*. New York: Lexington Books.

Kitzinger, J. (1994) The methodology of focus groups: the importance of interaction between research participants, *Sociology of Health and Illness*, 16(1).

Lazarsfeld, P.F. and Merton, R.K. (1950) *Proposal to Establish and Institute for Training in Social Science*. BASR Library.

Lunt, P. and Livingstone, S. (1996) Rethinking the focus group in media and communication research, *Journal of Communication*, 46(2).

Merton, R.K. (1957) *Social Theory and Social Structure*. Glencoe, IL: Free Press.

Merton, R.K. and Kendall, P.L. (1946) The focussed interview, *American Journal of Sociology*, 51.

Morgan, D.L. (1988) *Focus Groups and Qualitative Research*. Newbury Park: Sage Publications.

Morgan, D.L. and Spanish, M.T. (1984) Focus groups: a new tool for qualitative research, *Qualitative Sociology*, 7.

Patton, M.Q. (1990) *Qualitative Evaluation Methods*. Newbury Park, CA: Sage.

Tesch, R. (1990) *Qualitative Research: Analysis Types and Software Tools*. New York: Falmer Press.

ALL EARS

8

RADIO, RECEPTION AND DISCOURSES OF DISABILITY

Karen Ross

Media and the trope of disability

If radio as a medium has not enjoyed the same level of academic interest as its more flashy sister television since the latter became a mass medium, then disability[1] has also been almost totally ignored as a thematic of contemporary interest to mass media researchers, and what studies do exist are either content-driven (see, for example, Cumberbatch and Negrine 1992) or else focused on the views of non-disabled people (Broadcasting Standards Council 1994). It is only very recently that more nuanced accounts of disability and media portrayal have begun to be produced, most notably the very useful and comprehensive volume produced by Pointon and Davies (1997) but also Darke (1995) and Ross (1997a). What most of these studies show is that there is a dearth of images of disability in mainstream broadcasting and those that do exist are largely peripheral and stereotypical.

In some ways, this lack of focus on disability as an appropriate theme for media analysis parallels the difficulty that campaigners have had in getting issues relating to disability placed on the social, political and economic agenda, despite the fact that disabled people form the largest 'minority' group whose members consistently experience oppression and are denied fundamental rights. The fact that even at the time of writing, in 1999, Britain's Disability Discrimination Act (1995) still has significant elements

Karen Ross (2001) All ears: radio, reception and discourses of disability, *Media, Culture & Society*, 23(4): 423–36. Reprinted by kind permission of Sage Publications.

that have yet to come into force, provides a potent example of the way in which the rights of disabled people remain on the periphery of the collective political consciousness. So, if we believe, even if not fully consciously, that media messages have subtle effects on how and what we believe, if not determining the direction then at least framing the parameters, then how disability and disabled people's lives are portrayed in popular mass media is important.

Methods and process

The study that I describe in this essay aimed to explore what disabled listeners think about the way in which disability is treated on radio, both in terms of disability issues and their treatment, but also the ways in which disabled characters are portrayed. We also wanted to identify perspectives on the extent to which disabled people are included in radio programming, both as actors but also as presenters and contributors to shows. Although the original project idea originated with BBC Radio 4 and was initially conceptualized as an audience reception study of Radio 4 listeners with a disability, the parameters of the study quickly widened to include not just other BBC stations but the independent radio sector as well. This broadening of the original sample base proved to be an extremely worthwhile adjustment to the original design since it became clear during the fieldwork that audiences' listening behaviours were determined as much by what else they happened to be doing – 'I like Classic FM when I'm in the car', or 'I like to listen to the local news in the morning' – as their loyalty to particular programmes or stations. As with the previous studies I have carried out with/for the BBC (see, for example, Ross 1997b), there was again a conscious desire on the part of the project team to hear the views of 'ordinary' listeners rather than spokespeople for various pressure groups and campaign organizations. Not only do such spokespeople get many other opportunities to air their views, including access to the media, but many people with a disability are deeply suspicious of those they describe, often cynically, as part of the disability industry: '[they] speak for us, but are not one *of* us!' We therefore decided to use a variety of recruitment techniques to generate a sample that would have maximum diversity and geographical spread. Previous criticisms of audience work have often centred around the preponderance of participants from London, the South East or England more generally, and there was a genuine wish for the scope of the study to include other regions and nations.

We recruited the sample through several recruitment strategies including trails and interviews on network radio, notices in the disability press, a stand at a disability conference (SCOPE) and a questionnaire posted to the BBC's homepage. A total of 469 people with a disability took part in the study, including 82 participants in 15 group interviews, 85 individuals who completed questionnaires and 372 people who took part in a telephone interview. The principal criteria for participation were that individuals identified themselves as a person with a disability, that they were regular radio listeners and that they had a view on the way in which disability issues (in fact and fiction) are dealt with by that medium. What follows is an exploration of some of the key themes to emerge from the study and some suggestions about future strategies for producing more sensitive and informed broadcast narratives. Notwithstanding the discussion that is played out below concerning the nature of 'the audience', part of the method employed here in relation to talking to listeners can be seen to develop an ethnographic approach (following Ang 1991) which attempts to explore subjective meanings and context among media consumers in an effort to supplement the somewhat meagre and intrinsically superficial information which can ever be derived from the 'ratings' approach to audience appreciation and which tries to consider multi-significances in diverse reception circumstances (Moores 1993). While I am not suggesting that the subsequent narratives are necessarily more authentic or 'real' (see Nightingale 1996) than the data generated by the more quantitative techniques more routinely used by broadcasters, they are significantly *different* in their depth and breadth and do begin to offer a more complex analysis of relations between medium, message and consumer.

The usual suspects: stereotyping disability

There was a clear view among disabled listeners that there remain too many examples of stereotypical portrayal when radio deals with disability and disability issues, with many identifying the 'usual suspects' as 'tragic but brave', 'dependent and helpless', 'bitter and twisted', 'sexless and isolated' and so on. As well as these 'traditional' tropes of disability, the sanitizing of disabled people's lives, the infantilizing of disabled people and the inappropriate use of non-disabled actors for disabled character parts were also mentioned. These issues mirror more or less exactly those found in other studies of disability and broadcast media (see Gartner and Joe 1987; Karpf 1988; Barnes 1992; Davies 1997; Pointon and Davies 1997; Ross 1997a) but are no less potent for the repetition. For many respondents, their various impairments were not the most important aspect of their personalities in terms of how they think about themselves, but rather it is the social label of 'disabled' which actually limits their lives in real terms (Shakespeare 1994; Karpf 1997). It is precisely the figuring of disability within the dual tropes of disease and dependency that encourages the perpetuation of demeaning and outmoded perspectives on disability which deny the possibility of autonomous action or even an 'ordinary' life.

> We're always portrayed either as victims or as super humans – as two extremes – not as an ordinary person with a visual impairment. (Steve)[2]

> I think [portrayal of disability] it's patronizing, you think, oh god, it really is atrocious because it's so patronizing ... just because you're physically disabled, there's nothing wrong with the way you think but people just talk down to you. (Marilyn)

Listeners were irritated by the way in which one person's battle to fight a particular impairment becomes the benchmark for everyone else with that particular disability. As Shaban (1996) argues so persuasively, the conventional media strategy of framing disabled people as either 'rejects' or 'supercrips' persistently forces disabled people to conform to one or other constructed 'type' which, at the same time, rests blame or accolade at the door of the individual: it is personal, not political. Not only are these kinds of assumptions insulting to the individual concerned, but they carry with them the expectation that *all* disabled people can overcome the various vicissitudes of their disability and that those who don't, aren't really trying. A less common but alternative construction on achievement was one that offers exaggerated praise for minor successes where expectations of disabled people are so low that their subsequent achievement is noteworthy.

> Patronizing as well ... things are made simple for us so that we can appear to 'succeed'. Or they [the media] think that they can't put in that character in that situation because they are disabled. And we're not seen as people who have relationships, get married, have children. I know from my own experience of having a family and driving a car how that's seen as out of the ordinary, like you're so wonderful that you can work and have an ordinary life. (Sarah)

The way in which the lives of people with impairments is routinely santized and made 'palatable' for a predominantly non-disabled audience was an issue that was discussed many times during the group interviews.

Without wanting every portrait to be boringly 'warts and all' – there are, after all, only so many times that the problems of accessing public lavatories in a wheelchair or making coherent conversation with a speech impediment or looking after an incontinent relative needs to be signalled – the blithe disregard for the very real difficulties that people with disabilities routinely face gives the lie to well-researched and sensitive programme-making. This sanitizing of disability, including rendering it entirely unproblematic (because *invisible*) for non-disabled society, can be seen as part of a larger malaise which is fundamentally rooted in a (seemingly deliberate) lack of interest in and ignorance of disability and disability issues by researchers, producers and directors which shows itself through unrealistic (and sometimes physically impossible) portraits of the lives of disabled people in radio outputs. As Gregory (1991: 294–5) argues in the specific context of deafness, 'They [deaf] characters are not real people who happen to be deaf but deaf characters who, on the whole, appear not to be real people.' Where are the *real* (never mind realistic) representations of disability, of disabled people running homes, bringing up families, having loving relations and being ordinary people, rather than being constantly framed by the label of disability? Why are disabled characters so often left as two-dimensional ciphers, peripheral to the narrative thrust – unless the story turns to a disability theme – and isolated as (dis)embodied bit players on the margins of the action? Penny Boot, a disabled writer who recently took part in a TV programme, screened as part of the *Hidden Love* series, which explored the taboo subject of sex and disability (*A Love Less Ordinary*, 31.8.99, Channel 4), has argued that her participation in the programme was partly to assuage her own self-declared vanity but mostly because

> we must speak out for our right to be sexual, to be human. In expanding boundaries and addressing sexuality with fun and pride, we have much to offer the world. Disabled people have no history of representation as fleshed-out, three-dimensional human beings: we do not appear to exist in the wider community. Apparently, we do not slog industriously, we do not fuck, we do not raise families and so on – we are merely pitiable and jealous shadows of our non-disabled betters. (Boot cited in the *Guardian*, 20.8.99)

Part of the problem with 'fantasy' portraits of disability lies, arguably, with programme-makers: with their concern with the limits of 'acceptability' (at least for non-disabled audiences); the scope of their own imaginations; their poor (if any) contact with disabled people as contributors to story development; and their propensity for casting non-disabled actors in 'disabled' roles on the grounds that it is not necessary to have actually *had* particular experiences in order to be able to write convincingly about them – although I believe that this, in itself, is a moot point – but artistic licence and the creative imperative are meagre proxies for informed comment and the experiential evidence provided by those who live the life every day.

Whose life is it anyway?

Studies of visual media and disability (see, for example, Hevey 1992; Shakespeare 1997; Ross 1997a) consistently show that only a highly restricted repertoire of disability 'types' routinely receive an airing and that these tend to be those that are deemed the most 'acceptable' to non-disabled audiences, that is, they 'look normal' ('there but for the grace of god …') and therefore unlikely to be offend the gentle sensibilities of the mainstream audience. But there was a much greater expectation (and therefore a similarly sized disappointment) among radio's listeners that, as a *non*-visual medium, programme-makers might be prepared to take a few more risks in terms of range and scope of disability and disability narratives, be a bit more radical, to dare to be different. Listeners were in little doubt about which disabilities were more 'popular' and these tended to be the ones that were easily understood and easy to signify at least in narrative terms, such as physical or sensory impairments: more complex and/or multiple impairments were not seen as part of the 'routine' figuring of disability in radio programmes.

> Blindness seems to get a monopoly – you tell *me* why! It's over-balanced. What happened to Brian Aldridge's epilepsy? And how is it that that incredibly nice Phil Archer is still doing a full day's work after *how* many years with a hip replacement? (Carol)

> Obvious, visible disabilities – wheelchairs especially. I think they get more coverage because the public has been educated that it should be sympathetic to disability and something as obvious as a wheelchair shouts 'disabled!' and everyone knows how they are supposed to respond. There is even a traffic sign showing a stylized wheelchair which means disabled crossing or parking or what-have-you, applied to all sorts of situations. (Diana)

But what is required is not some kind of simplistic replacement of 'positive' for 'negative' images, since there is no agreement (and how could there be, really?) over what 'good' and 'bad' portrayal might actually be like (see Hevey 1993; Darke 1997). Thinking about portrayal as having a simple binary logic, positive vs. negative, is neither a cultural nor a political advance, and quite apart from generalized arguments relating to authenticity and diversity in disability portrayal are issues of signifying all those other cross-cutting variables which comprise our various selves such as gender, ethnicity, sexuality and age. Indeed several of the most powerful critiques of disabling and disablist imagery presented by mass media have come from feminists identifying as disabled, who have been particularly concerned with the construction of oppositional versions of femininity (see Morris 1991; Meekosha and Dowse 1997), with the 'good' female body being young, vital, seductive and 'whole' and her 'bad' sister counterpointed as sexless, unattractive and dependent.

The language of disability

When asked specifically about their views on the language of disability on radio, there were very mixed views on this subject. Some people believe that radio has embraced and incorporated an understanding of disability issues which has resulted, especially in factual programming, in a more sensitive and aware use of language. On the other hand, many other people believe that radio professionals are lagging some considerable way behind 'society' in their understanding of the issues and the importance of using anti-oppressive and sensitive language in reporting. These contradictory views are, obviously, hardly unexpected – there is, after all, no reason to imagine that people with a disability are a homogenous group (see, for example, Peters 1996) – but it does make hard the task of trying to respond, in broadcasting terms, to what are entirely diametrically opposed views, a difficulty that has not escaped the notice of the commissioners of this particular research.

> I hear the occasional play which characterizes mental illness in very odd ways, negative, old hat but there has also been the occasional thing which has been good. (Jamie)

> The problem is that the people working in the media aren't disabled themselves, so what you get are sensational terms but no understanding of what lies behind them. I think terms like 'cripple' still hang on because it's easier to write 'crippled' than 'a disabled person'. (Joan)

None the less, regardless of whether listeners believe that radio gets it mostly 'right' or mostly 'wrong', there were specific issues around language and terminology which were routinely articulated, especially when discussing fact-based programmes. For example, many listeners made comments about the offensive way in which 'appeals' programmes construct disabled people as objects of pity requiring 'our' help, through the use of derogatory terms such as 'wheelchair bound', 'crippled', 'handicapped' or the most frequently heard, 'the disabled'. Hevey (1992) suggests that what such 'disability' charities are actually engaged in is a 'branding' exercise, promoting their particular impairment by an appeal to our sympathies but where the autonomy and agency of disabled people must be denied in order that the (non-disabled) public can believe in the goodness of its benevolence. The perpetuation of the tragic/courageous myth peddled by many charities through braveheart media campaigns such as *Children in Need* and *Telethon* have been roundly and consistently criticized by commentators (see for example Oliver 1990; Doddington et al. 1994; Drake 1994; Shakespeare 1994; Devereux 1996) not only for the demeaning reinforcement of the dependency model but also because of the risks of internalizing such negative values among disabled media consumers. However, this is not to say that charity advertising (or indeed other media genres) is static and recently two of Britain's biggest charities, SCOPE and Mencap, have begun to introduce more complex and 'political' images into their campaigns (Barnes et al. 1999).

But even when media practitioners do try to provide less stereotypical and more genuinely 'human interest' stories about the lives of disabled people, they will often entirely negate their 'good' efforts by their lack of sensitivity over terminology. For example, one of the *Guardian*'s sports journalists, Phil Revell, recently wrote an interesting piece about disabled athletes competing in the 1999 London marathon – the fact that the paper carried the report at all especially in a mainstream section such as sport, is in itself a step in the right direction – but it was partly undone by his use of terms such as 'able-bodied' or 'wheelchair-bound' in his report (Phil Revell, *Guardian*, 13.4.99). In a moment of real irony, Revell states that 'basketball, tennis and rugby can all be played by wheelchair-bound athletes and to watch a wheelchair basketball game is to realise that the words disabled and wheelchair-bound are entirely inappropriate' (Revell, *Guardian*, 13.4.99) But what Revell (probably) meant was not that a term such as 'wheelchair-bound' is inappropriate because of its offensiveness but because of its inaccuracy, that is, because athletes can reach 'out' of their wheelchairs rather than being 'bound in' by them. So while he celebrates the skill displayed by disabled athletes, he is blissfully unaware of the offence he causes by using outdated terms.

Disability portrayal and non-disabled society: cause and effect?

A strong driver for carrying out studies with audiences is to try to identify cause and effect relationships between medium and audience, to explore in what ways (if any) media consumers comprehend aspects of their social world as a direct consequence of what they hear on radio or see on television. Disabled listeners in this study were very clear that the ways in which they are portrayed in broadcast media such as radio *do* have an effect on non-disabled people's understanding of disability and disability issues which in turn has an effect on how they treat disabled people in the real world. Although most estimates of Britain's 'disabled' population suggests 16 per cent[3] and therefore most people will know at least *one* disabled person as a friend, colleague or family member, there still seems to be much mystification, misunderstanding and fear surrounding both the idea and the reality of disability. While there is still considerable debate about what effect the exposure to media messages really has on attitude and behaviour, and although we have moved beyond the model of inert media consumer passively and unreflexively accepting whatever she is given, there is, none the less, some evidence to suggest that media messages are effective as reinforcers of people's views on particular social issues (Philo 1996; Kitzinger 1999), if not as catalysts for change. So, a disablist hegemony could be (and, I argue, *is*) promoted through the frame of 'normality' where each (re)articulation of what is 'normal' also reinforces the potency of its opposite by figuring what it is *not*. The narrow range of characterizations, plot and storylines involving disabled characters and the absence of disabled people from most programmes and genres, therefore, does very little to address the problem of poor knowledge levels, and it is this aspect, the education-giving potential of radio, that individuals in this study are keen to encourage the industry to explore.

Putting the 'new' into 'new millennium': an agenda for change

Notwithstanding the earlier caution over the 'I/we' problematic, there were sufficient instances of shared views relating to disability and portrayal to be able to suggest a tentative agenda for action, and a few thoughts on what such an agenda could include are given below. Crucially, the issue is as much (perhaps more so) about omission as comission, that is, much of the difficulty around portraying disability on radio lies in what is absent, what is missing rather than what exists.

For fictional programmes, a number of suggestions were made. There was a view that in too many instances radio professionals lagged far behind public opinion in terms of what 'the public' (i.e. non-disabled society) will 'accept' as far as the portrayal and inclusion of disability in radio programming is concerned. Many people mentioned how the non-visual aspect of radio lends itself much more readily to a more 'risky' format or narrative, since the audience cannot 'see' the disability in question and so would not be 'appalled' by the actual appearance of someone with, say, a speech impairment or poor muscle control but rather would be able to empathize with such a character in ways that would be much easier than having to engage at a more visual level. The two-dimensionality of many disabled characters, where individual lives are only partially explored, and the very real problems that many disabled people face at the mundane (albeit immensely frustrating) level of the everyday need to be addressed. The points that people identified often related to access issues. For example, we are never told how individuals with mobility difficulties suddenly 'arrive' at the top of a flight of stairs or sit on the top of a double-decker coach. The possibilities afforded by more contemplative material on disability and/or more radical narratives and/or more 'incidental' inclusivity were consistently mentioned and listeners believe that 'improvements' can be encouraged in at least three ways: making disability 'ordinary' by introducing a disabled character or two into long-running dramas such as soaps but where the character does not wear the badge of disability (Shakespeare 1997); introducing a calamitous element into a long-running drama whereby a favourite character becomes disabled and does *not* recover (see Karpf 1988); and introducing a variety of characters into a variety of programme formats as background.

> There's a tendency for disabled characters to get better or die. They seldom just live ordinary disabled lives like most of us. Mrs Antrobus in *The Archers*, for instance, is her eyesight going? Couldn't she get a guide dog? Some children with Stills disease live with a level of mobility impairment or even visual impairment and the latter possibility wasn't even mentioned when Daniel Hebden was ill. Couldn't Jamie, Daniel or Pip have some disabled playmates, etc? (Helen)

In fact-based programmes, attention needs to be paid to the language associated with disability and disability issues, and more and better consultation needs to take place with disabled people themselves. More generally, disability needs to be routinized across all genres and all programme types; the talents of disabled media professionals should be utilized more often; and disabled media professionals need to be involved in all areas of programme production, not sidelined into 'disability' slots or series. If disability is to be successfully integrated across the spectrum of radio programming, this means both preserving disability-specific shows such as *In Touch*, which appear to genuinely meet an identified need, but mostly including disability as a routine element in mainstream consumer shows such as *You and Yours*.

In this chapter, I have argued that, for the most part, radio does not offer a range of diverse portraits of disability and that many programmes continue to treat the issue in highly partial terms. Areas of contention include: characterization and genre range in fictional programming; language and authority in fact-based shows; and structure, agency and employment in the industry more generally. But although there are problems associated with the ways in which disability is represented and treated on and in radio broadcasts, I believe there is a much more fundamental and profound problem associated not with what *is*, but rather with what is *not*. In other words, I have a much greater issue to take with the routinized invisibility of disability – as fictional construct and as lived reality – which, whether wilful or unintentional (and in any case, either motivation results in the same outcome), serves to exclude disabled people from the routine radio landscape: disability is less a blot than a crater. It is in working to address the absences as much as the presences with which radio professionals should perhaps be engaged, rather than attempting to provide an imaginary (and, as it turns out, entirely mythical) disabled audience with programmes that they think they might want and enjoy but which they neither need nor appreciate. The employment of more people with disabilities in the industry would certainly be a good first step because different perspectives necessarily bring change and such a strategy would also allow diversity of expression (see Mulhern 1997; Vasey 1997; Rothwell 1997). As Morrison and Finkelstein (1997) argue, much work produced by disabled artists and media practitioners has tended to place its emphasis on 'educating' non-disabled people rather than providing a vehicle through which disabled people can communicate with each other, and they argue that introducing disabled people to the social role of artistic creativity and opening a debate about disability culture is a dynamic way of assisting disabled people to challenge their assumed dependency and place in mainstream society. If these acts of recuperation, transgression, challenge and celebration can be facilitated via the medium of radio emancipating disabled performers and at the same time 'educating' non-disabled listeners – and *Yes Sir, I can Boogie*[4] (director: Ash Atela, BBC Radio 4) is a good example of the power of radio to do precisely this politicizing work – then we will all be the richer for it.

More people with disabilities working in all sections of production, i.e. background as well as more people with disabilities featured 'on air'. (Graham)

All they've got to do is portray disability realistically, warts and all ... we might not be the most attractive people but we do have something to say. (Rebecca)

Notes

1   I use the term 'disabled people' following Pointon and Davies (eds) (1997) who use it in preference to 'people with disabilities' so as to make clear the fact that *society* disables people, rather than an individual's particular impairment.
2   All the material in quotation marks are quotes provided either verbatim by interviewees or else text-based responses from the postal questionnaire phase: all names have been changed.
3   The latest available statistic for the percentage of disabled people in Great Britain is 8.6m (DSS 1999).
4   *Yes Sir, I Can Boogie* was a short-run comedy series broadcast by BBC Radio 4 in early 1999. Each show comprised a series of short sketches which Williams (1998: 21), having attended the recording of the pilot suggests shows, 'disabled and non-disabled performers ... pulling apart the social model of disability [which provided] a pleasant and refreshing look at the images we are all lead to believe are 'the disabled.' Once on air, the show attracted mixed reviews as many people were simply unsure about how to 'take it', unsure whether to laugh at some of the crass comments and 'jokes' which litter the show, but which aim to provoke and question deep-seated assumptions of disability as other and different.

References

Ang, I. (1991) *Desperately Seeking the Audience*. London: Routledge.

Barnes, C. (1992) *Disabling Imagery and the Media: An Exploration of Media Representations of Disabled People*. Belper: British Council of Organisations of Disabled People.

Barnes, C., Mercer, J. and Shakespeare, T. (1999) *Exploring Disability: A Sociological Introduction*. Cambridge: Polity Press.

Broadcasting Standards Council (1994) *Annual Report*. London: BSC.

Cumberbatch, G. and Negrine, R. (1992) *Images of Disability on Television*. London: Routledge.

Darke, P. (1995) *'LINK': An Evaluation*. Leeds: University of Leeds Press.

Darke, P. (1997) Eye witness, in A. Pointon and C. Davies (eds) *Framed: Interrogating Disability in the Media*. London: British Film Institute.

Davies, C. (1997) Window on the world (almost), in A. Pointon and C. Davies (eds) *Framed: Interrogating Disability in the Media*. London: British Film Institute.

Devereux, E. (1996) Good causes, God's poor and Telethon television, *Media, Culture & Society*, 18(1): 47–68.

Doddington, K., Jones, R.S.P and Miller, B.Y. (1994) Are attitudes to people with learning disabilities negatively influenced by charity advertising? An experimental analysis, *Disability & Society*, 9(2): 207–22.

Drake, R.F. (1994) A critique of the role of the traditional charities, in L. Barton (ed.) *Disability & Society: Emerging Issues and Insights*. London: Longman.

Gartner, A. and Joe, T. (eds) (1987) *Images of the Disabled, Disabling Images*. New York: Praeger.

Gregory, S. (1991) Deafness in fiction, in S. Gregory and G.M. Hartley (eds) *Constructing Deafness*. London: Pinter in association with the Open University Press.

Hevey, D. (1992) *The Creatures that Time Forgot: Photography and Disability Imagery*. London: Routledge.

Hevey, D. (1993) From self-love to the picket line: strategeies for change in disability representation, *Disability, Handicap & Society*, 8(4):423–9.

Karpf, A. (1988) *Doctoring the Media*. London: Routledge.

Karpf, A. (1997) Crippling images, in A. Pointon and C. Davies (eds) *Framed: Interrogating Disability in the Media*. London: British Film Institute.

Kitzinger, J. (1999) A sociology of media power: key issues in audience reception research, in G. Philo (ed.) *Message Received: Glasgow Media Group Research 1993–1998*. Harlow: Addison Wesley Longman,

Meekosha, H. and Dowse, L. (1997) Distorting images, invisible images: gender, disability and the media, *Media International Australia*, 84 (May): 91–101.

Moores, S. (1993) *Interpreting Audiences: The Ethnography of Media Consumption*. London: Sage.

Morris, J. (1991) *Pride Against Prejudice*. London: The Women's Press.

Morrison E. and Finkelstein, V. (1997) Broken arts and cultural repair: the role of culture in the empowerment of disabled people, in A. Pointon and C. Davies (eds) *Framed: Interrogating Disability in the Media*. London: British Film Institute.

Mulhern, K. (1997) The only cripple in the room, in A. Pointon and C. Davies (eds) *Framed: Interrogating Disability in the Media*. London: British Film Institute.

Nightingale, V. (1996) *Studying Audiences: The Shock of the Real*. London: Routledge.

Oliver, M. (1990) *The Politics of Disablement*. Basingstoke: Macmillan.

Peters, S. (1996) The politics of disability identity, in L. Barton (ed.) *Disability & Society: Emerging Issues and Insights*. Harlow: Addison Wesley Longman.

Philo, G. (ed.) (1996) *Media and Mental Distress*. Harlow: Addison Wesley Longman.

Pointon, A. and Davies, C. (eds) (1997) *Framed: Interrogating Disability in the Media*. London: British Film Institute.

Ross, K. (1997a) But where's me in it? Disability, broadcasting and the audience, *Media, Culture & Society*, 19(4): 669–77.

Ross, K. (1997b) Two-tone telly: black minority audiences and British television, *Communications*, 22(1): 93–108.

Rothwell, J. (1997) Whose project, in A. Pointon and C. Davies (eds) *Framed: Interrogating Disability in the Media*. London: British Film Institute.

Shaban, N. (1996) *Supercrips and Rejects*. Without Walls. London: Channel 4.

Shakespeare, T. (1994) Cultural representations of disabled people: dustbins for disavowal, *Disability and Society*, 9(3): 249–64.

Shakespeare, T. (1997) Soaps: the story so far, in A. Pointon and C. Davies (eds) *Framed: Interrogating Disability in the Media*. London: British Film Institute.

Vasey, S. (1997) Sorry, I can't make the tea, in A. Pointon and C. Davies (eds) *Framed: Interrogating Disability in the Media*. London: British Film Institute.

Williams, D. (1998) Review of *Yes Sir, I Can Boogie*, *Disability Arts in London*, 139 (September): 21.

TRANSNATIONAL COMMUNICATIONS AND DIASPORA COMMUNITIES

9

Marie Gillespie

Introduction

This chapter is based on ongoing research into transnational networks of communications and diaspora communities. It focuses on everyday cultural and discursive practices among British Asian youth living in Southall, a multi-ethnic suburb of London, and a major commercial and cultural centre of the South Asian diaspora. The first section explains how transnational media play a role in sustaining South Asian diaspora formations and consciousness. The second section explains why and how anthropology provides useful tools for studying transnational communications networks among diaspora communities. Finally, in order to illustrate the theoretical and methodological approach, I briefly outline the findings of a case study of the reception of two TV versions of the Mahabharata, a foundational text of Indian society and culture, widely viewed in India and in the diaspora. The case study, which draws upon other similar work, shows how, even though representations of femininity in the epic are intricately interwoven with discourses of patriarchal and religious nationalism, Hindu women in London and Delhi selectively appropriate and contest key narratives for their own purposes, and in doing so subvert patriarchal and nationalist discourses in the construction of their own world-views and identities.

Marie Gillespie (2000) Transnational communications and diaspora communities, in Simon Cottle (ed.) *Ethnic Minorities and the Media*. Buckingham: Open University Press, pp. 164–78. Reprinted by kind permission of McGraw-Hill/Open University Press.

The key argument is that young people who are part of the South Asian diaspora make shared use of the increasingly transnational array of TV programmes and video films available to them, not only to lubricate their daily social interactions, but also to compare and contrast, judge and evaluate the culturally different social worlds that appear on their TV screens (Gillespie 1995). TV talk, though seemingly trivial and inconsequential, is enacted in a variety of private and public arenas, and in some cases constitutes an embryonic public sphere (Gillespie 1998a). It is both a form of self-narration, and a forum in which different vantage points and identities are experimented with and performed. TV talk among Southall youth revolves around issues and concerns which are common to most teenagers today: friends and family, school and locality, growing up and becoming adult, dating, sex and body culture, taste in style, fashion, food and other consumption preferences (Gillespie 1998b). But it is also shaped by the multiethnic and diaspora contexts in which they live, and the culturally diverse media which they consume. Thus subjects of TV talk may include a local racist murder, sex and gender in the latest Bombay blockbuster and in the Australian soap *Neighbours*, the irreverent and subversive humour of the BBC's British Asian comedy sketch series *Goodness Gracious Me*, the lyrics of a Cornershop hit, and the politics of religious nationalism and communalism.

The juxtaposition of representations of very distinct cultural and social practices, and different ways of life, on TV screens in Southall sitting rooms encourages cross-cultural, comparative analyses of media representations. The adoption of such a comparativist and culturally relativist perspective in interpreting different social worlds by youth in diasporas tends to heighten an already well-developed sense of culture consciousness. Those who have the necessary cultural capital can translate with ease across and between distinctive social worlds, languages and cultural spheres and acquire the status of a familial cultural broker. Such everyday analyses of transnational TV are highly contradictory in nature. They often express a cosmopolitan world-view, and articulate shared cultural spaces in which ideas, values, knowledge and institutions undergo processes of convergence, hybridization, synchronization and change (Werbner and Modood 1997). Transnational youth programming, dominated by Americanized teen consumer culture (MTV's 'McCulture'), encourages a self-perception as a world teenager, and mobilizes transnational identifications around consumption practices. Southall youth often voice strong sympathies with environmentalist, feminist and Human Rights movements – generated partly by television coverage of disasters, wars and famines, as well as by various kinds of global totemic media events, such as *Live Aid*, and national charity fund-raising appeals like *Comic Relief*.

National identifications are also important. The ritual enjoyment of *East-Enders* as a 'national soap', or of the evening national news bulletins, tends to affirm, even momentarily, a sense of belonging to a shared British culture. But a heightened and sharpened awareness of racism in the media and in the wider society engenders feelings of disaffection which often results in a hardening of cultural boundaries, the construction of exclusivist identities, or protestations about essentialist definitions of Britishness or Englishness. Religious sectarianism and bigotry, in Southall, in South Asia, in the diaspora and elsewhere, generate fierce criticism of the politics of religious nationalism, and a suspicion of religious absolutism among youth. But an Islamophobic British media may encourage a defensive affirmation of Islam (Islamism). Racism, and the limited sense of belonging to any particular nation or culture, often generate the desire for new kinds of transnational and diaspora identification (Brah 1996).

Diaspora identifications and connections are greatly strengthened by modern communications technologies. The connections may be simply symbolic links between viewers of the same blockbuster Bombay movies, or fans of the same popular music genres or acts; or they may be more concrete links between kin and friends, for example in the form of 'video letters' and home videos of weddings and other rites of passage, especially coming of age celebrations. Such videos serve a range of social, cultural and political functions. They enable families to maintain contact with distant kin; they may be used to introduce eligible marriage partners and theri families to each other; they may familiarize Punjabi families in, say, Yuba Valley, California, with the lives of their kin in Southall and vice versa – which amounts to a form of video tourism as well as a cultural exchange. Video (as well as audio) cassettes also serve to construct political and religious communities, in the form of globally circulating propaganda for the Khalistan (Land of the Pure) movement – the campaign for the creation of a separate, sovereign Sikh nation in the Punjab – or documentaries on the life and works of a Sikh sant (holy man), used in religious worship and instruction.

Transnational networks of media and communication are undoubtedly sustaining diaspora formations and enhancing a sense of diaspora consciousness (Cohen 1997). At the same time they are catalysing and accelerating processes of cultural change in a highly differentiated South Asian diaspora, hardening some boundaries while opening up others (Vertovec 1996). Various kinds of transnational ideologies and identifications, some progressive and some regressive, are disseminated in the South Asian diaspora by global communications with unprecedented scope, scale, speed and intensity. It remains to be seen how these varied and contradictory forces will be played out in different locations in the global South Asian diaspora.

Meanwhile Southall youth engage in a process of ongoing negotiation and creative reinvention of their identities. It is these processes of socio-cultural recreation and reinvention that form the focal point of my work. I believe that some of these creative multicultural and anti-racist practices point the way forward for us all, regardless of background, in an increasingly interdependent and interconnected world where racism, religious bigotry and ideologies of separation need to be contested and fought.

Electronic capitalism and imagined diaspora communities

In post-colonial Britain, established notions of national culture and national belonging – of what it means to be British and of who belongs – have been challenged and transformed in response to post-war migration and to the increased globalization of economic, political and cultural life. Media and cultural consumption – the production, 'reading' and uses of representations – play a key role in contesting and reconstituting national, religious, gender and ethnic identities. The role of media in the construction of national identities today has been quite well explored in media studies (see, for example, Schlesinger 1987; Morley and Robins 1989). The enormously influential work of Anderson (1983) argues from a historical perspective that 'print capitalism' was instrumental in forging the 'imagined community' of the nation. The widespread dissemination of newspapers (and the modern novel) led to a heightened awareness of the 'steady, anonymous, simultaneous experience' of communities of readers (Anderson 1983: 31). The notion of simultaneity was thus crucial to the construction of national consciousness in its early modern forms as it is today. The earliest newspapers connected dispersed people to particular discourses of the nation, and the mass ritual and ceremony of reading the newspaper continues to contribute to the construction of ideas of national community. The fact of engaging, in private isolation, in a joint public ritual with significant though absent others, may be as important culturally as any information conveyed.

If the imagined community of the nation became possible because of the advent of newspapers, then this is still more true of the contemporary regulation of simultaneous experience through broadcast media schedules (Cardiff and Scannell 1987), perhaps especially as regards the evening broadcast news on TV and, as we shall see later, soap operas (Morley and Robins 1989). But what kinds of imagined communities may be created as well as eroded by modern TV satellite technology? Satellite TV stations like

Zee TV and AsiaNet are already generating complex flows of images and narratives between Indians in India and in the diaspora (there are approximately 20 million Indians living in the diaspora). We are just begining to explore the ways in which diaspora communities use transnational communications networks. For example, a new and vibrant independent transnational cinema in which Indians in the diaspora are tackling highly controversial issues of sexual and religious politics. Some of these films would never get past the censors in India, but are being shown at film festivals in India, given media coverage, and generating debate (Triparthi 1997). Yet it is important to bear in mind that ethnic-based transnational audiences are lucrative niche markets, and very much the targets of transnational media corporations. It is important not to exaggerate or romanticize the progressive uses of transnational communications by diaspora communities. It is also premature to announce the end of the nation-state as does Appadurai (1996), but the emergence of an embryonic transnational public sphere of democratic debate is clearly visible, if not inclusive at this stage.

By articulating new kinds of spatial and temporal relationships, communications technologies can transform the politics of representation and the modes of identification available to migrant and diaspora groups. New developments in media are arguably now reducing the importance of geopolitical borders and spatial and temporal boundaries, and so threatening the vitality and significance, even the viability of national cultures, at the same time as they increase the significance of diaspora cultures (Clifford 1997). As Clifford points out, the language of diaspora appears to be replacing, or at least supplementing, minority discourse. However, the term is under-theorized and overused, and frequently conflates important distinctions between immigrants, guest-workers, ethnic and 'racial' minorities, refugees, expatriates and travellers. This threatens the term's descriptive usefulness (Safran 1991).

We need to recognize patterns of difference and similarity. For example, despite differences in development between different parts of the Hindu diaspora, in nearly every context outside India, Hinduism has emerged as a core feature of ethnic consciousness and community mobilization among Indian immigrants and their descendants (Vertovec 1996: 5). However, a huge diversity of Hindu beliefs and practices have come to pass in different parts of the world which forbids an absolutist or unified definition of Hinduism, and which must alert us to the importance of the comparative study of the structural, contextual and subjective factors which shape patterns of similarity and difference, and different trajectories and strategies of adaptation.

A diaspora perspective, one which situates British Asians in relation to the very complex web of transnational cross-connections in South Asia and in the wider diaspora, is needed to further our understanding of some of the consequences of media and migration in an age of globalization. Many British Asian families have kin not only in India and/or Pakistan but elsewhere in Asia, in the Middle East, in North America, in Africa (many Southall families are 'twice migrants', having formerly lived in East Africa: Bhachu 1985) and also elsewhere in Europe. Bearing this complexity in mind, and the diversity it entails, may help to avoid the pitfalls of ethnic community studies that tend to reify and essentialize ethnic difference.

A diaspora perspective is also important because it acknowledges the ways in which identities have been and continue to be transformed through relocation, cross-cultural exchange and interaction (Hall 1990). The globalization of media and culture is deeply implicated in this process (Featherstone 1990; Hall 1992; Appadurai 1996; Hannerz 1997). Ever more sophisticated international communications technologies are used not only by transnational media corporations but also by smaller transnational enterprises serving dispersed ethnic markets, as well as by families, individuals and local communities and groups maintaining and creating specific ties (Gillespie 1997). These processes dissolve distances and suspend time, and in doing so create new and unpredictable forms of connection, identification and cultural affinity, but also of dislocation and disjuncture between people, places and cultures (Giddens 1990, 1991). Thus the new social and cultural conditions of transnationalism require a rethinking of conceptual and methodological tools. An ethnographic approach is in my view essential to tracking complex transnational connections, in order to assess the rapidly changing and augmented economic, political and sociocultural significance of transnational communities.

Media anthropology and cultural globalization

Media researchers are increasingly looking to anthropology for conceptual and methodological tools to study the ways in which new media markets are transforming national and cultural boundaries (Silverstone 1990; Morley 1991; Silverstone *et al.* 1991; Moores 1993). Anthropology has a long tradition of studying people and places in a cross-cultural and comparative manner. In the past, anthropologists pursued their central interest in human cultural diversity through the study of local cultures, often in remote places with pre-modern social formations. More recently, anthropologists have revised their conventional conception of cultures as immutable, unchanging, bounded wholes untouched by modernity (Clifford and Marcus 1986). They have had to recognize that all cultures are impure, hybrid and constantly changing. Anthropology has also had to reckon with its troubled history of collusion with the violence and deceits of colonialism and imperialism (Asad 1973). It has often been charged with exoticizing, orientalizing, as well as degrading, the people studied, and indeed with 'inventing' 'primitive society' in opposition to a spurious conception of European civilization (Said 1978; Kuper 1992).

This history of complicity with racism cannot be ignored, especially when studying changing cultural and media boundaries. It is an enduring problem for us all, in our daily and in our academic lives, that the labels, categories, systems of classification that we use, and the hierarchies of value that we explicitly or implicitly adopt in our studies, often simplify human and cultural complexity and essentialize cultural difference. The politics and practices of research, and of representation, are very much at the heart of current debates in anthropology. As this agenda is shared by many media studies scholars, anthropology and media studies have much to learn from each other.

Ethnography enables us to track, with rich empirical detail, how global media are used and interpreted by particular people in specific local contexts. Ethnography aims at understanding the world from the point of view of the subjects of research through a long and engaged participation in their everyday lives and practices. It uses a variety of research strategies which, as far as possible, seek to gather data in natural settings. Ethnographic studies contribute to a rich understanding of what people actually do with the media, rather than predictable 'findings' about what the media do to people. Of course this is not meant to imply that media institutions are either benign, or impotent – far from it. Nor do I choose to ignore the many problems that arise from fieldwork experiences and ethnographic practice, not least the difficulties of linking micro-scale and macro-scale analyses of social phenomenon in ethnography (Hammersley 1992). But I do wish to argue the case for the adoption of a more actor-centred approach, for the use of more socially sensitive research tools for studying cultural change today, for the usefulness of multi-sited ethnographies of reception, and for the importance of transnational studies of the media. It remains for you to decide whether the very abbreviated summaries of research presented here live up to the challenge.

Mapping a Hindu nation through sacred TV epics: the Mahabharata in London and Delhi

When two of the most sacred texts of the Hindu religion, the Ramayana and the Mahabharata, were serialized as 'sacred soaps' by the purportedly secular state TV channel Doordarshan, the ratings broke all records in the history of Indian TV. Broadcast consecutively over a four-year period (1988–92), these were the most popular serials ever shown on Indian television and the viewing of them quickly became a ritualized event. All over India, Hindus performed purification rituals, garlanded their TV sets, observed ritual taboos, and participated in what became a national religious ceremony. From 9.30 to 10.15 every Sunday morning for these four years all India stood still. Never before had Indians in such large numbers (80–100 million as compared with a normal daily viewership of 40–60 million) simultaneously communed and consumed a narrative of the nation. Never before had it been possible: television on a mass scale came to India only in the mid-1980s. The television serials were widely perceived not only as sacred epics, but also as domestic/kinship melodramas, and as accurate accounts of ancient Indian history – as 'authentic' sacred narratives 'telling themselves' through the medium of television. Through viewing the serialized episodes in a devotional manner (as in acts of worshipping deities in a temple), viewers found a regular port of entry to a sacred world inhabited by splendid Gods in a Golden Age set in the mists of time in Indian history, prior to the Mughal invasions and to British colonial rule when India was Hindu India. The serials contributed to cementing the belief among vast numbers of Indians that to be truly Indian was to be Hindu. In so doing, they helped to mobilize considerable anti-Muslim sentiment (Singh 1995; Rajagopal 2000) in India and in the Hindu diaspora. This was exploited by the Hindu nationalist political party, the Bharatiya Janata Party (BJP), and several of its sister organisations. This mobilization, which took place on a transnational scale, involved political controversy over a site of worship in Ayodhia (purportedly the birthplace of the God Rama, the hero of the Ramayana), resulting in the deaths of thousands of people, mainly Muslims, in communalist slaughters on and after 6 January 1992. It also heightened tensions between Hindus and Muslims in the South Asian diaspora.

Why and how these serials were open to such exploitation, and how they provoked such a staggering and unanticipated response among viewer-devotees has been the subject of much debate (Lutgendorf 1990; Barucha 1991; Mishra 1991). Their huge popularity in India and the diaspora has been attributed variously to the mesmerizing power of television itself, to the enduring significance of sacred narratives, to the soap operatic ingredients, and/or to the unique manner in which they assisted in the reconstruction of an idealized 'imagined community' of the nation, which generated profound feelings of belonging. But these 'sacred soaps' have been regarded with the utmost disdain by most cultural critics, for whom they spell above all the demise of a long history of rich and diverse linguistic and artistic performance traditions.

There is but a short (and essential) step from discussing performance traditions to exploring the performance of tradition: mobilizations of cultural and religious nationalism which (re-)invent traditions in order to serve particular current political interests (Hobsbawm and Ranger 1983); performances of national ceremonies (Dayan and Katz 1992); and narrative performances of nationhood (Bhabha 1990). New media technologies very frequently serve in the reinvention of tradition (Gillespie 1989). The appropriation of the symbolic imagery and the narratives of impending social chaos and disorder in the Mahabharata by the BJP had devastating consequences for some. But in parts of the diaspora, the TV epics were appropriated in more positive ways. In order to understand more fully the discursive and hegemonic power of these TV performances of the Hindu nation in transnational networks of communications though, we need to examine their reception in the various local contexts in which they are used and interpreted, and to avoid monolithic accounts of 'the meaning' of the epic. For, as we shall see, the bringing together of ethnographic studies in various locations can help build up a much more differentiated and nuanced picture of the consequences of these TV epics.

The data for my study were gathered in the homes of Hindu families in Southall and based on my viewing of the TV epics with the family, usually in all-female viewing groups, as well as on extended interviews with women and girls locally. In earlier articles (Gillespie 1989, 1993, 1994), I elaborated how the Ramayana and Mahabharata have long played a central role in Indian popular culture where the narratives are reinscribed and reinvented a new in all art forms and performative genres, not least in every Bombay movie (Mishra 1985). The films and the comic books of the epics are exploited by parents, mothers especially, for didactic purposes in the post-migrant situation. The films especially have provided grandparents and parents with a colourful and lively way of teaching their children about the religious knowledge, beliefs and practices which are integrated into the everyday life-world of all Hindus. They have also been used for language learning and to foster a Hindu world-view more generally, and to catalyse familial debates about issues of cultural continuity and change. I also drew attention to the continuities of devotional viewing in India and the diaspora, the purification rituals, domestic worship and ritual taboos which accompany the viewing of film and TV texts perceived as sacred, and the notion of 'divine vision' (darshan/bhakti) which is seen to connect the devoted believer to the Gods and bestow blessings (Eck 1985).

The TV epics were widely viewed by Hindu families in Southall on local cable TV and/or video. The Mahabharata was also broadcast by BBC2 with subtitles on Saturday afternoons (1990–2). Though the serial in the UK was running well behind India, the sense of 'nearly' simultaneous viewing of a serial from among families in the diaspora and 'back home' was something novel, and much remarked upon by viewers. Time and again families told me that, apart from the pleasures of the serial itself, they enjoyed each episode because, when they were watching it, they felt such a close connection to the relatives back home. What is remarkable here is not only the way the viewers support Anderson's (1983) stress on the significance of imagined temporal identity (simultaneity) in constructing (trans)national community, but also the way in which the TV epics represent national, kinship and religious ties as primary and primordial, equivalent and indeed identical. The mass consumption of mediated performances of sacred texts in India and its diaspora has, in fact, generated the kind of powerful nationalist sentiments which Anderson sought to explain, though this nationalism now takes a religious form. Certainly, we now witness the strengthening of religious forms of nationalism in many contexts, which need to be studied comparatively and transnationally (van der Veer 1995).

The discursive power of the TV epics was greatly assisted by the genre of melodrama. The centrality in the serial, as in all melodrama, of kinship relations and of domestic life and conflicts affirmed connections between discourses of kinship and religion in a nationalized context, and brought to the fore the crucial importance of maintenance of the moral order in the past and in the present (Singh 1995). The TV epics also drew on age-old iconographic conventions. Although the performances of the TV epics take place in the rarefied world of the Hindu gods, these gods have long been domesticated and humanized through the use of popular iconography and performance styles with which Indian viewers are deeply familiar, not least the mythological film genre. The sacred world of the gods is apprehended through narratives of kinship set in a moral order that has to be maintained by Dharma (moral/divine law). The narratives of Hindi melodrama centre around a moral disorder, rather than a narrative enigma which has to be resolved. Viewers are less concerned about what will happen next than how (Thomas 1986). The key narrative question is: how will the moral order be maintained when threatened with chaos? This universalist theme is a screen on to which viewers project their present-day hopes and fears, anxieties and personal conflicts. The BJP was able to use effectively this threat of social and moral disorder to advance their own political purposes. They used the epic to preach that unless India returned to its pristine state as a purified Hindu nation then chaos would reign.

While Ramayana was being widely viewed in Southall, Peter Brook's controversial production of the Mahabharata was screened on British TV. I watched part of it with the mother and daughters of a local Hindu family, the Dhamis, who were to become key informants for my study. Only part of it, because it was met with incomprehension, indeed with revulsion, and switched off after about 20 minutes, whereupon Mrs Dhami and her eldest daughter left the sitting-room to perform a purification ritual upstairs. Before we examine the ways in which processes of identification are mobilized by the TV epics themselves, it is useful to explain why the Brook version was met with revulsion, not only by this family, but much more widely The Brook version disrupted the identificatory processes typical of the TV epics, and unlike the Indian TV serials, it could not be viewed in a devotional manner. Numerous dichotomies which crystallize the differences between the two versions immediately spring to mind: Indian versus European contexts of production and reception; televised theatre aimed at metropolitan, middle-class elite audiences versus a soap/mythological hybrid genre aimed at mass, largely illiterate Indian audiences at home and abroad; Brook's multicultural casting and interpretation versus a performance and iconographic style which are distinctively Indian; didactic narrative exposition via a 'cosmic' narrator for Hindus, versus 'universalist' mysticism for westerners. Now while all the above go some way to explaining the family's revulsion, they do not tell the whole story and bear the limitations of all binary thinking.

Empirically, deeper and more subtle answers to the question only began to emerge when, several weeks after the screening of the Brook version, Doordarshan's version of the Mahabharata began to be screened on BBC2. There began a long friendship and conversation with the Dhami family, and a long-term engagement with the Mahabharata which we watched together (almost) every week for two years. Over this period we explored many features of different versions of the Mahabharata. Quite spontaneously we performed a contrastive analysis of what the Dhamis referred to as the 'Indian' and 'English' versions. We started a long conversation about the world and the epic texts, about the sacred and the everyday and it became clear that these TV epics served quite a different set of uses.

In the context of Southall where Hindus are a somewhat beleaguered minority in a predominantly Sikh community (celebrations were held on the streets when Indira Gandhi was shot, for example), the TV epics where used in a much more benign assertion of diaspora religious identity. They helped young Hindus articulate a Hindu consciousness and world-view with remarkable sophistication and philosophical depth (see Gillespie 1993, 1994). This sophistication was achieved in part by the contrastive, cross-cultural analyses of the Indian and English versions, and perhaps also by the dialogic nature of the long conversation.

One episode in particular, Draupadi's disrobing (vastraharan), which recounts the public humiliation of one of the key female protagonists of the epic, was discussed at length and in depth over several weeks. It highlights some of the differences between the Indian and English versions which made the latter so distasteful to the Dhami family. It also shows the ways in which the TV epics offer powerful representations not only of what it is to be a woman, but also of what it means to be a Hindu Indian woman in particular. Drawing upon Mankekar's (1993) ethnography of the reception of TV epic among young women in Delhi, it is possible to compare and contrast readings of Draupadi's disrobing by Hindu women and girls living in London and in Delhi. Mankekar's work provides a most useful comparison and contrast to my own work, and made apparent to me the fruitfulness of multi-sited ethnographies.

Draupadi's disrobing

Briefly, the narrative of the Mahabharata centres around the enduring conflict between two rival clans of cousins, the Pandevas and the Kauravas. Draupadi is the polyandrous wife of the five Pandevas brothers. Yudhishtira, the eldest Pandevas (resplendently dressed in white to symbolize his goodness), and Duryodhana (sinister and evil in black), the eldest Kauravas, are the chief protagonists. Duryodhana exploits Yudhishtira's weakness for gambling by tempting him into a game of dice, and so leads him to lose everything that the Pandevas possesses. He even bets and loses his wife Draupadi. The Kauravas then attempt to humiliate her and violate her honour in public by stripping off her sari in the court before the eyes of kings and gods. However, after a powerful display of rage and anger by Draupadi, the God Krishna (who is on the side of the Pandevas) intervenes and magically bestows upon her a sari of infinite length, thus safeguarding her honour. The dramatic intensity of the Doordarshan version is heightened by the use of melodramatic techniques and histrionic traditions typical of some forms of North Indian folk theatre (Lutgendorf 1990). This scene was exhaustively discussed in the Dhami family. The first response was to compare it with the English version. Here one gets a sense of the significance of culturally specific iconographic conventions, such as the semiotics of colour coding, as well as codes of godlike behaviour and dress, when the trauma of Draupadi's violation is discussed:

N: In the English version when they drag her into court, she lets everyone know that she shouldn't be seen in public because she has her period. In the Indian version they just hint at it. It's understood because she is wearing yellow clothes and she's segregated – normally she's all dressed up like a queen.

S: In the Indian version the true strength of her character comes out. She stands up to all the men and she questions all the men in the court...

R: And in the English one Bhisma looks at Duryodhana trying to strip her clothes off her but he would never do that.

N: They call her a prostitute and insult her really badly but the hurt of all this doesn't come across in the English one.

R: She swears that she will get her revenge and after that she keeps the wound alive.

S: It's this incident that leads to the war.

R: It's one of the most important moments in the whole Mahabharata – together with the Bhagavat Gita where Krishna tells Arjuna to kill his cousins for the honour of Draupadi and for a better world.

The Brook version did not work for the Dhami women. As the mother said: 'It left a bad taste in my mouth'. One of her daughters added: 'The English version borrowed the story, not the culture'. The dramatic weight and moral significance of this was not properly understood by Brook.

In contrast, the readings of this scene in Doordarshan's version among Hindu women in London and Delhi suggest that it opened up a space for specifically female concerns, and a feminine/ist consciousness to express itself. Draupadi is admired and revered as a symbol of female strength and vulnerability. She is admired because she exposes and challenges the men who attempt to exploit her sexual vulnerability in such a powerful manner. According to Mankekar (1993), watching her disrobing compelled the young women that she worked with to confront and think about their familial and financial, emotional and sexual vulnerabilities. The parallels in the readings of Mankekar's informants and my own are striking. The fact that Draupadi was disrobed by her brother-in-law, in front of all her in-laws signalled a dread. The fact that the ties of kinship could not protect Draupadi from such abuse resonated strongly with a fear that in-laws might fail to protect the best interests of their daughter-in-law in their home. This is a deep-seated anxiety among many young women in India and in the diaspora. Conventionally, the new bride lives with her in-laws where typically she has little power or status, at least until she either provides sons or devises other strategies for overcoming the weakness of her structural position as the property of her husband and his family (Ballard 1982). Despite enormous variations in practices, there is still a dread among many young girls, and this was often expressed to me in Southall and to Mankekar in Delhi, that things may not work out with in-laws.

Draupadi symbolizes that fear and dread. But she also represents a powerful manifestation of female empowerment and rage – an enviable assertiveness that many young women feel is denied to them on the family stage. Yet, some of our informants, both in London and Delhi, point out that her rage, though explosive and absolutely central to the entire narrative in that it leads directly to 'global' war between the two sets of cousins, is ultimately contained within the overarching ideology of family loyalty, respect and honour (izzat), and so is not entirely empowering or subversive. In fact the story of the Mahabharata culminates in a war to end all wars which is fought in the name of Draupadi. The God Krishna actually incites the Pandevas to kill their kin in the name of female honour and chastity – the highest of all moral values. Readings of this scene brought to light, to Mankekar and myself, the many personal battles in the family that women fight for independence, autonomy and individuality. Young women in London and Delhi thus converge in their expression of fears and anxieties and to negotiate identities and gendered subjectivities, and in doing so they rupture the hegemonic nationalist discourse at one moment, only to reinstate it in the next (see Gillespie 1993, 1994).

In another context, as Rajagopal's excellent study of the rise of Hindu nationalism in India highlights, the incitement to war in the world of the Gods can very easily be recontextualized to justify political Hindu violence by young, poor, urban Hindu men disenchanted with the unfulfilled promised of modernity (Rajagopal 2000). The affirmation of India as a Hindu nation (an entirely racist imagining) in the TV epics may be accepted in primordialist manner as a 'true' account of Indian history. Yet, the horrors of the religious violence and slaughter in India among the Hindu youth with whom I worked, have led to a rejection of the kind of racist imagining of the nation, in favour of a more benign cosmological imagining of Hindusim itself. Hinduism is an integral part of the ethnic consciousness and identity of all my Hindu informants (but by no means all Hindus) in the British context, but it coexists alongside a multiculturalist and an anti-racist sensibility, and a cosmopolitan world-view which reacts against rising communal tension inside the town, as well as outside it.

Young people employ various strategies to reconstruct their identities in the post-migrant situation. One of these is to find comfort and solace in a cosmic and religious view of the world which transcends and redefines the problems of everyday life in the real world – problems such as the vulnerability of women, communal tensions, class inequalities, ill health, poverty, alienation at work, consumerist materialism and environmental destruction – all issues which were much discussed by families and young people in Southall in relation to the TV epics. Discourses inherent in the TV epics on the fragility of the social fabric, threats to moral order, or the importance of Dharma (divine law) can equally be applied in Delhi and in London.

Conclusion

The emergence of digital technologies enables diaspora communities to expand and accelerate their communication networks and activities on a global scale with often unpredictable and unforeseen consequences. Old and new media, however, are not universally available and so diaspora communications tend to privilege the affluent, and the flows between different parts of highly differentiated diaspora locations are highly uneven. Huge disparities in education, wealth and social status have profound effects on diaspora politics, formations and consciousness. Nevertheless, the forms of creativity displayed in both cultural production and consumption by members of diaspora groups is often at the cutting edge or avant-garde of media and literary cultures today.

The Indian diaspora also present itself to transnational media companies as a very lucrative market ready to be exploited commerically, and as we have seen, compromised and co-opted by politico-religious movements. But new media, Internet included, may also be used by diaspora communities to foster a concern with human and cultural rights, environmental issues and new forms of cosmopolitan democracy. To understand these contradictory tendencies we need more analyses of how transnational communiciations are being used by diaspora communities, and their consequences for nation-states, cultural policies and marginalized groups. This might be achieved through transnational studies of media that effectively combine political economy perspectives with the kind of culturalist approaches to media outlined here. This is as yet an aspiration which awaits realization.

Further reading

Appadurai, A. (1996) *Modernity at Large: The Cultural Dimensions of Globalization*. Minnesota, MN: University of Chicago Press.

Clifford, J. (1997) Diasporas, in J. Clifford, *Routes: Travel and Translation in the Late Twentieth Century*. Cambridge, MA: Harvard University Press.

Cohen, R. (1997) *Global Diasporas*. London: Routledge.

Gillespie, M. (1995) *Television, Ethnicity and Cultural Change*. London: Routledge.

Hall, S. (1992) The question of cultural identity, in S. Hall, D. Held and T. McGrew (eds) *Modernity and its Futures*. Cambridge: Polity.

Morley, D. and Robins, K. (1995) *Spaces of Identity: Global Media, Electronic Landscapes and Cultural Boundaries*. London: Routledge.

References

Anderson, B. (1983) *Imagined Communities: Reflections on the Origin and Spread of Nationalism*. London: Verso.

Appadurai, A. (1996) *Modernity at Large: The Cultural Dimensions of Globalization*. Minnesota, MN: University of Chicago Press.

Asad, T. (ed.) (1973) *Anthropology and the Colonial Encounter*. New York: Humanities Press.

Ballard, R. (1982) South Asian families in Britain, in R. Rappoport (ed.) *Families in Britain*. London: Routledge & Kegan Paul.

Barucha, R. (1991) A view from India, in D. Williams (ed.) *Peter Brook and the Mahabharata: Critical Perspectives*. London: Routledge.

Bhabha, H. (ed.) (1990) *Nation and Narration*. London: Routledge.

Bhachu, P. (1985) *Twice Migrants*. London: Tavistock.

Brah, A. (1996) *Cartographies of Diaspora: Contesting Identities*. London: Routledge.

Cardiff, D. and Scannell, P. (1987) Broadcasting and national unity, in J. Curran, A. Smith and P. Wingatee (eds) *Impacts and Influences*. London: Methuen.

Clifford, J. (1997) Diasporas, in *Routes: Travel and Translation in the Late Twentieth Century*. Cambridge, MA: Harvard University Press.

Clifford, J. and Marcus, G.E. (eds) (1986) *Writing Cultures: The Poetics and Politics of Ethnography*. Berkeley, CA: University of California Press.

Cohen, R. (1997) *Global Diasporas*. London: Routledge.

Dayan, D. and Katz, E. (1992) *Media Events: The Live Broadcasting of History*. Cambridge, MA: Harvard University Press.

Eck, D. (1985) *Darshan: Seeing the Divine Image in India*. Chambersburg, PA: Anima.

Featherstone, M. (ed.) (1990) *Global Culture: Nationalism, Globalisation, Modernity*. London: Sage.

Giddens, A. (1990) *The Consequences of Modernity*. Cambridge: Polity.

Giddens, A. (1991) *Modernity and Self-Identity*. Cambridge: Polity.

Gillespie, M. (1989) Technology and tradition: audio visual culture among South Asian families in West London, *Cultural Studies*, 3(2): 226–39.

Gillespie, M. (1993) From Sanskrit to sacred soap: a case-study in the reception of two contemporary TV versions of 'The Mahabharata', in D. Buckingham (ed.) *Reading Audiences*. Manchester: Manchester University Press.

Gillespie, M. (1994) Sacred serials, devotional viewing and domestic worship, in R. Allen (ed.) *To Be Continued: Soap Operas Around the World*. New York: Routledge.

Gillespie, M. (1995) *Television, Ethnicity and Cultural Change*. London: Routledge.

Gillespie, M. (1997) Multicultural broadcasting in Britain, in K. Robbins (ed.) *Programming for People: From Cultural Rights to Cultural Responsibilities*. United Nations World Television Forum Report, Rome: European Broadcasting Union/RAI.

Gillespie, M. (1998a) Media, minority youth and the public sphere, in *Zeitschift für Erziehungs-wissenchaft*, vol. 1. Berlin: Verlag Leske + Budrich, Opladen.

Gillespie, M. (1998b) Being cool and classy: style hierarchies in a London Punjabi peer culture, *International Journal of Punjab Studies*, 5(2): 160–78.

Hall, S. (1990) Recent developments in theories of language and ideology: a critical note, in S. Hall, D. Hobson, A. Lowe and P. Willis (eds) *Culture, Media, Language*. London: Hutchinson.

Hall, S. (1992) The question of cultural identity, in S. Hall, D. Held and T. McGrew (eds) *Modernity and its Futures*. Cambridge: Polity.

Hammersley, M. (1992) *What's Wrong with Ethnography?* London: Routledge.

Hannerz, U. (1997) *Transnational Connections*. London: Routledge.

Hobsbawm, E. and Ranger, T. (eds) (1983) *The Invention of Tradition*. Cambridge: Cambridge University Press.

Kuper, A. (1992) *The Invention of Primitive Society*. London: Routledge.

Lutgendorf, P. (1990) Ramayan: the video, *The Drama Review: A Journal of Performance Studies*, 34(2): 127–77.

Mankekar, P. (1993) Television tales and a woman's rage: a nationalist recasting of Drupadi's disrobing, *Public Culture*, 5(3): 469–92.

Mishra, V. (1985) Towards a theoretical critique of Bombay cinema, *Screen*, 26(3–4): 133–49.

Mishra, V. (1991) The great Indian epic and Peter Brook, in D. Williams (ed.) *Peter Brook and the Mahabharata: Critical Perspectives*. London: Routledge.

Moores, S. (1993) *Interpreting Audiences: The Ethnography of Media Consumption*. London: Sage.

Morley, D. (1991) Television and ethnography, *Screen*, 3(1): 1–15.

Morley, D. and Robins, K. (1989) Spaces of identity, *Screen*, 20(4): 3–15.

Rajagopal, A. (2000) *Politics after Television: Religious Nationalism and the Retailing of Hindutva 1987–1993*. Cambridge: Cambridge University Press.

Safran, W. (1991) Diasporas in modern society: myths of homeland and return, *Diaspora*, 1: 83–99.

Said, E. W. (1978) *Orientalism: Western Conceptions of the Orient.* London: Routledge & Kegan Paul.

Schlesinger, P. (1987) On national identity: some conceptions and misconceptions criticised, *Social Science Information,* 26(2): 219–64.

Silverstone, R. (1990) TV and everyday life: towards an anthropology of the TV audience, in M. Ferguson (ed.) *Public Communication.* London: Sage.

Silverstone, R. *et al.* (1991) Listening to a long conversation: an ethnographic approach to the study of information and communication technologies in the home, *Cultural Studies,* 5(2): 204–27.

Singh, S. (1995) The epic on tube: plumbing the depths of history: a paradigm for viewing the TV serialization of the Mahabharata, *Quarterly Review of Film and Video,* 16(1): 77–99.

Thomas, R. (1986) Indian cinema: pleasures and popularity, *Screen,* 26(3–4): 116–32.

Triparthi, S. (1997) The march of Vishnu, *Index on Censorship,* 26(6): 84–9.

van der Veer, P. (1995) *Religious Nationalism: Hindus and Muslims in India.* Berkeley, CA: University of California Press.

Vertovec, S. (1996) Comparative issues in and multiple meanings of the South Asian religious diaspora. Paper presented to the Comparative Study of South Asian Diaspora Religious Experience in Britain conference, London, 4–6 November.

Werbner, P. and Modood, T. (1997) *Debating Cultural Hybridity: Multicultural Identities and the Politics of Anti-Racism.* London: Zed Books.

10 | CHILDREN AND TELEVISION
A CRITICAL OVERVIEW OF THE RESEARCH

David Buckingham

One of the most immediately striking things about research into children and television is the sheer quantity of it. At a conservative estimate, there have probably been over seven thousand accounts of research in the field published since the introduction of television in the 1950s, ranging from brief reports of one-off experiments to extensive and lavishly funded surveys. So why has the relationship between children and television been such a major focus of research? Why have children been singled out for attention, and considered separately from adults? Why has television been chosen from among the myriad of other factors in children's lives? And why has so much of the research concentrated on the potential harm which television might cause them?

There are no easy answers to these questions. On one level, the research might be seen simply as a response to the relative importance of television. Thus, it is frequently pointed out that children today spend more time watching television than they do in school, or indeed on any other activity apart from sleeping – although elderly people are in fact the heaviest viewers, while teenagers watch the least of all. Yet the identification of children as a 'special audience' for television is not simply a matter of viewing figures. On the contrary, it invokes all sorts of moral and ideological assumptions about what we believe children – and, by extension, adults – to be.

David Buckingham (1998) Children and television: a critical overview of the research, in Roger Dickinson, Ramaswami Harindranath and Olga Linne (eds) *Approaches to Audiences: A Reader*. London: Hodder Arnold, pp. 131–45. Reprinted by kind permission of Hodder Arnold.

Defining 'the child'

As histories of childhood have shown, the definition and separation of children as a distinct social category are a relatively recent development, which has taken on a particular form in Western industrialized societies (Ariès 1973; James 1993). This process has been accompanied by a veritable explosion of discourses, both *about* childhood and directed *at* children themselves. The emergence of developmental psychology, and its popularization in advice literature for parents, for example, indicates some of the ways in which norms about what is 'suitable' or 'natural' behaviour for children have been enforced. Likewise, the production of children's literature and children's toys – and eventually of children's television – has invoked all sorts of assumptions about what it means to be a child.

As these examples imply, this construction of 'the child' is both a negative and a positive enterprise: it involves attempts to restrict children's access to knowledge about aspects of adult life (most obviously sex and violence), and yet it also entails a kind of pedagogy – an attempt to 'do them good' as well as protect them from harm. The constitution of children as a media audience, and as objects of research and debate, has been marked by a complex balance between these positive and negative motivations. In the early days of television, for example, one of the primary advertising appeals made by the equipment manufacturers was on the grounds of the medium's educational potential for the young (Melody 1973); and while some have argued that this pedagogical motivation has increasingly been sacrificed to commercialism, it remains a central tenet of public service provision for children. Likewise, early debates about the role of television in the family, both in the UK and in the US, were characterized by genuine ambivalence about its potential, as either an attack on family life or as a means of bringing about domestic harmony (Spigel 1992; Oswell 1995).

This definition of what it means to be a child is an ongoing process, which is subject to a considerable amount of social and historical variation. Policies on the regulation of children's programming (Anderson *et al.* 1982), for example, often reflect much more fundamental assumptions about the nature of childhood. Likewise, the struggle between parents and children over what is 'appropriate' for children to watch and to know is part of a continuing struggle over the rights and responsibilities of children; and yet the definition of what is 'childish' or 'adult' is also a central preoccupation among children themselves, not least in their discussions of television (Buckingham 1994).

Public debates

While there is certainly a considerable amount of diversity in the actual uses of television, the dominant assumption in public debates is that children's relationship with the medium is a fundamentally negative and damaging element in their lives. In this respect, it is important to locate the concern about television historically, in the context both of evolving definitions of childhood and of recurrent responses to the advent of new cultural forms and communications technologies. Concern about the negative impact of the media on young people has a very long history (Lusted 1985; Buckingham 1993a). Over 2000 years ago, the Greek philosopher Plato proposed to ban dramatic poets from his ideal Republic, for fear that their stories about the immoral antics of the gods would influence impressionable young minds. In more recent times, popular literature, music hall, the cinema and children's comics have all provoked 'moral panics' which have typically led to greater censorship designed to protect children from their allegedly harmful effects. In this respect, more recent controversies such as the 'video nasties' scare of the 1980s or the debates about screen violence that followed the killing of James Bulger in 1993 can be seen as merely heirs to a much longer tradition (Barker 1984; Buckingham 1996).

These different areas of concern share a fundamental belief in the enormous power of television, and in the inherent vulnerability of children. Television has, it would seem, an irresistible ability to 'brainwash' and 'narcotize' children, drawing them away from other, more worthwhile activities and influences. From this perspective, children are at once innocent and potentially monstrous: the veneer of civilization is only skin deep, and can easily be penetrated by the essentially irrational appeals of the visual media (Barker 1984). Such arguments often partake of the fantasy of a 'golden age' before television, in which adults were able to 'keep secrets' from children, and in which innocence and harmony reigned. By virtue of the ways in which it gives children access to the hidden, and sometimes negative, aspects of adult life, television is accused of having caused the 'disappearance of childhood' itself (Postman 1983).

To a large extent, what appears to be occurring here is a process of displacement. Genuine, often deep-seated anxieties about what are perceived as undesirable moral or social changes lead to a search for a single causal explanation. Blaming television may thus serve to deflect attention away from other possible causes – causes which may well be 'closer to home' or simply much too complicated to understand (Connell 1985). The symbolic values that are attached to the notion of childhood, and the negative associations of an 'unnatural' technology such as television, make this a particularly potent combination for social commentators of all persuasions. Yet they also make it extremely difficult to arrive at a more balanced and less sensationalist estimation of the role of television in children's lives.

All research is based on epistemological and theoretical assumptions, even if these are not always made explicit. Not least because of the intense emotions that often surround the issue of children's relationship with television, and because of the quantity and diversity of the work itself, it is thus extremely difficult to produce definitive statements about what 'research has shown'. The review which follows, therefore, is organized in terms of the different research paradigms – that is, the broad theoretical orientations – which have guided and informed specific research projects. As I shall indicate, there are several fundamental incompatibilities between them, not only in what they take to be valid knowledge, but also in terms of the questions they have chosen to address in the first place.

The search for negative effects

Research into the effects of television violence on children has remained the most prominent preoccupation in this field. Yet the search for negative effects has also encompassed other areas, some of which I go on to consider here. Broadly speaking, this research regards the relationship between television and children as one of cause and effect: the 'messages' contained within the medium are assessed in terms of their quantifiable impact on viewers' attitudes or behaviour. Nevertheless, research has gradually moved away from the cruder form of behaviourism (the so-called 'magic bullet theory') which was apparent in some of the early research on children's responses to television violence. While the influence is still seen to flow in one direction, the emphasis now is on the range of 'intervening variables' which mediate between the stimulus and the response. In the process, effects researchers have tended to adopt rather more cautious estimates of the influence of the medium. Brief accounts of research in two areas will serve to illustrate some of these developments.

Advertising

Advertising is perhaps a 'special case' in communications research, in that its intention is clearly and explicitly to persuade, and hence to produce specific behavioural effects – namely, purchasing. Of course, advertising may have broader effects, for example in terms of encouraging more generalized forms of 'consumerism' or 'materialism', or in terms of ideology: advertising is often accused of promoting 'false needs' and irrational fantasies, or reinforcing exaggerated gender stereotypes. Nevertheless, it is often children who are seen to be particularly at risk here, precisely because of their apparent inability to recognize the persuasive intentions of advertising. Even researchers who reject more exaggerated notions of advertising as 'manipulation', and of audiences as simply 'malleable consumers', have made a special case when it comes to children: unlike adults, children are seen here as lacking in 'the level of conceptual and experiential maturity needed to evaluate commercial messages rationally' (Leiss *et al.* 1990: 365), and hence as especially vulnerable to influence.

In fact, research has largely failed to substantiate many of the more exaggerated claims about the effects of advertising on children. As with the violence research, this is partly because of methodological limitations (Goldberg and Gorn 1983). For example, most children are likely to respond positively to a question like 'would you like to have most of the things they show on TV commercials?' (Atkin 1980), but this can hardly be said to prove the advertising stimulates these desires, or that they are necessarily 'false' – or indeed, that such responses can be taken as evidence of a more general set of 'materialistic' values (Greenberg and Brand 1993). Similarly, while it might be proven that 'heavy viewers' are likely to eat more Hershey bars or to use more mouthwash or acne cream than 'light viewers' (Atkin 1980), this does not necessarily prove anything about the *causal* role of advertising.

As such, much of the evidence here remains equivocal. For example, researchers have tended to conclude that advertising has a relatively weak influence on nutritional knowledge, and that parental attitudes and socio-economic status are more important (Young 1990). While advertising may influence preference for individual brands, there is less evidence that it causes children to consume more of any given *type* of product (Goldberg and Gorn 1983). Indeed, research would suggest that television is a less significant source of product information than other sources, such as visits to the shops (Wartella 1980).

Despite these qualifications, the dominant view which informs the research here is one that has been aptly characterized by Brian Young (1986) as 'child-as-innocent and advertiser-as-seducer'. Children tend to be defined here as passive victims of persuasion, as essentially trusting and uncritical viewers. In fact, there is a good deal of research which points to children's growing cynicism about the claims of advertising. While estimates vary, it seems that children become aware of the persuasive intentions of advertising at an early age (Gaines and Esserman 1981; Dorr

1986), and that by the time they reach middle childhood an intense scepticism becomes the order of the day (Young 1990; Buckingham 1993b). From a psychological perspective, these 'cognitive defences' are seen as intervening variables which moderate the impact of advertising – although the fact that children possess such defences does not necessarily mean that they will be used (Brucks *et al.* 1988). Here again, the significance that is attributed to such defences is heavily dependent upon the methods used to measure them: performance data should not be confused with competence data (Young 1990).

Young (1990) reformulates this issue in terms of the notion of 'advertising literacy', arguing that children's growing awareness of the functions of advertising, and their increasing scepticism about it, can be seen as part of a more general development in 'metacommunicative' abilities. In middle childhood, he suggests, children become much more capable of standing back from language and other forms of communication, and reflecting upon how they work. For example, they increasingly recognize that utterances may not be intended literally, that they may be inconsistent or indeed deliberately ambiguous; and they become much more sensitive to metaphor, irony, humour and other non-literal uses of language – precisely those which are so central to advertising. Young's argument here usefully moves beyond the behaviourist assumptions of effect research, and towards a 'constructivist' position (to be considered in more detail below); although in common with that research, it tends to neglect the social and interpersonal dynamics that surround the viewing process (and indeed the purchasing process), and to leave aside the considerable pleasures which are involved (Buckingham 1993b).

Stereotyping and 'social learning'

Similar assumptions would seem to inform research on children's social learning from television – that is, its contribution to forming their attitudes and beliefs about society. Television is routinely cited as a powerful influence on children's political socialization (Chaffee and Yang 1990), and on their beliefs about social institutions such as the family (Dorr *et al.* 1990), the police (Murray 1993) and government (Conway *et al.* 1981). While there is a limited amount of research on the 'pro-social' or educational effects of television, much of the work in this field has concentrated on the influence of negative 'stereotyping' of particular social groups. Thus, many studies have concluded that television is a powerful source of children's beliefs about gender roles (Morgan 1987; Signorielli 1993), about other ethnic groups (Graves 1993) and about the elderly (Kovaric 1993); and in each case, it is suggested that television causes them to adopt beliefs which are inaccurate, intolerant or otherwise negative.

Here again, however, there are significant methodological problems, which are perhaps more acute than in the other areas discussed so far. One tendency here – which is also characteristic of a great deal of public debates in this field – is to assume that effects can simply be 'read off' from the analysis of content. Statistical studies of the representation of particular social groups on television, for example, are often implicitly taken as evidence of its influence on children's beliefs about those groups (Berry and Asamen 1993). Such analyses frequently seem to take the form of a simplistic 'head count', or a reductive (and sometimes very impressionistic) analysis of characters' attributes (Palmer *et al.* 1993). In-depth analysis of television, and particularly of children's television, is conspicuous by its absence here.

Of course, it is much more difficult to gather evidence about attitudes or beliefs than about aggressive behaviour or purchasing decisions; and establishing proof of the *causal* role of television in such longer-term processes is bound to be fraught with problems. 'Before-and-after' studies which attempt to quantify the effects of exposure to a 'stereotypical' stimulus (e.g. Tan 1979) are perhaps particularly inappropriate in this respect. Yet even much more elaborate forms of 'cultivation analysis' which have attempted to correlate attitudes with levels of television exposure have encountered considerable difficulties in establishing evidence of causality (Wober and Gunter 1988). For example, dividing people into 'light viewers' and 'heavy viewers', which is characteristic of this approach, implicitly assumes that television is all the same, and neglects the diversity of material to which viewers might be exposed. For example, 'heavy viewers' may be more likely to encounter 'counter-stereotypical' representations; and since these are exceptions to the norm, they may well have more impact upon some viewers.

Kevin Durkin (1985) provides a valuable critique of this approach, which focuses particularly on television's contribution to children's learning of 'sex roles'. While he agrees that television tends to provide 'stereotyped' representations of male and female roles, he rejects the view that these are somehow 'burned' into the viewer's unconscious, or that they necessarily have a cumulative effect. Durkin argues that the 'direct effects' approach tends to neglect the relationship between television and other factors which contribute to sex role socialization; and that it ignores developmental changes in children's understanding and use of the medium as they mature. While he does not go so far as to question the more fundamental assumptions which are at stake here – notions such as 'stereotyping' and 'sex role', for example, have been heavily contested elsewhere (e.g. Barker 1989; Davies 1990) – Durkin does point to the need to locate children's responses to television within their social context, and to acknowledge the ways in which they actively make sense of what they watch. This emphasis is one which will be pursued later in this chapter.

Active audiences?

While advocates of the 'magic bullet' theory are still to be found, the development of effects research has largely been in the direction of emphasizing the role of 'intervening variables' which mediate between television and its audience. Far from seeing the audience as a mass of undifferentiated individuals, the focus has increasingly been on 'individual differences' which lead viewers to respond in different ways to the same messages. Over the past two decades, this tradition has been joined by newer perspectives, which have defined children as 'active viewers'. The notion of 'activity' here is partly a rhetorical one, and it is often used in rather imprecise ways. Yet what unites this work is a view of children, not as passive recipients of television messages, but as active interpreters and processors of meaning. The meaning of television, from this perspective, is not delivered *to* the audience, but constructed by it.

Uses and gratifications

Two distinct traditions of research can be identified here. The first is that of 'uses and gratifications'. In practice, uses and gratifications research has tended to focus largely on adults, although there are some important studies which focus on children and young people. Rosengren and Windahl (1989), for example, paint a complex picture of the very heterogeneous uses of television among Swedish adolescents, and its interaction with other media such as popular music. In the process, they challenge many general assertions about media effects, for example in relation to violence and displacement, arguing that the socializing influence of television will depend upon its relationship with other influences, and upon the diverse and variable meanings which its users attach to it. Thus, for example, television viewing or popular music will have a different significance depending upon the child's orientation towards the school, the family and the peer group. As they indicate, the influence of variables such as age, gender and social class means that different children can effectively occupy different 'media worlds' – an argument which clearly undermines any easy generalizations about 'children' as an homogenous social group.

Constructivist perspectives

Uses and gratifications research also has a great deal in common with the 'constructivist' or cognitive approach, which is the second major perspective I shall discuss here. This tradition is both extensive and diverse, yet the shared emphasis here is on the psychological processes whereby viewers construct meaning from television. Rather than simply responding to stimuli, viewers are seen here as consciously processing, interpreting and evaluating information. In making sense of what they watch, viewers use 'schemas' or 'scripts', sets of plans and expectations which they have built up from their previous experience both of television and of the world in general (for a review, see Dorr 1986). In studying children's understanding of television, cognitive psychologists have tended to concentrate on the 'micro' rather than the 'macro' aspects – on detailed aspects of mental processing, rather than on questions about television's role in forming attitudes or beliefs. The following sections offer brief 'snapshots' of some of the principal concerns.

Attention and comprehension

The work of Daniel Anderson and his colleagues (e.g. Anderson and Lorch 1983) illustrates the ways in which research in this area has increasingly come to regard children's relationship with television as an active, rather than merely a reactive, process. Anderson refutes the idea that attention is a kind of conditioned reflex which will be produced automatically by certain stimuli, such as rapid movement or loud sound effects. On the contrary, he argues that children actively choose to pay attention to television, and that the choices they make depend upon their efforts to understand what they watch, and on the other activities which are available in the viewing environment. According to Anderson, comprehension does not follow automatically from attention: rather, children's attention is partly determined by their comprehension processes.

Anderson's focus is primarily on visual attention, and he tends to neglect the role of auditory or linguistic factors – not least because auditory attention is far more difficult to identify simply by observation. Nevertheless, the argument that children actively choose the amount of mental effort they invest in television has been strongly supported by the influential work of Gavriel Salomon (e.g. 1983). Significantly, Salomon argues that these choices may be affected by children's preconceptions about the medium as a whole, which may themselves be culturally specific: his comparative research with Israeli and North American children indicated that the latter's view of television as a 'less demanding' medium led them to invest less mental effort, and hence to learn less (Salomon 1984).

Children's understanding of narrative

While studies of attention and comprehension have tended to focus on a fairly limited range of 'formal features' (Meyer 1983), there has been some cognitive research into broader aspects of television, such as narrative. W. Andrew Collins (e.g. 1981) and his colleagues have looked at the ways in which children's understanding of narrative varies according to the 'world knowledge' which they bring to it, and also according to their past experience of television itself (their 'television literacy'). As they develop, children acquire an increasingly flexible knowledge of 'common event sequences' which enable them to predict and interpret narrative.

One problem with this approach – and indeed with most studies of comprehension – is that it implicitly assumes the existence of an 'objective' meaning within a given text. Thus, Collins evaluates children's ability to distinguish between 'central content' and 'peripheral content', or between 'essential' and 'non-essential' features, although the distinctions between them are made by the researchers (or by other adult subjects) rather than by children themselves. Likewise, his judgement of children's ability to make inferences, for example about characters' motivations and feelings, depends upon a comparison with the 'correct' inferences which are made by the researchers (see Buckingham 1993b). In common with much cognitive research, there appears to be an implicit view here of the child as a 'deficit system': children at certain ages are seen to be unable to accomplish the 'logical' sequencing of visual images, to recall the 'essential' features of a narrative, or to 'correctly' distinguish between positive and negative characters – which of course implies that adults' responses to such things are taken as the norm (Anderson 1981).

Developmental studies

One of the major concerns of the constructivist approach is with the ways in which children's understanding of television changes along with their general intellectual development. Much of the research in this area has been heavily informed by the work of Piaget, which is perhaps surprising given the extensive critiques to which it has been subjected in other areas of psychology (e.g. Donaldson, 1978; Walkerdine 1984). Grant Noble (1975), for example, is one of many researchers who seeks to provide an account of the televiewing styles of children at each of

Piaget's developmental stages, which represents a steady progression towards 'the sophistication which will take final shape at the University film club' – an approach which may seem to neglect those who only get as far as the local video shop.

One particular concern here is with the development of children's ability to distinguish between reality and fantasy on television. According to Hawkins (1977), children's judgements of television depend both on their knowledge of the constructed nature of the medium (which he terms 'magic window' knowledge), and on their knowledge or 'social expectations' about the world in general. As Dorr (1983) indicates, such judgements depend both on children's general cognitive development and on their experience of the medium: children use formal or generic 'cues', and build up a growing body of knowledge about the processes of television production. 'Judging reality' is a complex and multi-faceted process, which involves the application of a wide range of different (and sometimes conflicting) criteria.

Some qualifications

While the theoretical basis of this research is outwardly very different from that of the more behaviourist effects studies, several limitations can be identified. Indeed, in some respects, the 'cognitive revolution' which was so apparent in other areas of psychology has remained incomplete here. Cognitive researchers have often continued to rely on behaviourist hypotheses and methods, for example about the negative effects of television viewing on mental processes. Cognitive processing is often seen merely as an 'intervening variable'; and meaning continues to be seen as something which is inherent in the text, which can be objectively identified and quantified.

As in many other areas of psychology, cognitive researchers have focused almost exclusively on the intellectual aspects of children's relationship with television. This focus on the individual's internal mental processes has made it difficult to assess the role of social and cultural factors in the formation of consciousness and understanding. While some cognitive researchers do acknowledge these factors in theory, much of the research itself appears to function with a notion of 'the child' which is abstracted from any social or historical context. Factors such as gender, 'race' and social class tend to be bracketed off, or regarded as influences which only come into play when the already-formed individual enters the social world.

Both within effects research, and in the constructivist approach, the relationship between children and television has thus predominantly been conceived in *psychological* terms, as a matter of the isolated individual's encounter with the screen. The central questions are about what television does to the child's mind – or, more recently, about what the child's mind does with television. In the process, television itself, and the social processes through which its meaning is established and defined, have often been neglected. These are central issues in the third research paradigm I shall consider here.

Cultural studies: an emergent paradigm?

Studies of children's relationship with television have been a relatively marginal concern in Media and Cultural Studies. To some extent, this may reflect a wider division of academic labour, whereby the study of children is still largely seen as the proper domain of psychology. At the same time, the study of audiences in general has been a relatively recent development in Cultural Studies; and while there is now a growing body of debate about the issue, there are still very few substantial empirical studies. While it is not necessarily incompatible with many of the concerns and theoretical perspectives discussed above, the Cultural Studies approach would appear to go beyond many of the limitations both of effects research and of 'active audience' theories.

Cultural Studies is itself a rather broad area, whose boundaries are far from well defined. Yet it has often been conceptualized in terms of an interaction between *institutions, texts* and *audiences* (e.g. Johnson 1985/86); and it is under these three headings that I will offer a brief review of its potential contribution to the study of children's relationship with television.

Institutions

Accounts of children's television written from within the industry have perhaps inevitably tended towards public relations (e.g. Home 1993; Laybourne 1993). Yet the study of the institutional context of children's television production has been a relatively marginal concern within communications research generally. Early studies such as Melody (1973) and Turow (1981) adopted a broad 'political economy' approach, focusing on questions of ownership, marketing and regulation. With the exception of Palmer (1987), there has been very little analysis of producers' assumptions and expectations about their child audience; and while there has been some historical work on the evolution of regulatory policy on children's television (e.g. Anderson *et al.* 1982; Kunkel and Watkins 1987), this also has remained under-researched.

More recently, however, the increasing 'commercialization' of children's television and the apparent retreat from the public service tradition have generated a growing body of academic research and debate (e.g. Engelhardt 1986; Blumler 1992; Kline 1993; Seiter 1993; Buckingham 1995a). On the one hand, there has been concern about the decline in factual programming for children, and the extent to which production is increasingly tied in with merchandising; yet there have also been calls for a more positive (or at least less Puritanical) account of 'consumption', and a more thoroughgoing discussion of what is meant by 'quality'. The highly 'gendered' nature of a great deal of children's television has been a particular focus of analysis here; although such studies implicitly raise some very challenging questions about the 'taste cultures' of children, and the ways in which their specific needs as an audience are to be defined.

Texts

As I have implied, the study of television texts within the mainstream communications research tradition has been dominated by statistical content analysis. Television is typically seen to contain fixed 'messages' which can be objectively identified and quantified. This is most obvious in the case of effects research, for example in the 'head counts' which have characterized research into social learning from television. Yet despite the much more sophisticated approach to 'mental processing' within the constructivist tradition, cognitive psychologists' analysis of television texts frequently appears to neglect the complexity of even the most simple programmes (Livingstone 1990). Ambiguity, 'openness' and contradiction, which many analyses of popular television have shown to be fundamental to its success (e.g. Fiske 1987), have effectively been ignored.

By contrast, researchers in Media and Cultural Studies have tended to adopt much more complex forms of *textual* analysis, which are variously informed by semiotics, structuralism, psychoanalysis and post-structuralist theory. Until recently, there has been very little attempt to extend this approach to the study of children's television, although in many respects this would seem to provide an important testing ground for wider arguments about television's role in 'positioning' the viewer (Buckingham 1987a, b). Thus, analysis has focused on the ways in which children's television provides opportunities for 'para-social interaction' (Noble 1975), how it handles the relationship between 'information' and 'entertainment' (Buckingham 1995b), and how it addresses the child viewer (Davies 1995). As in children's literature, the position of television as a 'parent' or 'teacher' and the process of attempting to 'draw in' the child is fraught with uncertainties (cf. Rose 1984).

Audiences

As I have indicated, Cultural Studies offers a perspective on the audience which is significantly more 'social' than that of the research discussed above. At least in principle, viewers are seen here not as unique and coherent individuals, but as sites of conflict, 'points of intersection' between a variety of potentially conflicting discourses, which in turn derive from different social locations and experiences (for example, in terms of social class, gender and ethnicity) Different discourses will be mobilized in different ways by different viewers in different contexts; and the production of meaning is therefore seen as a complex process of social negotiation (for a review, see Moores 1993).

Hodge and Tripp (1986) apply a social semiotic perspective, both to the analysis of children's programming, and to audience data. The central focus here is on the social processes through which meaning is constructed, and the power-relationships which inevitably characterize them. This approach has been pursued in my own work, where there is a central emphasis on the ways in which children define and construct their social identities through talk about television (Buckingham 1993b, 1996).

In parallel with this work, it is possible to identify a more strictly 'ethnographic' approach to studying children's viewing, both within the context of the home (e.g. Palmer 1986; Lindlof 1987; Richards 1993) and in the context of the peer group (Willis 1990; Wood 1993). Marie Gillespie's (1995) study of the use of television among a South Asian community in London, for example, integrates an analysis of the role of television within the dynamics of the family and the peer group with an account of children's responses to specific genres such as news and soap opera. Television is used here partly as a heuristic means of gaining insight into 'other' cultures, although (as with the work discussed above), there is a self-reflexive emphasis on the role of the researcher, and on the power-relationships between researchers and their child subjects, which is typically absent from mainstream research.

The work discussed here is both new and comparatively tentative in its claims, and it would be false to claim that it has resolved the problems it has set itself. In particular, the challenge of *integrating* the different areas of concern – with institutions, texts and audiences – remains a central priority in future work, and indeed in media research more broadly. This is not, I would argue, simply a matter of balancing the equation, and thereby finding a happy medium between the 'power of the text' and the 'power of the audience'. Nor is it something that can be achieved in the abstract, through the application of theory. Like many other areas considered in this book, the relationship between children and television can only be fully understood in the context of a wider analysis of the ways in which both are constructed and defined.

References

Anderson, D.R. and Lorch, E.P. (1983) Looking at television: action or reaction? in J. Bryant, and D.R. Anderson (eds) *Children's Understanding of Television*, New York: Academic Press.

Anderson, J.A. (1981) Research on children and television: a critique, *Journal of Broadcasting*, 25(4): 395–400.

Anderson, J.A., Meyer, T. and Hexamer, A. (1982) An examination of the assumptions underlying telecommunications social policies treating children as a specialized audience, in Burgoon, M. (ed.) *Communication Yearbook 5*. New Brunswick: Transaction Books.

Ariès, P. (1973) *Centuries of Childhood*. Harmondsworth: Penguin.

Atkin, C.K. (1980) Effects of television advertising on children, in E.L. Palmer and A. Dorr (eds) *Children and the Faces of Television: Teaching, Violence, Selling*. New York: Academic Press.

Barker, M. (ed.) (1984) *The Video Nasties*. London: Pluto.

Barker, M. (1989) *Comics: Ideology, Power and the Critics*. Manchester: Manchester University Press.

Berry, G.L. and Asamen, J.K. (1993) *Children and Television: Images in a Changing Socio-cultural World*. London: Sage.

Blumler, J. (1992) *The Future of Children's Television in Britain: An Enquiry for the Broadcasting Standards Council*. London: Broadcasting Standards Council.

Brucks, M., Armstrong, G.M. and Goldberg, M.E. (1988) Children's use of cognitive defences against advertising: a cognitive response approach, *Journal of Consumer Research*, 14: 471–82.

Buckingham, D. (1987a) The construction of subjectivity in educational television. Part one: towards a new agenda, *Journal of Educational Television*, 13(2): 137–46.

Buckingham, D. (1987b) The construction of subjectivity in educational television. Part two: You and Me – a case study, *Journal of Educational Television*, 13(3): 187–200.

Buckingham, D. (1993a) Introduction: young people and the media, in D. Buckingham. (ed.) *Reading Audiences: Young People and the Media*. Manchester: Manchester University Press.

Buckingham, D. (1993b) *Children Talking Television: The Making of Television Literacy*. London: Falmer Press.

Buckingham, D. (1994) Television and the definition of childhood, in B. Mayall (ed.) *Children's Childhoods Observed and Experienced*. London: Falmer Press.

Buckingham, D. (1995a) The commercialisation of childhood? The place of the market in children's media culture, *Changing English*, 2(2): 17–41.

Buckingham, D. (1995b) On the impossibility of children's television, in C. Bazalgette, and D. Buckingham (eds) *In Front of the Children*. London: British Film Institute.

Buckingham, D. (1996) *Moving Images: Understanding Children's Emotional Responses to Television*. Manchester: Manchester University Press.

Chaffee, S.H. and Yang, S-M. (1990) Communication and political socialization, in O. Ichilov (ed.) *Political Socialization, Citizenship Education and Democracy*. New York: Teachers College Press.

Collins, W.A. (1981) Schemata for understanding television, in H. Kelly and H. Gardner (eds) *Viewing Children Through Television*. San Francisco: Jossey-Bass.

Connell, I. (1985) Fabulous powers: blaming the media, in L. Masterman (ed.) *Television Mythologies*. London: Comedia/MK Media Press.

Conway, M.M., Wyckoff, M.L., Feldbaum, E. and Ahern, D. (1981) The news media in children's political socialization *Public Opinion Quarterly*, 45(2): 164–78.

Davies, B. (1990) *Frogs and Snails and Feminist Tales*. Sydney: Allen & Unwin.

Davies, M.M. (1995) Babes 'n' the hood: pre-school television and its audiences in the United States and Britain, in C. Bazalgette and D. Buckingham (eds) *In Front of the Children*. London: British Film Institute.

Donaldson, M. (1978) *Children's Minds*. London: Fontana.

Dorr, A. (1983) No shortcuts to judging reality, in J. Bryant and D.R. Anderson (eds) *Children's Understanding of Television*. New York: Academic Press.

Dorr, A. (1986) *Television and Children: A Special Medium for a Special Audience*. Beverly Hills: Sage.

Dorr, A., Kovaric, P. and Doubleday, C. (1990) Age and content influences on children's perceptions of the realism of television families, *Journal of Broadcasting*, 34(4): 377–97.

Durkin, K. (1985) *Television, Sex Roles and Children*. Milton Keynes: Open University Press.

Engelhardt, T. (1986) The strawberry shortcake strategy, in T. Gitlin (ed.) *Watching Television*. New York: Pantheon.

Fiske, J. (1987) *Television Culture*. London: Methuen.

Gaines, L. and Esserman, J.F. (1981) A quantitative study of young children's comprehension of television programs and commercials, in J.F. Esserman (ed.) *Television Advertising and Children*. New York: Child Research Service.

Gillespie, M. (1995) *Television, Ethnicity and Cultural Change*. London: Routledge.

Goldberg, M.E. and Gorn, G.J. (1983) Researching the effects of television advertising on children: a methodological critique, in M.J.A. Howe (ed.) *Learning from Television: Psychological and Educational Research*. London: Academic Press.

Graves, S.B. (1993) Television, the portrayal of African Americans, and the development of children's attitudes, in G.L. Berry and J.K. Asamen (eds) *Children and Television*. London: Sage.

Greenberg, B.S. and Brand, J.E. (1993) Television news and advertising in schools: the 'Channel One' controversy. *Journal of Communication*, 43(1): 143–51.

Hawkins, R.P. (1977) The dimensional structure of children's perceptions of television reality, *Communication Research*, 4(3): 299–320.

Hodge, B. and Tripp, D. (1986) *Children and Television: A Semiotic Approach*. Cambridge: Polity Press.

Home, A. (1993) *Into the Box of Delights: A History of Children's Television*. London: BBC Books.

James, A. (1993) *Childhood Identities*. Edinburgh: Edinburgh University Press.

Johnson, R. (1985/86) What is Cultural Studies anyway? *Social Text*, 16, 38–80.

Kline, S. (1993) *Out of the Garden: Toys and Children's Culture in the Age of TV Marketing*. London: Verso.

Kovaric, P. (1993) Television, the portrayal of the elderly, and children's attitudes, in G.L. Berry and J.K. Asamen (eds) *Children and Television*. London: Sage.

Kunkel, D. and Watkins, B. (1987) Evolution of children's television regulatory policy, *Journal of Broadcasting and Electronic Media*, 31(4): 367–89.

Laybourne, G. (1993) The Nickelodeon experience, in G.L. Berry and J.K. Asamen (eds) *Children and Television*. London: Sage.

Leiss, W., Kline, S. and Jhally, S. (1990) *Social Communication in Advertising*, London: Routledge.

Lindlof, T. (ed.) (1987) *Natural Audiences*. Newbury Park, CA: Sage.

Livingstone, S. (1990) *Making Sense of Television*. Oxford: Pergamon.

Lusted, D. (1985) A history of suspicion: educational attitudes to television, in D. Lusted and P. Drummond (eds) *TV and Schooling* London: British Film Institute.

Melody, W. (1973) *Children's Television: The Economics of Exploitation*. New Haven: Yale University Press.

Meyer, M. (ed.) (1983) *Children and the Formal Features of Television*. Munich: Saur.

Moores, S. (1993) *Interpreting Audiences*. London: Sage.

Morgan, M. (1987) Television, sex-role attitudes and sex-role behavior, *Journal of Early Adolescence*, 7(3): 269–82.

Murray, J.P. (1993) The developing child in a multimedia society, in G.L. Berry and J.K. Asamen (eds) *Children and Television*. London: Sage.

Noble, G. (1975) *Children in Front of the Small Screen*. London: Constable.

Oswell, D. (1995) Watching with mother, in C. Bazalgette and D. Buckingham (eds) *In Front of the Children*. London: British Film Institute.

Palmer, E., Smith, K.T. and Strawser, K.S. (1993) Rubik's tube: developing a child's television worldview, in G.L. Berry and J.K. Asamen (eds) *Children and Television*. London: Sage.

Palmer, P. (1986) *The Lively Audience*. Sydney: Allen & Unwin.

Palmer, E. (1987) *Children in the Cradle of Television*. Lexington, MA: Lexington Books.

Postman, N. (1983) *The Disappearance of Childhood*, London: W. H. Allen.

Richards, C. (1993) Taking sides? What young girls do with television, in D. Buckingham (ed.) *Reading Audiences: Young People and the Media*. Manchester: Manchester University Press.

Rose, J. (1984) *The Case of Peter Pan: Or the Impossibility of Children's Fiction*. London: Macmillan.

Rosengren, K.E. and Windahl, S. (1989) *Media Matter: TV Use in Childhood and Adolescence*. Norwood, NJ: Ablex.

Salomon, G. (1983) Beyond the formats of television: the effects of students' preconceptions on the experience of televiewing, in M. Meyer, (ed.) *Children and the Formal Features of Television*. Munich: Saur.

Salomon, G. (1984) Television is 'easy' and print is 'tough': the differential investment of mental effort as a function of perceptions and attributions, *Journal of Educational Psychology*, 76: 647–58.

Seiter, E. (1993) *Sold Separately: Parents and Children in Consumer Culture*. New Brunswick: Rutgers University Press.

Signorielli, N. (1993) Television, the portrayal of women, and children's attitudes, in G.L. Berry and J.K. Asamen (eds) *Children and Television*. London: Sage.

Spigel, L. (1992) *Make Room for TV: Television and the Family Ideal in Postwar America*. Chicago: University of Chicago Press.

Tan, A.S. (1979) TV beauty ads and role expectations of adolescent female viewers, *Journalism Quarterly*, 56: 283–8.

Turow, J. (1981) *Entertainment, Education and the Hard Sell*. New York: Praeger.

Walkerdine, V. (1984) Developmental psychology and the child-centred pedagogy, in J. Henriques *et al.* (eds) *Changing the Subject*. London: Methuen.

Wartella, E. (1980) Individual differences in children's responses to television advertising, in E.L. Palmer and A. Dorr (eds) *Children and the Faces of Television: Teaching, Violence, Selling*. New York: Academic Press.

Willis, P. (1990) *Common Culture: Symbolic Work at Play in the Everyday Cultures of the Young*. Milton Keynes: Open University Press.

Wober, M. and Gunter, B. (1988) *Television and Social Control*. Aldershot: Avebury.

Wood, J. (1993) Repeatable pleasures: notes on young people's use of video, in D. Buckingham (ed.) *Reading Audiences: Young People and the Media*. Manchester: Manchester University Press.

Young, B.M. (1986) New approaches to old problems: the growth of advertising literacy, in S. Ward, T. Robertson and R. Brown (eds) *Commercial Television and European Children*. Aldershot: Gower.

Young, B. (1990) *Children and Television Advertising Oxford*. Oxford University Press.

RATINGS ANALYSIS IN ADVERTISING

James G. Webster, Patricia F. Phalen and Lawrence W. Lichty

Audience research comes in many forms having a wide variety of applications. At first glance, this abundance may be overwhelming. How does one make sense of all those numbers? What is a high rating, or what is a low one? What is an unusual or important feature of audience behavior, and what is routine? This chapter offers a framework for evaluating and analyzing the information contained in audience data, with an emphasis on broad concepts and theories. This approach is intended to give readers a sense of perspective on the audience – to help them see the forest instead of an endless succession of trees.

The information collected by the research firms is conceptually straightforward. At their core, databases simply record people's reported exposure to media. Databases reveal nothing about the effects of that exposure or motivations for listening or viewing. Any useful framework for analyzing these data, then, requires understanding the complexities of how people use media. If researchers know what determines exposure to media and can predict patterns of use likely to emerge under given circumstances, then they have a way of interpreting the numbers that confront them.

The chapter contains four sections. First, we take a closer look at just what a ratings analyst is trying to assess – exposure to media. We categorize

James G. Webster, Patricia F. Phalen and Lawrence W. Lichty (2000) Ratings analysis in advertising, *Ratings Analysis: Theory and Practice*. Hillsdale, NJ and Hove, London: Lawrence Erlbaum Associates, pp. 158–64, 179–84. Reprinted by kind permission of Lawrence Erlbaum Associates.

and discuss the principal measurements of audience behaviour. Second, we review the most common theories for explaining people's choice of media offerings. These rely heavily on individual preferences to explain what the audience is doing. Third, we introduce factors that seem critical to understanding audience formation. Finally, we present a model of audience behavior that reflects all of these considerations and offers a more complete way to understand exposure to media. This is the key to interpreting audience information.

Exposure to media

As noted previously, most commercial audience research is simply a record of what kinds of people are exposed to what kinds of media. The practice in the television and radio industries has been to define exposure as program choice, or tuning behavior, rather than as attention or involvement. By studying a properly drawn sample of individuals and accurately measuring each one, researchers can have considerable confidence in their ability to describe exposure to media, using various definitions of exposure. Of course, research firms encounter myriad problems in sampling, measurement, and data processing. These exact a toll on accuracy. But even experienced users who are aware of data error tend to take numbers at face value in their day-to-day work. For the most part, that is our approach. When substantial methodological problems or biases suggest a qualified interpretation of the data, it is noted; but otherwise, we treat audience ratings as valid measures of exposure.

We have already encountered ways to measure or somehow quantify media audiences – some are reported by ratings services, others are calculated by ratings users. It is useful, at this point, to draw a broad distinction between these various measurements and indices. One type is called *gross measures* and the other *cumulative measures*, depending on whether the behavior of individuals is tracked over time. If an audience statistic does not depend on tracking, it is a gross measure. If it does, it is cumulative. This temporal quality in the data defines a fundamental distinction that is carried through the rest of this volume.

Gross measures of the audience

Gross measures of exposure include estimates of audience size and composition made at a single point in time. The best examples are audience ratings and market shares, although summaries like the circulation of print media or total sales (e.g., movie ticket or record sales) are also gross measures of the audience. Even the number of hits on a Web site would seem to qualify. In effect, the gross measures are snapshots of the population that give no clear sense of the number of repeat customers involved.

Electronic media take these snapshots with the greatest rapidity. Ratings services estimate how many people listened to a station in an average quarter hour or watched a program in an average minute. As projections of total audience size, HUT and PUT levels belong in this category as well. Gross measures of exposure can also include secondary calculations derived from other measurements. Gross rating points (GRPs) – a summation of individual ratings over a schedule – are such calculations. Simple cost calculations, like cost per point (CPP) and cost per thousand (CPM), can also be thought of as gross measures.

Gross measures are the most common audience summaries, and comprise most of the numbers reported in syndicated research reports. As a result, they are the best known and most widely used of audience measurements. Useful as they are, however, they fail to capture information about how individual audience members behave over time. That kind of behavior is expressed in cumulative measures.

Cumulative measures of the audience

The most familiar example of the second group of audience measurements is a station's cumulative audience, or *cume*. To report a weekly cume audience, a ratings company must sort each person's media use for a week and summarize how many used the station at least once. Analogous summaries are *reach* and *unduplicated audience*. A closely related cumulative measure increasingly familiar to advertisers is *frequency* – how often an individual sees a particular advertising message over time. Studies of program audience duplication, likewise, depend on tracking individual media users over time.

With the exception of the various cume ratings, cumulative measures are less commonly reported by syndicated research services than are gross measurements. Customized studies of audience duplication, however, may be useful in a variety of applications. For example, a programmer studying audience flow, or an advertiser tracking the reach and frequency of a media plan, is concerned with how the audience is behaving over time. Indeed ... this sort of tracking can be illuminating for social scientists interested in any number of questions. Table 11.1 lists the most common gross and cumulative measures of media exposure.

Table 11.1 – Common measures of exposure to media

Gross measures	Cumulative measures
Audience ratings	Cume ratings
Market shares	Reach
Circulation	Frequency
Web-site hits	Audience duplication
Sales	Inheritance effects
Attendance	Channel loyalty
Rentals	Repeat viewing

Comparing gross and cumulative measurements

To get a clearer picture of the difference between gross and cumulative measures, and to begin to appreciate the analytical possibilities offered by such data, consider Figure 11.1. The large box in the upper left-hand corner represents a simplified ratings database. The data are from a hypothetical sample of 10 households, numbered 1 through 10, down the left-hand column. The media use of each household is measured at 10 points in time, from Time 1 to Time 10 across the top of the page. Both types of measures can be generated for such a database.

In practice a sample would include hundreds or thousands of units of analysis, which could be individual people or households, as indicated in the figure. There would also be many more points in time. For example, a standard television diary divides each of 7 days into 80 quarter hours. Each person is measured across 560 (i.e., 7 × 80) points in time, rather than the 10 illustrated in this example. Now try to imagine how many points in time could be identified in peoplemeter data that track viewing moment to moment over a period of years.

Figure 11.1 portrays household television viewing, but radio listening or Web-site visits could be conceptualized in the same way. This illustration assumes a 3-station market, which means that each household can be doing one of four things at each point in time. It can be turned to Channel A, Channel B, Channel C, or nothing at all. These behaviors are indicated by the appropriate letters, or a blackened box, respectively.

The most commonly reported gross measures of exposure are shown in the box directly under the database. ... Hence, Channel A has a rating of 20 and a share of 40 at Time 4. All one needs to do is look down the appropriate column. Unlike the calculation of a cume, whatever happened before or after that time period is irrelevant to the calculation of a rating.

The box on the right-hand side of the page includes common cumulative

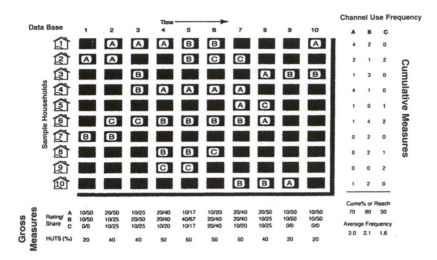

Figure 11.1. Gross vs. cumulative measures in ratings data

measures. To calculate these, an analyst must first examine each household's viewing behavior across time. That means moving across each row in the database: The first household watched Channel A 4 times, Channel B 2 times, but never watched Channel C. Each channel's column of cumulative viewing indicates its reach, or cume. Each channel's cumulative audience is expressed as a percentage of the sample who viewed it at least once over the 10 points time. Therefore, the first household would be included in the cume of A and B, but not C. Furthermore, the analyst can report mean frequency of viewing among those who viewed a channel by computing the average of numbers in the column. This is essentially what an advertiser does when calculating reach and frequency, with the relevant points in time being determined by when a commercial message runs.

Studies of program audience duplication can also be executed from this database. An analyst might be interested in how well Station A retains an audience from one show to the next. This can be determined by seeing how many people who watched Station A at one point continued to watch the program that aired after it. The analyst could also compare any pair of program audiences to assess repeat viewing, audience loyalty, and so on. Each case requires tracking individual households across at least two points in time, which would be a cumulative measure of exposure.

Depending on the question, ratings analysts would interpret gross measures, cumulative measures, or numbers derived from these two ways of defining exposure. A large number of analytical techniques can be organized in this way. In fact, these techniques are likely to maintain their usefulness even as the new technologies develop. Whether audiences are reached through the Internet, DBS, or traditional over-the-air broadcasting, the concepts of gross and cumulative measurements convey important information to programmers and advertisers. Exploiting those analytical techniques to their fullest, however, depends on a better understanding of the factors that shape audiences from moment to moment.

Common theories of media choice

The question most often asked by students of audience behavior is, 'why do people choose specific media content?' The answer most commonly provided is, 'they choose what they like.' This reasoning is typical of industry practice, communications policy, and most academic theories of choice. It suggests equivalence between program preferences and program choices. This section reviews four of the most popular theories of choice: working theories used by industry practitioners, economic models of program choice, selective-exposure theory; and uses and gratifications research. All are based heavily, if not exclusively, on the idea of preferences. They provide a background against which our framework can be better understood.

Working theories of program choice

Working theories are the principles and assumptions used by media professionals while conducting their jobs. These 'rules of thumb' may or may not have been subjected to systematic investigation. They may or may not correspond to academic theories of choice. But they certainly deserve attention. Programmers and media planners base these working theories on a day-to-day familiarity with how the audience responds to the media environment.

The people who craft media content monitor trends in popular culture in anticipation of audience behavior. Often, interest centers on what types of content people will like: in television – soap operas, cop shows, game shows, and situation comedies; in radio – station formats, like contemporary hits, country, new age, or all news. These are the familiar industry categories, but we can also define program types in other ways. For example, content could be grouped as entertainment or information, adult or children's, and so on.

It is widely assumed that media consumers will consistently prefer content of a type. Anecdotal evidence supports such reasoning within media industries. Popular movies become television series of the same sort. Hit TV programs are imitated on the assumption that there is an audience out there who likes that kind of material. In television, as one pundit put it, nothing succeeds like excess. Market researchers have conducted formal studies to identify the content characteristics that seem to polarize people's likes and dislikes. What they have generally discovered is that common sense industry categories come as close to a viewer-defined typology as anything. In simple terms, the people who like one soap opera do, in fact, tend to like other soap operas, and so on. Similar preferences for rap music, country-western, opera, and most other types of music are also common (MacFarland 1997).

An interesting facet of program preferences has emerged from this type of research: dislikes are more clearly related to program type than likes. In other words, what people like may be eclectic, but their dislikes are more readily categorized. A simple test involves listing the five TV shows one likes most, and the five one likes least. For some people, it is hard to express dislikes in anything other than program types. If program choice is as much a matter of avoidance as anything else, this could be an important insight.

Another significant feature of program type preferences is the linkage found between certain types of content and audience demographics. In television, it is well established that news and information draw an older audience. Similarly, men tend to watch more sports than women do, children are drawn to animation, and popular programs among African American feature Black characters. The same linkages exist in other forms of media. Women are the usual readers of romance novels. Young men prefer action-adventure films. Interent use also relates to age and gender. None of these associations is intended to suggest a lock-step connection between preferences and demographics, only correlations. But working professionals should certainly be aware of their existence.

As important as preferences are in determining people's choice of media materials, programmers know well that other factors enter the picture. Recall ... the importance of audience flow. Radio and television programs appear in a carefully crafted lineup. A program scheduled immediately after a popular show will enjoy a significant advantage in building an audience. Programming strategies such as lead-in effects and block programming depend on this reasoning.

It is also important to consider when the audience is likely to be using the medium in question. Conventional wisdom and some formal theories of audience behavior suggest that other factors than programming determine who is in the audience. In 1971, the late Paul Klein, then a researcher at

NBC, offered a tongue-in cheek description of the television audience. Struck by the amazing predictability of audience size, Klein suggested that people turn the set on out of habit, without much advance thought about what they will watch. After the set is on, they simply choose the *least objectionable program (LOP)* from available offerings. In effect, Klein suggested that audience behavior is a two-stage process in which a decision to use media precedes the selection of specific content. The tendency to turn on a set without regard to programming is often taken as evidence of a *passive audience*, although this seems a needlessly value-laden label. The conceptual alternative, a thoroughly *active audience*, appears to be unrealistic. Such an audience would turn on a set whenever favorite programs were aired, and turn off a set when they were not. It is known, however, that daily routines (e.g., work, sleep, etc.) effectively constrain when sets are turned on. It is also known that many people will watch or listen to programming that they are not thrilled with, rather than turning off their sets.

Of course, this is a broad generalization about audience behavior. It is not intended to rule out the possibility that people can be persuaded to turn their sets on by media content. Major events, like the Super Bowl or dramatic news stories, undoubtedly attract people to the media who would not otherwise be there. Promotion and advertising may also get the attention of potential viewers who then remember to tune in. It is also likely that levels of activity vary by medium. Print and the Internet may be intrinsically more engaging although they require more effort on the part of media consumers. Moreover, levels of activity can vary over time. The same person might be choosy at one time and a 'couch potato' the next. Overall, though, a two-stage process, including the role of habit, appears to explain audience behavior rather well.

An integrated models of audience behavior

Now that we have introduced the range of factors influencing audience behavior, we can try to forge an overall framework for examining media exposure. Using a comprehensive model of audience behavior, the job of summarizing, evaluating, and anticipating the data contained in the ratings will be more manageable.

Audience researchers have devoted much time and effort to understanding people's use of electronic media. Ad agencies and programmers have engaged in pragmatic studies of audience formation, economists have developed abstract theories of program choice, and social psychologists

Table 11.2 – Media factors affecting exposure

Structural	*Individual*
Coverage	Technologies owned
Household penetration	Radio & TV sets
Signal carriage	VCRs
Clearance	Computers
Content options	Subscriptions
Number of choices	Print media
Program schedules	Cable
Linked web sites	DBS
	Internet service
	Repertoires
	Channel repertoires
	Bookmarking

have performed a succession of experiments and surveys to reveal the origins of audience behavior. Despite this progress, there remains a tendency for each group to work in isolation. Collaborations among theorists and practitioners or even across academic disciplines are, regrettably, rare.

At the risk of oversimplifying matters, two distinct approaches to understanding the audience can be identified. The first emphasizes the importance of the individual factors, which is typical of work in psychology, communication studies, marketing, and economics. It has enormous intuitive appeal and is likely to characterize most commonsense explanations of the audience. Because audiences are simply collections of individuals, understanding behavior at the individual level helps explain patterns of mass behavior. To conceptualize audience behavior at the individual level, researchers try to explain what distinguishes one person from another. Preferences are usually invoked to explain behavior. But this focus misses trends that become clear at different levels of analysis. For instance, it is doubtful that any one television viewer chooses to create an 'inheritance effect,' yet night after night the audience manifests this form of behavior.

The second perspective emphasizes structural factors as key determinants of mass behavior. This approach is more typical in sociology, human ecology, and at least some forms of marketing and advertising research. It downplays individual needs and wants and concentrates on things like total audience size, coverage areas, and program schedules to understand behavior. Although this work can successfully produce statistical explanations of aggregate data, it often rings hollow, prompting questions like 'What does this mean in human terms – what does it tell us about ourselves?' Such explanations are usually possible, but not always apparent.

It is important to recognize that neither approach is right or wrong. They are simply different ways to know the audience. It is also important to note that neither approach stands alone. Models of audience behavior are sometimes advanced as mutually exclusive alternatives, but there is much to be gained by trying to integrate them. Specifically, analyses of individual behavior might be enhanced by a more deliberate consideration of the structural factors suggested here. Researchers know through observation that these variables are highly correlated with audience behavior, and weaving them into microlevel studies might increase the latter's power and generalizability. Conversely, research in mass behavior might be more explicit about its relationship to theoretical concepts central in the individual approach. This could improve its popular acceptance and utility. It is in this spirit that we propose the following model.

The model

The model presented in Figure 11.2 is intended to organize thinking about audience behavior as commonly defined in audience research. Although the model suggests broad relationships, it does not provide testable hypotheses. It certainly falls short of being a mathematical model ... We should also point out that this model focuses primarily on short-term features of audience behavior.

The central component to be explained is exposure to media. As argued [previously], audience analysts are interested in mass behavior, which can be categorized as gross or cumulative. Two broad categories are shown as the causes of exposure: audience factors and media factors. The shape of the boxes indicates the direction of influence. For example, the model suggests that audience factors help determine ratings, not vice versa. There are also cause–effect relationships among factors within each box. For instance, audience preferences probably contribute to patterns of availability, and cable subscription helps shape cable network coverage. We have opted to omit the arrows suggesting these interrelationships for simplicity.

To use the model, an analyst would identify the audience behavior he or she wished to explain. Is the researcher concerned with the size of an audience at a single point in time (i.e., a gross measure), or with how audience members behave across time (i.e., a cumulative measure)? To

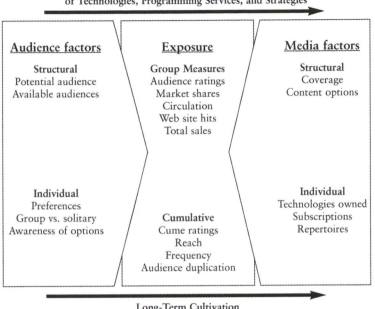

Figure 11.2. A model of audience behavior

begin the process of evaluating, explaining, or predicting that behavior, the analyst considers structural determinants first. We recommend this approach for three reasons. First, they begin at the mass level of analysis, like the measures of exposure being analyzed. Second, they are knowable from program schedules, network coverage, and audience research reports. Individual factors, like audience awareness and the use of remote-control devices, are harder to pin down. Third, we know from experience that structural explanations work well with most forms of audience data. If they fail to provide a satisfying answer, attention should be directed to the individual-level factors on either side of the model.

A sample scenario
While working through an example to get a better sense of the model, keep in mind it is not designed to provide quick answers to difficult audience research questions, but rather to guide the analyst in considering all the relevant factors. Consider, for instance, the ratings of a local television news program. Why do some stations have high ratings and others have low ratings? What factors will shape a station's audience size in the future?

Advertisers, as well as local station managers and programmers, would probably have an interest in this analysis. Imagine that you work for a station and want to assess its situation.

Remember that a rating is a gross measure of audience size. Local news ratings, in particular, have an important impact on station profitability. To explain the size of a station's news audience, we should first consider structural factors. If audience size is to be expressed as an absolute number, we would need to know the size of the potential audience defined by the population in the market. At the same time, we would want to consider the nature of the station's coverage area. Is it a VHF or a UHF station? If UHF, you are probably already at a disadvantage. Is there anything about the station's signal or local geography that would restrict its ability to reach the entire potential audience?

Next, we would want to know the size of the audience when the news is broadcast. An analysis of share data might overlook this, but since we are interested in ratings, the bigger the available audience, the better the chances of achieving a large rating. We might pay special attention to audience segments more likely to be local news viewers, usually older adults. Next, we would consider a variety of program scheduling factors.

The first scheduling consideration would involve assessing the competition. How many competitors are there? As they increase in number, your ratings are likely to decrease. Do other stations enjoy advantages in covering the market? To what extent has cable television penetrated the market? How many house-holds have access to the Internet, and what do the usage patterns look like? What are your principal competitors likely to program opposite the news? Will you confront only news programs, or will the competition counterprogram? Counterprogramming is more likely if you are a network affiliate with independents in the market. If the available audience contains a large segment unlikely to watch the news (e.g., children and young adults), that could damage your ratings. Consider the programming on before and after the news. A highly rated lead-in is likely to help your ratings, especially if it attracts an audience of news viewers. If you are an affiliate, pay close attention to the strength of your network's news program. Research has shown a strong link between local and network news ratings.

Usually, these structural factors explain most of the variations in local news ratings. A station can control some things, like lead-in programming. Other things, like the number of competitors, are beyond control. Because a single ratings point might make a substantial difference in a station's profitability, however, consideration of individual factors may be warranted, especially if these are things a station can manipulate.

Among the most likely candidates for consideration are viewer preferences and awareness. Are there certain on-air personalities or program formats that are more or less appealing to viewers? Every year, consultants to stations, called 'news doctors,' charge large fees to make such determinations. Are there certain news stories that will better suit the needs and interests of local viewers? In markets not measured continuously, stations often schedule sensationalist special reports to coincide with the ratings sweeps. A riveting investigative report is unlikely to boost a program's ratings, however, unless additional viewers are made aware of it. So stations must simultaneously engage in extraordinary promotion and advertising. Of course, all the stations in a market are probably doing the same thing. Therefore, although catering to audience preferences is very important in principle, in practice, it may not make a huge ratings difference. Even so, a small edge can be crucial to profitability.

The analysis of radio audience behavior resembles that in television, except exposure is typically defined in terms of stations and dayparts rather than programs. Listeners occasionally tune to specific programs, but more often they select a station rather than a discrete radio show. The key determinants of radio audience size and flow are still structural, but individual factors take on added salience. Radio stations usually operate in competitive markets and specialize in one kind of programming. The choice of stations is more likely to be the decision of a single individual than a group. Radio listeners are also likely to select a station by searching through a limited repertoire. They may leave the radio tuned to a favorite station all the time or they may select a station by pressing a preset button instead of consulting a program guide. For all these reasons, people's preferences and awareness of a station's offerings weigh more heavily in the analysis of radio audience behavior.

There is more to learn about the behavior of Internet audiences. In a media environment where there are fewer structural constraints, it seems reasonable to expect that notions of selective exposure and related theories may gain new adherents. Web users are typically characterized as individuals actively seeking information, so a theory that posits an active audience seems to offer an appealing interpretation of behavior. Even the term 'user' implies a more actively engaged individual than does the more passive term 'viewer.'

Finally, consider the long-term nature of exposure to media. One danger of characterizing audience behavior as the result of nicely drawn arrows and boxes is that things are made to seem simpler than they are. For instance, the model defines exposure as the result, not the cause, of other factors. Over a period of months or weeks, ratings can have a substantial effect on the structure of the media. Programs are canceled, new shows developed, schedules altered, and clearances changed, often on the basis of audience behavior. Such relationships have been the subject of a number of interesting investigations. Similarly, the model, as we have presented it, suggests a high degree of independence between audience and media factors. In the short term, that seems to be a workable assumption. Over time, however, it could distort the picture of audience behavior.

To address these issues, we have specified some long-term relationships between audience and media factors. For example, the growth of potential audiences and patterns of availability clearly affect the development of media services and programming strategies. Conversely, the structure and content of the media undoubtedly cultivate certain tastes, expectations, and habits on the part of the audience. These are important relationships, but not central to our purpose. Bearing such limitations in mind, we hope the model can provide a useful framework for evaluating ratings data and exploiting the analytical techniques discussed in the remaining chapters. We also hope that it dispels the myth that preference translates easily into choice.

Related readings

Barwise, P. and Ehrenberg, A. (1988) *Television and its Audience*. London: Sage.

Bower, R.T. (1985) *The Changing Television Audience in America*. New York: Columbia University Press.

Comstock, G., and Scharrer, E. (1999). *Television: What's on, Who's Watching, and What it Means*. San Diego, CA: Academic Press.

Goodhardt, G.J., Ehrenberg, A.S.C. and Collins, M.A. (1987) *The Television Audience: Patterns of Viewing*, 2nd edn. Aldershot, UK: Gower.

Heeter, C. and Greenberg, B.S. (1988) *Cable-viewing*. Norwood, NJ: Ablex.

MacFarland, D.T. (1997) *Future Radio Programming Strategies: Cultivating Listenership in the Digital Age*. Mahwah, NJ: Lawrence Erlbaum Associates.

McPhee, W.N. (1963) *Formal Theories of Mass Behavior*. New York: The Free Press.

McQuail, D. (1997) *Audience Analysis*. Thousand Oaks, CA: Sage.

Neumann, W.R. (1991) *The Future of the Mass Audience*. Cambridge: Cambridge University Press.

Owen, B.M. and Wildman, S.W. (1992) *Television Economics*. Cambridge: Harvard University Press.

Rosengren, K.E., Wenner, L.A. and Palmgreen, P. (eds) (1985) *Media Gratifications Research: Current Perspectives*. Beverly Hills: Sage.

Steiner, G.A. (1963) *The People Look at Television*. New York: Alfred A. Knopf.

Webster, J.G. and Phalen, P.F. (1997) *The Mass Audience: Rediscovering the Dominant Model*. Mahwah, NJ: Lawrence Erlbaum Associates.

Zillmann, D. and Bryant, J. (eds) (1985) *Selective Exposure to Communication*. Hillsdale, NJ: Lawrence Erlbaum Associates.

HEADS OF HOUSEHOLD AND LADIES OF THE HOUSE

GENDER, GENRE AND BROADCAST RATINGS, 1929–1990

Eileen R. Meehan

In 1928, advertisers, national radio networks, program producers, and ratings firms divided the adult audience for broadcasting into two categories: heads of household and ladies of the house. The former category comprised male wage earners whose productive labor allowed the latter category to stay home as unpaid (hence, in capitalist terms, unproductive)[1] housekeepers, baby sitters, nannies, and domestic purchasing agents. Based on this division of labor, the broadcasting industry developed its own forms of industry wisdom and traditional practices.[2]

In this essay I will examine the political economy of ratings in order to add to our understanding of the business practice of categorizing people as ladies or heads or working women, as well as the programming practice of selecting genres for genders and discriminating by parts of the day. I will analyze how the audience figures in the transindustrial market where ratings firms sell to advertisers, networks, and program producers the documents that define, describe, and measure the audience. At stake are the definitions of *audience, women's concerns, men's genres, children's television*, and similar terms that imply our personal and collective responsibility for the content of broadcasting.

The historical context and corporate struggles transformed wireless into radio and the listening audience into the commodity audience. In that

Eileen Meehan (1993) Heads of household and ladies of the house: gender, genre and broadcast ratings 1929–90, in Robert McChesney and William Solomon (eds) *Ruthless Criticism*. Minneapolis: University of Minnesota Press, pp. 204–21. Reprinted by kind permission of University of Minnesota Press.

context and those structures are rooted the modern structure of television, whether broadcast or cable. I begin by tracing the history of the ratings industry, with particular attention to the effects of demand on methodology and definitions of demographics. Next, I will contextualize the ratings industry within the larger transindustrial structure of broadcasting, which is organized around two levels of activity. Finally, I will consider changes in the consumerist caste, the emergence of the 'working woman' as a ratings category, and the relationship between industrial culture and popular culture.

From audience to commodity audience

The modern structure of the broadcasting industry emerged in the period directly after World War I and was consolidated by 1928. National net-works comprised local radio stations interconnected by AT&T and earned revenues through the sale of time slots to advertisers, which had designed programs in an attempt to influence the purchasing habits of the audience.[3] The business of broadcasting had apparently become the business of selling time to advertisers.

If advertisers were really buying time, however, one would expect that the cost of any particular time slot should be the same, regardless of day-part. That is, fifteen minutes on Sunday at 7:00 p.m. should cost the same as fifteen minutes on Monday at noon or Tuesday at midnight or Wednesday at 5:30 a.m. However, each of these time slots had a different price. Clearly, advertisers were not buying time, but rather access to an audience. And advertisers did not want to pay for just anybody who happened to tune in; they targeted the consumerist caste,[4] which was but one part of the vast listening public.[5] Thus, toll broadcasting earned its revenues from an invisible commodity, as the consumerist caste became the commodity audience.

Advertisers had to be convinced that the size and quality of broad-casting's product – the commodity audience – were sufficient to balance the costs of programming and the costs of access over the network. Both NBC and CBS produced materials designed to assure advertisers that the networks attracted huge audiences of dedicated consumers: Mrs. Consumer listened to the programs of soap manufacturers during the day, Mr. Con-sumer took control of the radio set at night, and the little Consumers sat glued to the set from after school to bedtime.[6] Advertisers distrusted these 'studies' as self-serving, since NBC and CBS also based their prices on these reassuring measurements of consumerist audiences.[7] Yet advertisers needed information about demographics to select the proper times for their commercial-length programs and to evaluate the efficiency of those programs to reach the right audiences. Advertisers also needed information on the sizes of the targeted audiences, to evaluate the prices charged by networks.

In 1928, the Association of National Advertisers (ANA) hired Archibald Crossley to design a measurement technique that would provide advertisers with their own proprietorial information about audience quality and quantity.[8] A year later, Crossley unveiled his method: telephone interviews soliciting respondents' reports on what shows with which sponsors they listened to yesterday. The ANA embraced this approach, creating a subsidiary organization, the Cooperative Analysis of Broadcasting (CAB), to produce audience measurements for circulation only among advertisers. By 1930, CAB provided its ANA subscribers with ratings that showed radio programs drew a high-quality, low-quantity audience.

Crossley's method favored advertisers' interests. First, it relied on telephone interviews to inquire about radio use. By 1929, radio was well on its way to becoming a ubiquitous feature of American life: 13 million radio sets had been sold.[9] With penetration rates of more than 50 percent in households and radios situated in many public places (diners, soup kitchens, department stores, taverns, and so on), radio's status as a mass medium was undisputed. While anybody might have a radio or have consistent access to radio broadcasts, however, residential telephones remained rather a luxury. Although 41 percent of the private homes in the United States subscribed, being listed in the telephone book was still a mark of social status. During the Great Depression, households often cut back on luxuries; between 1929 and 1931, residential telephone subscriptions fell 10 percent. In contrast, radio presented no subscription costs; while radio homes might lack telephony, telephone homes were likely to have radios. In this way, Crossley sampled not radio homes, but telephone homes that had radios. To be included in the sampled radio audience, a household had to have sufficient income to afford monthly telephone charges, had to desire the social status signaled by a telephone listing, and had to live in an area deemed sufficiently profitable for AT&T to provide service. In short, Crossley's method ensured that he counted only the consumerist caste.

But if CAB was guaranteed high-quality audience by Crossley's telephone sample, it also was guaranteed low-quantity audience by Crossley's questions. In 1929, most radio programs ran fifteen minutes; asking someone to recall an entire day's listening was certainly an imposition. More important, the imposition was targeted at a social stratum that valued the symbols of middle-class status at a time when the middle-class code of conduct emphasized indirection and politeness as ways to avoid conflict and maintain face. Confronted by an unreasonable imposition, one might correctly extract oneself by deploying the social lie. Asked to remember twenty-four hours of programming for a perfect stranger on the telephone, one could easily escape the unpleasantness by suddenly 'remembering' that one had not listened yesterday. Crossley could not separate true reports of no listening from white lies about not listening.

Unsurprisingly, Crossley and CAB 'found' that radio audiences were indeed small. Further, households that either could afford luxuries such as the telephone or were unwilling to lose the social status associated with telephone subscription might also have been able to finance the middle-class ideal of the 'unproductive' wife. Calls, then, could be timed to reach the particular gender targeted by the particular daypart. Measuring Mrs. Consumer would mean daytime calls; measuring Mr. Consumer would require evening calls and specific requests to speak with the head of the household.[10] In any case, Crossley's methodology produced ratings that defined the audience as the consumerist caste while delivering estimates of audience size that suited advertisers' vested interest in lowering networks' prices.

High quality, high quantity

As networks sought some way to counter the CAB ratings, the C. E. Hooper Company (CEH) was designing a methodology that would be attractive to *both* advertisers and networks. When Hooper began to consider challenging the CAB in 1930, that task must have seemed almost impossible. How could one resolve the contradictory demands of advertisers for low quantity and of networks for high quantity? How could one persuade advertisers to buy ratings from an independent firm when their own ANA ran a ratings operation? Yet, by 1932, CEH had developed a strategy based on measurement technique and on the syndication of ratings reports that would secure a monopoly over ratings production for CEH by 1936.

With telephone subscription dropping in the early 1930s, a sample based on telephone subscribers was an even better guarantee that radio listeners in such households would have sufficient disposable income and desire to qualify as bona fide consumers. Those in such a sample also were more likely to maintain the middle-class ideal of housebound wives and day-working husbands, thus satisfying advertisers' demand for women during the day and for men at night. CEH – like CAB – used telephone directories as the basis for its audience measurements. To CAB's design, however, CEH added the fillip of using urban directories, thus ensuring that the sample would have easy access to national brands through large retailers in cities and suburbs. During the Depression, middle-class folks in small-town and rural America simply were less desirable as members of the audience. They might maintain their telephones, consumerist ideology, and disposable income, but their access to national brands was through mom-and-pop retailers or mail-order catalogues. During the Depression, the constriction of national distribution to rural areas further decreased the attractiveness of these middle-class populations. This slight narrowing of the sample promised a higher-quality audience than that measured by CAB.

A more significant departure from CAB's approach was incorporated into CEH's telephone interview. Called the 'telephone coincidental,' this interview was a model of efficiency and ease. Respondents were asked if the radio was on when the telephone rang. A positive answer triggered a simple request for the name of the program and the sponsor. This was followed up by soliciting the demographics of the respondent and any other listeners. Finally, the respondent was queried about the fifteen minutes prior to the telephone call. This produced information about listening immediately before, and coincidental to, the telephone call. The task required little effort, but it yielded important results: suddenly, radio audiences were gigantic.[11] Thus, CEH could offer an increase in audience quantity to networks and significantly more accurate information about the listening habits and availabilities of the consumerist caste for advertisers. This improved information was but one element designed by CEH to offset the higher prices that networks would demand, given higher quantity of audience. The second element was CEH's decreasing costs of audience measures for advertisers. Because CAB's ratings were circulated only to subscribing advertisers, those sponsors paid all of CAB's operational costs through the price of their subscriptions. In contrast, CEH offered its reports to any firm that could pay the price. Termed 'syndicated' ratings, these reports were sold to all comers, including advertisers, networks, program producers, and stations. This allowed CEH to spread its costs of operation over considerably more purchasers, hence lowering the cost per purchaser on any ratings report.

Consumerist caste versus listening public

From 1936 to 1942, CEH's monopolization of ratings suggests that the company's strategy for measuring high-quality consumers, who replicated the idealized middle-class division of labor by gender, was successful. The C. E. Hooper Company monopolized the most profitable niche in the ratings industry – the production of ratings for national advertising over radio networks. This position also gave CEH an edge in the production of ratings for local markets.

During this period, radio's listening public clearly was larger and more diverse than the commodity audience reported in the ratings.[12] Then as now, the listening public included households where men were unemployed or absent, where the primary wage earners were women or children. Then as now, some people rejected consumerism in favor of self-sufficiency; others embraced the ideology of consumption but lacked either the money or the access to enact it. Then as now, U.S. culture comprised multiple heritages; society was divided along lines of gender, class, race, ethnicity, religion, and sexual orientation. This diversity, however, was not reflected in the ratings.

Rather, as commodities themselves, the ratings were constructed in response to market pressures, including competition and monopolization as well as continuities and discontinuities in demand. The ratings producer was no scientist motivated by curiosity, but rather a company seeking its self-interest through the profitable manipulation of demand. By targeting the consumerist caste, the new broadcasting industry adopted the ideals of that caste as an operational definition of internal divisions in the commodity audience: the employed male as head of household, the unpaid wife as lady of the house, and their requisite children. In this way, ideology and economics interpenetrated to 'naturalize' both the consumerist ideal of domestic division of labor and the artificial market definition of the 'real' audience for radio.

This raises questions about the appropriate use of language in discussions of industrialized popular culture. To whom does a genre belong? Scholars of popular culture generally have divided genres by gender, speaking of womens' genres, men's genres, even juvenile genres.[13] The use of the possessive suggested that the particular gender was intimately linked to the particular genre. From that perspective, one could interpret audience research or sales figures as feedback mechanisms for industrialized popular culture. If many women found pleasure in radio soap operas, then the soap operas earned high ratings; this encouraged soap manufacturers to produce soap operas that connected strongly to women's lives, so that women listened to radio soaps, and so on. From this perspective, the industrialization of culture did not interfere with relations between the populace and culture. Popular culture still belonged to the people, despite the presence of Procter & Gamble, Lever Brothers, RCA's NBC, CBS, and the C. E. Hooper Company. The companies remained in the cultural system, but their influence was limited by audience measures that accurately identified what people liked.

Such a position has long marked the public discourse of program producers, advertisers, networks, and ratings firms. However, the discourse is seriously undermined by the market structures that define the ratings commodity and the commodity audience. Women's genres are designed to target the women in the consumerist caste, and ratings are designed to measure only those ladies of the house. Similarly, men's genres target men within that consumerist caste; 'kids' shows' target the offspring of the idealized middle-class household firmly rooted in a particular division of labor and a particular sexual orientation.

This is not to argue that women, men, and children outside the consumerist caste were unmoved by *Ma Perkins, Suspense,* or *The Shadow.* Rather, one must recognize that their listening and their pleasures were economically irrelevant. For industrial purposes, such folks were eavesdroppers who simply could be picked up as an incidental, secondary, and free audience. Because they lacked any value in the market, such listeners were literally priceless. Advertising vehicles (programs) were not designed for the public, but the technology of broadcasting and the costing of radio receivers did not bar the public from listening. People outside the consumerist caste might produce alternative or oppositional readings of the radio texts, but such increased cultural labor would not bar the listening public from escaping into the future via *Buck Rogers* or finding inspiration in *Mary Noble, Backstage Wife* or identifying with the suave Philo Vance.

Changing players on a constant field

With CEH's success in 1936, the transindustrial market structure for broadcasting was fully articulated and firmly in place. That structure would persist until the introduction of peoplemeters in 1987, although surface changes did occur in the 'players' and the 'rules of the game.' This section discusses such changes in terms of the continuing deep structure of broadcasting.[14] That structure was organized into two levels. The first determined how broadcasting functioned as a programming service; the second determined how audiences were defined, measured, and commoditified. The second level provided the rationale behind and empirical justification for programming policies guiding decisions in the first level.

On the first level, ownership of networks and broadcast technology changed. NBC was forced to divest its second radio network to ABC in 1943, which subsequently followed NBC and CBS into television. Radio was replaced by television as the technology of national network broadcasting. The new technologies of television emerged from government contracts for wartime research in radar granted to RCA and CBS, indicating the persistence of broadcasting's ties to the military.

Another organizational shift was triggered by combined economic and political pressures that emerged around the innovation of television. Television meant higher production costs for programs, with low rates of viewership until television sets were widely purchased for household use. The networks recruited some new sponsors, which typically used inexpensive genres such as game shows. Indeed, the desire to keep costs low while attracting increasingly larger audiences resulted in the systematic rigging of game shows. Revealed in a dramatic congressional hearing, the resulting 'quiz show scandals' rocked network television.[15] Networks took over program selection and programming costs, gaining the ability to control their own schedules. Advertisers gave up sponsorship and programming costs, gaining access to the entire broadcast day by buying thirty-second or one-minute slots. This rearrangement of responsibilities persists to the present day. Thus, the period 1936 to 1987 saw shifts in responsibilities, technology, and firms on the first level, where programs were selected, advertisers and networks interacted, and national distribution was achieved via AT&T.[16]

The second level organized relations among advertisers, networks, and ratings producers. Continuities in demand for quality audience limited ratings methodologies to measurement of the consumerist caste. Discontinuities in demand over quantity of audience, rooted in the conflicting interests of advertisers and networks in price for the broadcast audience, opened up the possibility of some independence from demand for ratings producers. In the 1930s, this opening was used by CEH to rebalance relations between advertisers and networks, and to gain monopoly over national ratings production. That monopoly was protected by an ancillary need: advertisers and networks needed a 'floor' upon which to stand when buying and selling broadcast slots. In terms of capitalist economics, it simply was irrational to start every deal for every broadcast slot by negotiating which ratings report from which ratings company would be used to set prices. Over time, companies challenged or replaced a ratings monopolist through the use of measurement methods that rebalanced discontinuities in demand. In 1942, CEH was seriously challenged by the A. C. Nielsen Company (ACN), which achieved monopoly over national ratings production by 1950. From 1959 to 1965, ACN faced challenges from two rivals (Sindlinger & Co. and ARB) and congressional hearings, which pressured ACN into changing its sample in 1970 and installing its Audimeters in a more urban and youthful sample.[17] These combined pressures and ACN's careful adaptations resulted in ACN's continued dominance over national ratings, ARB's emergence as 'the' local rater, and creation of the Broadcast Ratings Council by the National Association of Broadcasters to protect ratings from government regulation.

During the post-World War II period, the consumerist caste expanded appreciably as the economy boomed. ACN's measurement methods suited the wider definition of the caste as well as the networks' new position as schedulers and programmers. For ACN's Audimeters, any television set that was turned on became a television set that was carefully watched. ACN gathered its demographics from diaries kept by viewers who were not in the Audimeter sample and then mapped the demographics from the diaries onto the Audimeters' reports of tuning. From 1965 to 1987, ACN weathered various challenges from ratings firms and from increasing penetration rates for cable television.

Starting in 1975, the U.S. economy underwent periodic recessions that triggered a slow decline in the consumerist caste.[18] This contraction in the consumerist caste set the stage for an expansion in the types of 'players' measured by ACN. The rating firm had long resisted pressure from cable networks, which wanted inclusion in the national ratings. This policy changed as the Turner Broadcasting System subsidized ratings for its cable-distributed superstation. Rising interest from advertisers encouraged the full-blown measurement of cable, which by definition meant a decrease in network audiences as the same ACN sample was split across more television channels.[19] With the introduction of its peoplemeter in 1987–89, ACN achieved a rebalancing of advertisers and networks, plus the introduction of cable networks as a major source of demand for ratings. The expansion of ratings buyers and the replacement of CEH by ACN are surface changes on the second level of organization; they are not structural changes. Differences in pricing still trigger discontinuities in demand over audience quantity: advertisers seek lower quantity to lower network prices, and networks still seek to increase quantity.

In this regard, cable presents an interesting case of pressure and adaptation. New networks (satellite/cable channels) have used a new technology in attempting to increase their audience quantity at the expense of old networks using an old technology. At the same time, old networks have joined in ventures that have founded new networks and have purchased stock in the companies that own new networks. Despite this rivalry on the surface of the market, the deep structure of the market remains the same: the network oligopoly may have expanded, but it remains an oligopoly. The constraints at this level produce the immediate conditions in which audiences are measured and ratings are produced. The interaction of advertisers, networks (broadcast or cable/satellite), and the ratings monopolist generate the definition of the commodity audience, which is then operationalized through the ratings.[20]

The two levels intertwine to create the transindustrial market that constitutes broadcasting, a market in which manufacturers of nationally advertised brands interact with a network oligopoly, an interconnection monopolist,[21] and a ratings monopolist in order to deliver commercials to the consumerist caste via broadcast and telecommunications technologies.[22] While the first level manufactures, sells, and purchases the commodity audience, the second level proves that the commodity audience has been duly manufactured and sells that proof primarily to those companies that operate on the first level.

Yuppies versus yuffies: peoplemeters 1987–90

Broadcasting, then, revolves around the commodity audience. Absent from this ratings process is the actual audience – the audience that comprises actual listeners or actual viewers, regardless of their relationship to the consumerist caste. This realization is borne out by ACN's response to major social trends encouraged by the Reagan administration: increasing class stratification, downward social mobility, and increasing participation in the labor force by middle-class women.[23] The periodic recessions starting in the mid-1970s were exacerbated by the economic policies of the Reagan administration in the 1980s. As with Thatcherism, some corporations and segments of cities boomed under policies fostering speculation, deregulation, privatization, deindustrialization, and militarization. But the bulk of the population experienced significant loss of income in terms of real dollars. Some also lost employment as unionized manufacturing jobs were exported. Replacement jobs developed in an expanding service sector generally paid low wages with no medical benefits. Further, the service sector did not grow sufficiently to absorb all displaced workers, and the Reagan administration's anti-Keynesian policies severely limited the federal role in job creation. The result was significant transfer of wealth from the middle class and working class to the ruling class.

For the consumerist caste, this made the concept of 'the lady of the house' increasingly anachronistic. Most nuclear households simply could not afford a division of labor in which women worked without pay. This pushed increasing numbers of women into the labor force. Multiple low-paying jobs and teenage employment became facts of life. In the 1980s, the economic status of the consumerist caste was more akin to its status during the Great Depression than during the postwar boom when economic growth had been generalized across classes.

For the transindustrial market constituting broadcasting, these changes posed serious – but not radical – problems. Changes in methodology were necessary to ensure the quality of the commodity audience measured by ratings. Similarly, methodological changes were necessary to respond to pressures from cable networks for inclusion in the official ratings. When this connected with increasing interest among advertisers in cable audiences and the shrinkage of the consumerist caste, it culminated in a shift in demand: cable households began replacing television households as the population from which the peoplemeter sample was drawn. Like telephone subscription during the Great Depression, cable subscription during the current depression signaled a household's place in the consumerist caste. Despite cable's penetration rate of roughly 50 percent, cable subscription still effectively separates consumers from public, particularly as fees for basic service easily have doubled under deregulation. Further, working women were added to the ratings as economics dislodged the middle-class ideals regarding division of labor.

The resulting changes in the definition of the commodity audience, in the categories of women, and in the methods used to generate ratings were used by the ACN to fend off challenges from two rival firms that had proposed using peoplemeters. ACN's own version of the peoplemeter recorded television tuning and accepted input from viewers identifying themselves. Every fifteen minutes, a red light came on to remind viewers to touch the button that identified them to the machine. This simplified the construction of ratings by allowing demographics and tuning to be measured simultaneously.

It also depressed ratings by underreporting the quantity of viewers. For example, children often failed to respond, which resulted in wholesale drops in the quantity of the child audience for Saturday morning cartoons. Similarly, the engendering of household tasks affected peoplemetered ratings. Men responded to the technology; in diary studies, women had been the primary respondents. Further, broadcast networks questioned ACN's policy of installing a people-meter in a household for ten years. One would expect that a respondent's willingness to enter data every fifteen minutes would diminish as the decade wore on. For the interim, however, advertisers were well pleased with the new ratings, which ensured high-quality and low-quantity audience. Joining the advertisers were the cable network, which found their positions considerably enhanced as network ratings diminished. Only the networks complained, using TBS's tactic of paying ACN for the maintenance of a diary-meter sample and other considerations while adjusting to the new facts of the marketplace.

Those adjustments have been difficult indeed. Not only have the ratings been reshaped against the broadcast networks' main interests, but the overwhelming adoption of videocassette recorders has further decreased dependence on locally broadcast signals for televised entertainment during prime time. For some households, video stores and public libraries have become important sources of prime-time television. In others, the lady of the house has became a working woman, time-shifting her viewing of soap operas via a VCR to the evening. Surveys suggest that working women maintain some control over their incomes but also remain the primary house worker.[24] Such women have become sufficiently attractive to advertisers that ABC/Hearst designed the cable network Lifetime as a women's channel. In network broadcasting, ABC joined CBS, NBC, and newcomer Fox in the creation of mixed-genre programs designed to appeal to the consumerist couple. The logic was simple: build programs that combined male and female genres in order to attract heads, ladies, and working women who have missed or time-shifted their soaps.

A brief glance back at network television of the 1980s indicates broadcast schedules that combined gender-specific genres with gender-mixed genres. Let us consider *Hill Street Blues* and *Alien Nation* in terms of gender stereotypes. While he watched shoot-outs and car chases on *Hill Street Blues*, she watched the continuing stories of Renko and Bobby, Faye and Frank, Pizza Man and the Counselor. While he watched shoot-outs, car chases, and seminaked aliens simulating sex on *Alien Nation*, she watched the continuing stories of one man's family and its human friend as the Franciscos struggled to make a home and Matt struggled with his xenophobic upbringing, his partnership with George, his adoption by the family, and his increasing attraction to his alien neighbor.

Similarly, during daytime television, soap operas have been revamped in recognition of an audience beyond the housebound mother. Romantic melodrama has been extended to include relatively explicit depictions of sexual violence as well as consensual sexual liaisons. Among the standard population of soap opera doctors, nurses, lawyers, and extended families have been mixed urbane detectives, high-tech spies, international terrorists, European royalty, and industrial saboteurs. Higher production values, more on-location shooting, and a more expensive mise-en-scène have moved soap operas out of Ma Perkins's kitchen and into Scorpio's combination luxury home and high-tech control center.

As television's task became attracting the young urban professional and ignoring the young urban failure, the old genres became increasingly 'upscale' and increasing intermixed. The economic down-swing sharpened advertisers' demands for the consumerist caste and opened the way for an expansion in the network oligopoly to include cable networks. In the deep structure of the transindustrial market for broadcasting, the oligopoly in networking was expanded; the monopoly over ratings remained intact. As broadcast networks adjusted to the newly measured rivalry of cable channels and the new populations targeted by ratings, they built into their schedules new programs that combined old genres that had been reliable producers of either male or female audiences. This tactic sought to recapture the mass of the consumerist caste. However, in the 1990s, the very shape of the market for ratings has made it unlikely that network broadcasting will recapture its quantity audience.

Popular culture, industrial culture, people's culture

Neither commercial radio nor television, broadcast or cable, is a genuine mass medium. Nor are the cultural artifacts distributed via those media genuinely popular culture. Rather, the transindustrial structure that binds together these technologies and their artifacts is organized to tap and manipulate only one sector of the population – the consumerist caste. The artifacts manufactured within that structure are designed to assemble the consumerist caste for measurement and sale. Further, the programs themselves exist only as vehicles for advertisements targeting that caste. The industrialization of such artifacts differentiates them from popular culture: broadcast/cable materials are neither of the people nor by the people, and they are not intended to be popular with the people.

Yet people do derive something from radio and television, both broadcast and cable.[25] Although intended only for the consumerist caste, access to radio and television is not restricted to that caste. Broadcast media are almost universal in the United States; cable subscribers are not automatically compulsive shoppers in this period of the 'new frugality.' Despite differences of ethnicity, gender, race, sexual orientation, religion, and class, most people assume that all of us are familiar with the cultural products distributed by these technologies. Industrialized culture has become part of our lives, as constant companion, news source, least objectionable entertainment, favorite show, background noise, or focus for fandom. We seem to work very hard at producing the alternative and oppositional readings that transform industrialized culture into shared visions and acceptable representations. From a political economic perspective, our labor is unsurprising: the cultural products are not designed for us and so must be reworked to be used. However, the fact that we actually exert our labor on such objects is quite surprising. To understand the need of human collectivities to construct people's cultures from the products of culture industries, we must turn to cultural studies and social history. By taking a political economic approach, we can see that the industrialized culture distributed via media, as well as the gender-specified genres constituting much of that product, is not popular culture, people's culture, or mass culture. Public taste has little to do with the manufacture of commodity audiences, ratings, and programming.

Notes

1   For an analysis of domestic labor and gender, see Christine Delphy, *Close to Home: A Materialist Analysis of Women's Oppression*, ed. and trans. Diana Leonard (Amherst: University of Massachusetts Press, 1984).

2   For descriptions and chronologies of industrial wisdom regarding gender differentiation of audiences, compare Erik Barnouw, *The Sponsor: Notes on a Modern Potentate* (Oxford: Oxford University Press, 1975), 9–74, especially 68–73 on demographics; and Harry J. Skornia, *Television and Society: An Inquest and Agenda for Improvement* (New York: McGraw-Hill, 1965), 17–68, 88–142; with Hugh Malcolm Beville, Jr., *Audience Ratings: Radio, Television, Cable* (Hillsdale, N.J.: Lawrence Erlbaum, 1985) 1–82; and Karen S. Buzzard, *Chains of Gold: Marketing the Ratings and Rating the Markets* (Metuchen, N.J.: Scarecrow, 1990), 3–48, 86–96. The critical analyses presented by Barnouw and Skornia contrast sharply with the standard 'industry insider' account given by Beville or the nonanalytic historical account constructed by Buzzard. Both Beville and Buzzard naturalize industrial wisdom and traditional practices; Barnouw and Skornia use an analytic approach to uncover how and why such wisdom and practices have been constructed by firms in particular ways. This essay takes a similarly critical and analytic approach to the economic history of ratings, genre, and gender commodities.

3   During the Patent Pool's internal troubles, William Paley first purchased and then reorganized a third national network, dubbed the Columbia Broadcasting System. For greater detail on networks and network programming, see Barnouw's three volumes as well as Laurence Bergreen, *Look Now, Pay Later: The Rise of Network Broadcasting* (Garden City, N.Y.: Doubleday, 1980); A. Frank Reel, *The Networks: How They Stole the Show* (New York: Charles Scribner's Sons, 1979); J. Fred MacDonald, *One Nation under Television: The Rise and Decline of Network TV* (New York: Pantheon, 1990); Todd Gitlin, *Inside Prime Time* (New York: Pantheon, 1983).

4   By 'consumerist caste,' I mean persons who met three criteria: first, they had sufficient disposable income to afford a life-style based on the consumption of manufactures that were nationally distributed and advertised; second, they had adopted the ideology of consumerism over the ideology of self-sufficiency; and third, they had easy access to the developing system of national distribution and national retailing.

5   Compare Beville, *Audience Ratings*; and Buzzard, *Chains of Gold*; with Eileen R. Meehan, 'Why We Don't Count: The Commodity Audience,' in *Logics of Television: Essays in Cultural Criticism*, ed. Patricia Mellencamp (Bloomington: Indiana University Press, 1990), 117–37.

6   Early internal studies that were reprinted for advertiser consumption include *Does Radio Sell Goods?* (CBS, 1931); *Has Radio Sold Goods in 1932?* (CBS, 1932); *Ears and Incomes* (CBS, 1934); *Little Books on Broadcasting*, series 1–12 and A–F (NBC, 1927–31); and from the same period, *A New Measurement of the Size, Locations, and Occupations of NBC Radio Audiences, Supplemented by Dealers Opinions of Radio Advertising* (NBC, n.d.). Networks have continued to issue such promotional materials disguised as objective, neutral studies. Erik Barnouw features an especially interesting CBS brochure, called *Where the Girls Are*, in *Tube of Plenty: The Evolution of American Television*, 2d rev. ed. (Oxford: Oxford University Press, 1990). The CBS brochure included a dial that advertisers could turn to determine what age group among females purchased a product type, hence what age group should be targeted by the manufacturer of that product type. While one may be tempted to dismiss the obvious sexism of the brochure's title as an artifact of the 'bad old days,' it is note-worthy that the brochure is presented as an illustration of how networks and advertisers used demographic ratings in the 1970s.

7   For 'industry insider' discussions of ratings measurement techniques and advertiser interests, see Archibald Crossley, *Watch Your Selling Dollar* (New York: B. C. Forbes, 1930). An interesting comparison can be made with the apologia published by Crossley's successor, C. E. Hooper in Matthew N. Chapell and C. E. Hooper, *Radio Audience Measurement* (New York: Steven Daye, 1944) and later self-justifications published by A. C. Nielsen, Sr., *Greater Prosperity through Market Research: The First Forty Years of the A. C. Nielsen Company* (Northbrook, Ill.: A. C. Nielsen Company, 1963) and A. C. Nielsen, Jr., *If Not the People. … Who?* (Northbrook, Ill.: A. C. Nielsen Company, 1966).

8   Compare Mark James Banks, 'A History of Broadcast Audience Research in the United States, 1920–1980, with an Emphasis on the Ratings Services,' doctoral dissertation, University of Tennessee, Knoxville, 1981; with Beville, *Audience Ratings*; and Buzzard, *Chains of Gold*. Where Banks takes an entirely descriptive, chronological approach to the topic, Donald Lee Hurwitz adopts an idealist culturalist position in analyzing the rhetoric of ratings firms in 'Broadcast Ratings: The Rise and Development of Commercial Audience Research and Measurement in American Broadcasting,' doctoral dissertation, University of Illinois, Urbana, 1983. For an approach utilizing rhetorical analysis and political economic analysis, see Eileen R. Meehan, 'Neither Heroes nor Villains: Towards a Political Economy of the Ratings Industry,' doctoral dissertation, University of Illinois, Urbana, 1983. For an institutional approach, see Eileen R. Meehan, 'Ratings and the Institutional Approach: A Third Answer to the Commodity Question,' *Critical Studies in Mass Communication* 1 (1984): 216–25.

9   For penetration rates, see U.S. Bureau of the Census, *Statistical History of the United States from Colonial Times to the Present* (New York: Basic Books, 1976), 783–84, 796. For a discussion of radio sales, see Barnouw, *Tube of Plenty*, 30–40; and Frederick Lewis Allen, *Only Yesterday: An Informal History of the 1920s* (New York: Harper, 1964 [1931]), 137–39.

10   In telephone surveys, men are generally more difficult to reach than women. Researchers have coped with differential rates of answering the telephone by asking for the 'head of household,' which has traditionally meant the senior male. The practice is less efficacious now as a means of snagging male respondents, because of both changing consciousness and the feminization of poverty.

11   See C. E. Hooper and Matthew Chapell, *Radio Audience Measurement* (New York: Stephen Daye, 1944); *Hooperatings Hi-lites*, 1932–40, various volumes; Banks, 'A History of Broadcast Audience Research.'

12   Much current historical research documents the multiplicity of the 'American experience.' For example, the American social history project directed by Herbert G. Gutman published the first volume of *Who Built America? Working People and the Nation's Economy, Politics, Culture, and Society* in 1989 (New York: Pantheon). The volume's attention to the differentiated experiences of working people whose lived experience connected them to distinct subcultures based on gender, race, ethnicity, religion, and politics provides a sharp contrast to Daniel J. Boorstin's three volumes of *The Americans* (New York: Vintage, Random House, 1974), which posits a homogeneous nation awakened to consumerism and the good life.

13   Compare Tania Modleski, *Loving with a Vengeance: Mass Produced Fantasies for Women* (New York: Methuen, 1982), 11–34 on feminine forms and 85–109, on soap operas; Janice A. Radway, *Reading the Romance: Women, Patriarchy, and Popular Literature* (Chapel Hill: University of North Carolina Press, 1984), 3–45; John Fiske, *Television Culture* (London: Methuen, 1987), 179–223 on feminine and masculine television; Jackie Byars, *All That Hollywood Allows: Re-reading Gender in 1950s Melodrama* (Chapel Hill: University of North Carolina Press, 1991), 1–24.

14   I rely on the traditional methods of political economy that address the intertwining of macroscopic structures and systems, particularly institutional analysis and aggregate analysis. For examplars, see Adam Smith, *The Wealth of Nations*, ed. Edward Cannan (London: Methuen, 1961 [1776]); Karl Marx, *A Contribution to the Critique of Political Economy*, ed. Maurice Dobb (New York: International Publishers, 1981 [1859]); Rudolf Hilferding, *Finance Capital*, ed. Tom Bottomore (London: Routledge & Kegan Paul, 1985 [1910]); Gunnar Mydral, *The Political Element in the Development of Economic Theory* (New York: Simon & Schuster, 1969 [1954]); Howard J. Sherman, *Elementary Aggregate Economics* (New York: Appleton-Century-Crofts, 1966).

15   William Boddy, 'The Seven Dwarfs and the Money Grubbers: The Public

Relations Crisis of US Television in the Late 1950s,' in *Logics of Television: Essays in Cultural Criticism*, ed. Patricia Mellencamp (Bloomington: Indiana University Press, 1990), 98–116.

16 PBS's experiments in the late 1970s with satellite distribution of broadcast signal eventually opened the door for companies – including RCA – to sell interconnection services via satellite. By the late 1980s, satellite capacity was very much in demand. However, recent decisions by the Federal Communications Commission will allow telephone companies to deliver video over fiber-optic cable. It remains to be seen whether AT&T or the 'baby Bells' will attempt to monopolize interconnection through this newly sanctioned use of fiber optics, thereby respectively taking on satellite interconnection services and cable operating companies.

17 For a detailed account of these hearings and previous congressional inquiries into ratings, see Meehan, 'Neither Heroes nor Villains.'

18 For an authoritative account of this process, see Barry Bluestone and Bennett Harrison, *The Deindustrailization of America: Plant Closings, Community Abandonment, and the Dismantling of Basic Industry* (New York: Basic Books, 1982).

19 For an insider account, see Mark Christensen and Cameron Stauth, *The Sweeps* (Toronto: Bantam, 1985); see also Gitlin, *Inside Prime Time*, 325–35. Also, please note that the expansion of the ratings sample to include cable audiences automatically meant a decrease in network audience and corresponding increase in cable audience.

20 For advertisers, the ratings achieve three ends. First, ratings demonstrate the existence of the commodity audience. Next, ratings rationalize decisions about the purchase of advertising times and the placement of ads in particular genres targeted by demographics. Last, ratings justify network prices. For networks, ratings serve similar functions. Besides facilitating business relations with advertisers, ratings guide networks' scheduling decisions, identifying when the particular demographic group will be available for 'its' genres and determining if a particular example of the genre is delivering enough audience to warrant renewal. In this way, surface changes in the second organizational level had a direct impact on the business practices of the first organizational level.

21 As noted previously, the interconnection monopoly has come under recent pressure by the oligopoly in satellite ownership. However, demand for satellite capacity has outstripped the availability of satellites, leaving satellite-distributed cable channels rather at the mercy of the satellite divisions of AT&T, Western Union, and GE (including GE's RCA). It may well be that the monopoly in interconnection will also expand to an oligopoly. However, AT&T's new technologies and its divestment of regional operating companies may reinstate its old oligopoly.

22 Masking the basic structure, however, is a plethora of surface detail: ratings rise and fall; shows are canceled; fans protest; network executives bet their careers on the upcoming fall's lineup; commercials interrupt shows; new measurement

techniques are announced; once more, new technologies are touted as offering a whole new world of programming choice and efficient access to consumers. Beneath this avalanche of detail rests a bilevel market that has been constructed by multiple industries and in which these industries go about the business of broadcasting.

23 Bluestone and Harrison, *The Deindustrialization of America*, 25–48, 82–107.
24 For a full discussion of gender, class, consumerism, and deindustrialism, see Katherine S. Newman, *Falling from Grace: The Experience of Downward Mobility in the American Middle Class* (New York: Random House, 1988).
25 The concept of negotiated readings and a potentially obstreperous audience has attracted much attention from cultural theorists, textual analysts, and audience researchers. See Raymond Williams, *Marxism and Literature* (Oxford: Oxford University Press, 1977); Janet Woollacott, 'Messages and Meanings,' in *Culture, Society, and the Media*, ed. Michael Gurevitch, Tony Bennett, James Curran, and Janet Woollacott (London: Methuen, 1982), 91–111; Stuart Hall, 'The Rediscovery of 'Ideology': The Return of the Repressed in Media Studies,' in *Culture, Society, and the Media*, ed. Michael Gurevitch, Tony Bennett, James Curran, and Janet Woollacott (London: Methuen, 1982), 56–90; Charlotte Brunsdon and David Morley, *Everyday Television: 'Nationwide'* (London: British Film Institute, 1978); David Morley, *The 'Nationwide' Audience* (London: British Film Institute, 1980); Ien Ang, *Watching* Dallas: *Soap Opera and the Melodramatic Imagination* (New York: Methuen, 1985); Byars, *All That Hollywood Allows*, particularly 25–66.

INTERACTIVE AUDIENCES
FANS, CULTURAL PRODUCTION AND NEW MEDIA

It has become deeply fashionable to describe oneself as an interactive kind of person in much the same way as being a couch-potato in the 1990s was also modishly acceptable. But the chic thing in media in the twenty-first century is the notion of active engagement with the text or, more correctly in this consumerist age, the commodity. Of course, what is conveniently forgotten in this ahistoric insistence on giving old things new names, is that fan audiences have been interacting with the text and with each other for decades, from post-war outings to the cinema to catch the latest John Wayne or Audrey Hepburn film, to attending *Star Trek* conventions dressed as Mr Spock and learning Klingon.

Probably the best-documented fan communities, those celebrating Marilyn Monroe and Elvis Presley, can be seen as expressing the hopes and dreams of post-Second World War consumer culture. The untimely deaths of these media stars demonstrated that these hopes and dreams cannot be fulfilled, even if you are Marilyn or Elvis. In the first essay in this section, Virginia Nightingale (Chapter 13) draws attention to the improvisation and impersonation that characterized fan fascination with these early icons. She suggests that the choice of improvisation and impersonation deserves closer analysis, and that the reasons that these activities rather than others are so enjoyed by fan communities should be examined. The documentation of fan activities often stops at descriptions rather than actively analysing the sort of choices made and interpreting the cultural significance of the choices. In addition, the objects and people celebrated and commemorated by fans point to the deeper dilemmas of consumer culture that fans both celebrate and protest. Nightingale implies that all the choices that fans make merit close analysis and interpretation, since fans are reacting to the cracks and fissures in consumer culture.

Nancy Baym (Chapter 14), by contrast, considers the way in which soap fans appropriate the Internet and experiment with the new forms of community made possible by the nature of virtual space. She explores the processes that affect the development of fan communities as a consequence of using the Internet as a medium of fan-to-fan communication. In particular she explores the ways in which online talk is deployed to experiment with the expression of gender and identity played with, and played out, by online fans.

Annette Markham (Chapter 15) carried out an Internet ethnography, soliciting online conversations with other Internet users and interviewing them about their online activities. She explores the use of autobiographical and researcher-centred methods in the online environment. Markham takes us with her on her own research journey into the Internet and, along the way, introduces us to some of the people she meets in virtual space. Importantly, Markham's larger work asks extremely pertinent questions about the *real* innovations in audience research which will be required by the increasing fascination with the Internet – questions of authenticity, ethics and trust. And she frankly admits to the difficulties of negotiating her own role in the research process.

The range and nature of fan activities enabled by the technological expansion of communication media in the information age now make the nature of fan activity in previous decades, such as the circulation of handwritten and photocopied fanzines on *The Archers* or the sing-alongs of the convention delegates, seem somewhat amateurish. More recently, these activities have been replaced by much more ambitious and hi-tech expressions of fan attachment.

Henry Jenkins (Chapter 17) argues that, thanks to their early adoption of the Internet as a means of expanding and enhancing their communities, fandom is now a prototypical example of 'intelligent community' (Levy 1997) and that fans enable the development of new media commodities at sites where production and consumption meet in a sort of mutual development. Each contributing element enhances the knowledge and understanding of all the other participants in the site.

John Banks (Chapter 16) provides an excellent example of how this process works. Banks is well aware of the significance of the convergence of production and consumption in the activities of both fans, enthusiasts and developers, and he uses this understanding to document how this type of mutual production occurs. Banks was involved as a participant observer of the development of an Internet game called *Trainz*. This gave him a privileged position from which to observe the interactions of games fans and games developers as they worked together to create a new game product. Banks noted that most producers are simultaneously game players and producers, so the distinction between gamer and producer, enthusiast and entrepreneur, breaks down in the processes of sharing 'intelligence'. As both academic and industry insider, Banks's work meshes theory and practice, showing how the company for which he worked established a product network that embraced the skills and enthusiasms and intelligence of both 'ordinary' gamers, train enthusiasts and 'professional' developers.

Jenkins has argued that fans are at the forefront of breaking down the distinction between production and consumption in the new media environment. However, the readings in this final part demonstrate that new kinds of audience activity are emerging as significant aspects of the information age. The information age creates a voracious demand for intelligence, where audiences and fans alike are recognized as knowledge sources as well as consumers of intelligent work. All are consciously engaged in producing and consuming artefacts for wider circulation among themselves.

But the convergence of production and consumption is also problematic. The disintermediation of media industries precipitated by this convergence causes industrial instability. In order to restore the power balance of traditional media with their audiences, media industries have sought to reintroduce the distinction between production and consumption. The contemporary disputes over online sharing of music, films and other forms of electronic intellectual property demonstrate the countervailing force to the examples of mutual sharing documented by Jenkins and Banks. The economics of intelligence in the information age is therefore far from resolved, and the dependence of production companies on audience intelligence is increasing. As participation in audience events becomes the process of everyday life, the nature of the forms that production takes can be expected to continue to change dramatically – possibly just as dramatically as the importance of audience research.

Reference

Levy, P. (1997) *Collective Intelligence: Mankind's Emerging World in Cyberspace*. Cambridge: Perseus.

IMPROVISING ELVIS, MARILYN AND MICKEY MOUSE

Virginia Nightingale

Impersonating power structures

As a research object, the [audience-text] relation impersonates the power structures of the developing global metropolis and its cultural environments. Two aspects of this cultural environment particularly expressed through the [audience-text] relation are the dismantling of nations and the unity of the global market. The relevance of the concept *nation* has been diminished by the size, significance, and bargaining power of multi-national corporations. Until now this narrowing appears to have affected geo-politics, by which I mean the relations between nations, less than it has affected everyday life. The nation-state continues to negotiate on behalf of business and trade, to facilitate trade relations, and to protect the off-shore interests of its citizens. But at the level of everyday life, global commerce affects a realm of activities, ideas, and expectations which transcend national interests and present the global interests of multinationals and the personal interests of people as synonymous. Global ideas have replaced national ideas in the hegemonic struggle for dominance, and national interest is increasingly identified with the power to create possibilities for participation in the type of economic prosperity developed and perpetuated as a cultural ideal by the West in its representations of itself in the mass media. In this context, the global reach of the mass media assists the

Virginia Nightingale (1994) Improvising Elvis, Marilyn and Mickey Mouse, *Australian Journal of Communication*, 21(1): 5–20. Reprinted by kind permission of Queensland University Press.

gathering of all human activity into the one system of exchange and makes redundant the indigenous markets which once ensured diversity.

The [audience-text] relation, in this context, assumes importance as a way of identifying where either or both innovation and patronage might occur in a system of media products where there is no 'outside – merely opportunities for minor variation 'within'. Such a closed cultural system has probably never before existed. Cultural environments, as we have known them until now, valued, preserved, and celebrated ways of recognising and classifying ideas from outside – whether by orientalisation, annihilation, recuperation, or assimilation. In this context, the [audience-text] relation can be seen to possess both a market and policy relevance. It points to ways in which diversity can be created and encouraged within a closed system. The heterogeneity of the relation and the ways people perform it can demonstrate the cultural flexibility of Text – both as polyglossy and as polysemy. [Audience-text] allows as to embark on voyages of discovery within known territories rather than outside them.

The [audience-text] relation simulates the political unravelling of the nation-state – the technology which made modernisation, immense population growth, and unsustainable development possible in the West. It can be understood as a prototype for a politics of the 21st century. As control or management strategies, totalitarian perspectives like 'the mass audience' are increasingly experienced as irksome and unnecessarily limiting. Participation and negotiation, elevated from tactic to strategy in contemporary political action, become key aspects of the type of research consistent with an [audience-text] perspective. Identifying a broader range of media interests and commitments than ever imagined in the heyday of broadcast mass media has become the research challenge, as contemporary questioning of political power allocates renewed value and recognition to diversity, and as difference is cherished rather than abhorred. The global entertainment media, in turn, will be challenged to reconsider their totalitarian treatment of audiences. The challenge is sustained by the development of multimedia forms like interactive computer games and the seductive potential of cyberspace, which set new parameters for the meaning of 'entertainment'. Engagement rather than merely entertainment is now on the agenda as virtual worlds are created and appended to the 'real' everyday. Engaging media demands exploration of the full potential and specificity of the [audience-text] relation rather than being limited to its articulation as 'reception'. Instead of pursuing the politics of crowd control, as during the era of the mass audience, the [audience-text] relation suggests a politics more like multi-culturalism – the active pursuit of cultural diversity and difference.

The key to understanding [audience-text] lies in the recognition that it is a performance object like [self-everyday life]. As such, it is open to observation and 'text-ure'; it plays itself both as fantasy and documentary. Impersonation and fandom are key aspects of its manifestation, as demonstrated in the recent rush to publish work on fans and to chronicle the Elvis impersonation phenomenon (Fiske 1993; Harrison 1992; Jenkins 1993; Lewis 1992; Marcus 1991). Yet what is sometimes missed in this development is a sense of the broad cultural significance of such phenomena. Impersonation and fan communitas alike are signs of the culture and manifestations of broader engagement. They are globally recognisable genres of stylistic specialisation in a culturally homogenising world.

In this sense, the pursuit of [audience-text] leads to a new framework for discussing audience performances. [Audience-text] requires that its behavioural and textual ideas are examined in interaction in both their particular and homogeneous forms. The relation is cultural and requires semiotic analysis. It follows generic patterns. The most popular of these so far for cultural studies research have been the 'tribute' genres, mentioned above, which can range from impersonation to ventriloquism and parody. Yet the more prevalent pattern for the [audience-text] relation is improvisation, evident in the patchwork activities of everyday life and in the stylistics of identity – phenomena like quotation, poaching, translation, and transposition – the more difficult arenas visited by the early cultural studies audience experiment. The impersonator is easier to identify as text than as research object when the complexity of the persona produced as impersonation becomes evident. Improvisation is the 'dirtier', more difficult mode because it requires the co-optation of the researched as collaborator or co-researcher. The development of research strategies for the study of improvisation remains a major challenge in [audience-text] research because the research required defies the conventions of mainstream social science and questions its ideology.

Impersonation or 'Yes, Virginia, there is a Santa Claus!'

Impersonation is a component of all cultural production. Its accessibility as a research object, as a manifestation of the [audience-text] relation, is evident in perhaps the most publicised of [audience-text] performances – the star impersonation. The 'observations' of impersonation I will discuss here are press reports which document the spectacular activity at the 'fringe' of [audience-text]: its excesses. In the overall context of the newspaper, they are like reports of curiosities or freak shows, often meriting only a paragraph here or a snippet there, for in the quixotic character of impersonators, the press have discovered a news-worthy 'audience' theme – at first sight perhaps a positive side of the 'death metal' music or television addiction panics. The reported acts of impersonation are often unexpected, freakish, and enduring manifestations of devotion, presented as eccentric, slightly weird behaviour. They become newsworthy because of the presence of the impersonator as spectacle. By refraining, as they usually do, from interpretation of the 'weird' behaviour, the reporting journalists invite the act, the look, the gesture to speak for itself. Occasionally, the mocking tone of the journalist amplifies the contradiction inherent in the situation – the fans who exploit the Marilyn 'look' re-enact her exploitation by the press (Article 13.1). The impersonators, the fans who 'front' the press, represent a larger group of devotees who express themselves less spectacularly but with at least matching devotion (see *Couchman*, 1991). Fiske (1993, p. 117) has described the meaning of the activity of fans as *communitas*, invoking the Christian ideal of the Church, the Bride of Christ. In this context, fans take on the role of immortalising the body of the star as everyday activity. They actively produce its immortality in the combination of impersonation and patronage which constitutes their enactment of the [audience-text] relation. The 'Church' analogy proposes a priestly role for the impersonator, as demonstrated by both Fiske (1993) and Harrison (1992). The impersonator delivers the 'eucharist', the signs of an Elvis-christ: Elvis music, visual spectacle, kisses, and the sacred scarves distributed at impersonation concerts. Fiske's description of fan *communitas* reiterates the importance of service as a component of fan activity. The impersonation would not be complete without the service of those who offer themselves as worthy recipients of the touch, the kiss, the scarf – the Elvis blessings.

The analogy is useful since it can be so easily and widely understood in Christian cultures, but it is also limited. The most publicised examples of fan commitment invariably are case studies in intense identification – the desire to 'be' the lost love object, to replace the image, the star, with one's self – an almost invariably newsworthy image switch, especially with Marilyn or Elvis. The spectacle of the identification is important: impersonators strive to be instantly identifiable as the 'loved object'. Identity, not similarity, is desired. To be identical, to take the place of the other, to replace the original in the hearts and minds of those who love them – nothing less will satisfy. Impersonators willingly sacrifice their right to independent life in order to perform the life of the other. In this sense, impersonation is fraught with psychic danger – the danger of losing a

Article 13.1

Marilyn would have loved it. The fans were given shiny white souvenir programs as they shuffled into the gloomy church.

Two giant theatre spotlights hung from the ceiling to fill the crowded chapel with light for the benefit of television cameras and paparazzi squeezed in next to Marilyn lookalikes.

The All About Marilyn Fan Club, sponsor of the 30th anniversary memorial service at Westwood Memorial Park, promised a media circus and they delivered.

When the congregation, several hundred strong, shuffled into the hot Californian sunshine to unveil a monument at the site of her unglamorous grave, fans were close to tears – because the media scrum ensured they did not get a glimpse of her flower-strewn grave.

'I am just a fan', Ms Yvonne Deboer, 29, a travel agent from Santa Monica said.

'This isn't a memorial service. This is a zoo. She is being exploited again. Marilyn always said it was the public that turned her into a star', she added, wiping back a tear.

The memorial part lacks the mystique and glamour the blonde bomb-shell was known for, with a view of two high-rise office blocks and the dull roar of heavy traffic along trendy Westwood Boulevard.

Sitting in the VIP enclosure at yesterday's ceremony was Ms Susan Strasberg, daughter of Lee Strasberg, who was Marilyn Monroe's acting coach in Los Angeles.

She reached for her handkerchief and said: 'I hope her death has spurred sympathy and understanding for a sensitive artist and woman who brought joy'.

The voluptuous actress died aged 36 from an overdose of barbiturates, leading to speculation about whether she was murdered or committed suicide.

Monroe, born Norma Jean Mortenson, grew up in orphanages and foster homes in Los Angeles and was discovered by a photographer while working in an aircraft factory.

Her 97 cm bust and platinum dyed hair made her an instant sex symbol when she made her film debut with a cameo appearance in *All About Eve*. Her most successful films, including *Some Like it Hot*, *The Seven Year Itch* and *Gentlemen Prefer Blondes*, set box office records.

Cash, W. (1992), Fans lament the eternal exploitation of Marilyn, *The Australian*, 7 August.

perspective from which to remember the difference between self and star, the danger of a too complete reproduction of the life and death of the star. One can be deeply impressed, bedazzled by the bravado of such reckless-ness.

In a variation of this phenomenon such as in the demise or transformation of a show, for example, *Star Trek* or *Dr Who* (Tulloch and Alvarado 1983), the actors become impersonators of their younger selves, of themselves acting. In so doing they invariably maintain the social structure of the on-screen community and articulate it as an off-screen reality. Celebration of the body of the 'star' or the ageing corps of a show can be a source of delight, a refuge from the chaotic alienation generated by capitalism's indifference to community. The star's death, the show's demise, everyday events, assume a function of explaining the separation of the significant body from its followers – a separation often presaged 'unnaturally' by image makers and public relations advisers, by fame and by the frailty of the star's human body.

A real person can be in only one place at a time. However, through communal sharing of the impersonation, as demonstrated by the most classic example in Western culture, Santa Claus, the sense and sensibility, and real control of the original, pass back to the community. The impersonator demonstrates the literal 'lack' of the dead star by becoming the star's counterfeit; they sacrifice themselves to simultaneously cover up the real inadequacy, the mortality, of the scions of mass culture in defiance of the perpetual brightness of the image. In contrast to the image, the impersonation promises the star, but always delivers only the impersonator. Where the star, by definition, was more than the image but less controllable – always threatening to prove the image false by a bad performance, weight gain, drug addiction – the impersonator is less than the image but more amenable to regulation.

Death both completes the 'star's' story, and defines a predictable basis for future encounters. As Marcus has demonstrated (1991), this can become the basis for a new story – the story of the 'dead' star. This story evolves from the variety of ways real audiences perform the dead star – whether as alter egos, phantom lovers, recalcitrant fathers, or best friends. Invariably, in some manner, resuscitation (for example, 'Elvis in hiding', Article 13.2) or transmutation (c.f. contemporary speculation that the Sherlock Holmes character was 'real') is desired. When the representation of the 'star' can no longer be disrupted by the 'star' as referent – by the frail human body, susceptible to weight gain and ageing, with which the story began the dead star is incorporated into the living bodies of the former audience and lived as an [audience-text] relation.

Article 13.2

Hundreds of Elvis Presley devotees have flocked to a four-day seminar studying claims that 'The King' faked his own death.

Many attending the conference, held in Kingman, Arizona, carried mementos such as Elvis Presley snapshots and credit cards, locks of his hair, and scarves stained with his sweat.

One even claimed to have seen the performer after his death at Graceland on August 16, 1977.

'I saw him in Memphis in the 80s', said Maria Columbus, president of one of many Elvis fan clubs.

Mrs Columbus claims that a man who looked like Elvis pulled up in a car when she was manoeuvring out of a parking spot and gave her the right of way.

Speculation that Elvis is alive was reinforced during talks by self-described experts who claim to have researched official documents about him.

One such researcher, political adviser Luc Dionne, concluded that the singer may be hiding under the Federal Witness Protection Program. And handwriting expert Paul Weast, 70, said Elvis may have penned his own name on his death certificate.

Elvis 'in hiding', fans told. *Sunday Telegraph* (1991) 16 June, p. 43.

Article 13.3

More than 100 Sherlock Holmes fans celebrated the 100th anniversary of the great detective's death in Switzerland yesterday.

Members of The Sherlock Holmes Society from all over the world gathered at the Reichenbach Falls wearing full Victorian dress and re-enacted author Arthur Conan Doyle's 'killing off' of his greatest character.

On May 4th, 1891, Holmes was involved in a death struggle with the evil Professor Moriarty at the falls in the Bernese Oberland.

Condon, M. (1991) 100 years since Sherlock fell, *Sydney Morning Herald*, May 4.

Stories of capitalism

If we look at impersonation from a slightly different perspective than The 'Church' analogy, rather different qualities of the impersonator and fan performances become evident. While The 'Church' analogy sharpens focus on the details of impersonation as re-enactment, it also narrows our observations to the acts of sacrificial service which maintain the dead body. Semiotic analysis of the performance points to impersonation as inter- pretation in action. As the impersonator performs the nature, the psychology, and the spectacular manifestations of the 'star' as character, the impersonation generates another experience, a re-creation of the star not as an image but as a story about capitalism, often as the story of a contradiction in capitalism. As the 'star's' personal narrative is recreated and explored by the impersonator, another performance, another personal narrative is pursued – the impersonator's life as the star (see for example, *Impersonators* 1991). From the fan community as 'church' perspective, the community validates the worth of impersonation, sustains the image, and creates a reality in which the variety of the ways the 'truth', or meaning, of the star is experienced is publicly legitimated. The Elvis community, for example, catalogues sightings, endorses impersonations, and keeps alive a spirit of 'caring through Elvis'. The commemorative dimension of such phenomena maintains the 'image', guards it against debasement and frau- dulent use, and licenses the accepted policing of Estate Trustees and Fan Societies. From a semiotic perspective, the life of the impersonator is much more interesting. Between the impersonator's life as sign and the star's life as referent the differences of each as signifier and signified demand expla- nation.

The Marilyns, for example (see Article 13.1), attended a commemorative service to remember Monroe's exploitation, the wasting of her body, and were themselves exploited. They performed Marilyn by creating themselves as her look-alikes, and were exploited, just as she was, by the media's never-ending 'hijack' – of Monroe's body and 'their' event. The Marilyns perpetuate an ideal already demonstrated to be unlivable – the impossibly beautiful yet innocent, usually 'untouchable' image of woman.

> One day after class, we were walking down Broadway. No one was paying attention to Marilyn. Maybe a few eagle-eyed spirits would take a second look – 'Could that be ... no!' – and then go on their way.

> 'Do you want to see me be her?' she asked casually. Of course we did, though I wasn't sure what she meant. As we watched, she switched on some inner light, the hips swung, the body rhythm shifted. She whipped

off the scarf, revealing her tousled blond hair. It was as if she sent out some invisible signal, the way birds fly or bees find honey. 'Look! Oh, my God, it can't be! It *is*! Marilyn, Marilyn!'

She looked at us as if to say, See? As people started to close in, she was excited, in her element. She loved this display of power, and we were properly impressed. They loved her so much, were so fascinated by her. They wanted to touch her, not just look, the way they did with Garbo or the other stars I'd seen accosted. Then they would want a piece of her. It was scary (Strasberg 1992: 143).

Impersonation repeats a pattern, a way of being sometimes intially performed by the star for advantage or as 'self' protection. It 'renders visible the existential deadlock of its participants, the weight of decisions they were forced to assume in that unique constellation' (Zizek 1992: 79). The tragedy of Monroe's real-life marriages, her childless, child-like naivety, her personal unhappiness, her expressed desire not to be misunderstood, all were undone by the exploitation as image of the voluptuousness of her body. The impersonation at her commemoration service fails to convince that Monroe's story could ever have had a happy ending, yet it strongly recreated the dilemma her being suggested: the eternal confusion in capitalism between 'value' and 'exchange value', woman and woman-for-sale, so well demonstrated in Monroe by the lack of coherence between her person and her body's image.

A similar [value-exchange value] contradiction haunts the dead Elvis phenomenon. The Elvis suit, the ultimate constant of Elvis impersonation, and sign of the masculinity embodied as nature in his youthful performance becomes in impersonation a material representation of Presley's youthful sexuality. The suit also embodied the unacceptability of a life spent impersonating onself. It marks the beginning of impersonation. Putting on the suit signalled Presley's break with the given reality of his body and the beginning of his active re-production of the given characteristics which have become the central motifs of his contemporary impersonation. The suit, as talisman, belongs in the realm of impersonation, where it invokes not just the man but his dilemma. Like Monroe, Presley was alienated from his own image and ultimately from himself. As Strasberg reflected of Monroe,

It occurred to me that MM's *her* was her Frankenstein. She loved/hated it, but it was her own creation, and she was stuck with it, unless Pop or her doctor or her husband could help her get unstuck.

Writers say that sometimes their imaginary characters take over and they can't control them. It was the same for Marilyn – worse. She couldn't crumple the page and throw it away; it was her (Strasberg 1992: 144).

Of course, ultimately Monroe did 'crumple the page and throw it away'. The lives of both Monroe and Presley re-enact an older cultural concern outlined by Sontag (1977) in her description of the dangers of the image world. The fear of the stealing of souls by their creation as image, a fear contested by the cultivated realism of the photographic image, a fear of losing oneself in the alienating metropolitan environment of global capit-alism, the fear of the replacement of the real world by its image, by simulacra, is repeated as cautionary tale in acts of Elvis and Marilyn impersonation. The impersonation exceeds repetition or commemoration and points to the deeper psychic dangers of a world in which the image has assumed disproportionate power. The psychic power of the impersonator is linked to the courage with which they address such dangers.

If one considered only Elvis and Marilyn impersonations, one could assume that the impersonator as high priest(ess) was the significant per-former or even evidence of the cult, but this position cannot be sustained if extremely active character-based impersonations, like the Sherlock Holmes Society and the Star Trek fan clubs, are considered. I suggest two reasons for this. Firstly, the impersonator tends to have a specialised role but no authority within the fan community. The community produces the imper-sonator as a sign of itself.[1] The Elvis impersonator visits the fan community as an outsider, usually by invitation. He (or she) no longer belongs to a fan community, but to the entertainment industry (like Elvis). Secondly, the prevalence of character-based impersonations suggests that the narrative associated with the impersonated is more significant than the character per se. Characters are not real but fictional constructs. The Sherlock Holmes Society and the *Star Trek* examples foreground the importance of audience performance of character and narrative, and reverse the logic of the Elvis and Marilyn examples. There is no repetition of the real here, but a desire to prove the reality of fiction. Whether or not Holmes and Moriarty ever existed, their fictional dying is witnessed by mourners only in its replay. Its significance is sensually experienced, intellectually assimilatable, by the real fiction of the mourners who attest the significance of the event. The moment when the detective who enunciated the deductive method and lived rationality and individualism as a creed, and Moriarty, the man who matched him in these very qualities, were undone by natural elements (water and gravity) – a fictional encounter grounded in the nature/culture dialectic – is celebrated 100 years later. The fan community replays obsessively the moment of contradiction which undid these 'sovereign individuals of capitalism' – their own undoing of the myth of reason. Rationality after all is based on a fiction about truth. The Holmes community asserts the reality of the 'sovereign individual of capitalism' and the world he inhabited. They impersonate not only Holmes and Moriarty but the by-standers and passers-by assumed by their re-enactment and the reality they now claim for Holmes. The *Holmes* and *Star Trek* communities celebrate imaginary worlds: the imagined perfection of past or future communities. In Holmes, an Adorno-esque world where reason is supreme; in Star Trek, the future multi-cultural community where after each tribulation, the community recreates an ordered and benevolently administered environment; each example reminds that, in producing culture, we seek to demonstrate the plausibility of dreams.

In these brief and far from complete analyses, I have tried to demonstrate that the specificity of the [audience-text] relation always matters. Generalisations about 'impersonation' cannot tell the whole story of the [audience-text] relation as expression of the cultural realities in which ordinary people live. Spectacular audience performances, like spectacular youth sub-cultures, point to specific discursive locations and to the invocation of older, often psychically powerful, cultural dilemmas reactivated at a particular moment in history and attuned to, expressive of, its structure of feeling.

Improvisation

In the re-enactment of contradiction, in the multitudinous acts of commemoration, the system which produced the images is maintained. The sacrificial quality of fan community ensures the continuity of commitment. Yet fans also use the original to improvise, just as I use research interview transcripts as the basis for improvisation on existing knowledge – to produce new knowledge and to occupy a ground from which to speak. Effort by the entertainment industry can subdue the tendency to improvisation by engaging only the consumer potential of fans, by creating in the fan community a dependence on the industry, its re-releases, and its endorsed events. Priscilla Presley opens Graceland to the tourists and the trustees of the Elvis Estate police the impersonations, ensuring that they sound sufficiently like the original to keep selling the original records. Entrepreneurs make impersonation a business proposition, and the impersonators generate their own fan clubs. New commodities – like *Dead Elvis* (Marcus 1991), like recordings of new music by tribute bands or performers, or perhaps even like the ghost-writing of new works by Schubert or Mozart –

become commonplace. Impersonation points to its related mode of cultural engagement, improvisation.

In the context of contemporary mass communication research, both the press interest in fans and the commercial exploitation of tribute phenomena point to the adaptability of fans to the administrative ends of commerce. In just the way that spectacular youth subcultures (Hebdige) provided information about the dilemmas, ideals, and life experiences of youth in general, spectacular fan 'subcultures' draw attention to themselves, to the non-organic, often internationally dispersed and yet totally media-dependent communities formed through repeated performances by fans. The 'look' and other characteristics (ways of speaking, ways of writing, approaches to grooming, places frequented) are adopted. But each activity 'adopted' in this way is, as Hebdige demonstrated with Punk, a motivated sign, simultaneously signalling a commitment to accepted cultural ideals and a quest for personal identity. People perform Text simultaneously as impersonation and as improvisation; they repeat the cultural ideal and sacrifice themselves to it at the same time that they expand their consciousness of the world they inhabit and their relation to it.

Variations on a theme

'To sleep, perchance to dream'?

> I was in my room when Madonna jumped out of one of my posters and 'Into the groove' was playing. We started dancing and laughing and got to be really good friends. Jeanna, age 13, July 1991 (Turner 1993: 68).

Even in dreams we improvise. We create possibilities that are otherwise beyond belief. By focussing on improvisation, what is sacrificed for the repetition is less central than the manner in which the 'original' is made into something else – a quality, a philosophy of being, a moral or psychological dilemma, a statement, already lived but given new meaning with each articulation. The early cultural studies audience experiments were first attempts to explain improvisation. They drew attention to audience accounts of their improvisation (Hobson 1982; Ang 1985; Buckingham 1987) to the significance of the interpretive work undertaken in the course of such activity (Fish 1980; Said 1982), and to the power of the interpretive community to determine the meaning of such activities. This power was at first taken to demonstrate that media audiences retain an ability to resist domination, to subvert the meaning of the text, and to bend it to their own ends (Fiske 1987). The possibility of resistance through improvisation is beyond dispute, even though it rarely happens as social strategy, and the longevity of personal strategies of resistance as coherent and meaningful social action must be questioned. Resistance is one possible form of improvisation, and far from its more radical modes which include parody, defamiliarisation, and combinations of both. Improvisation, as suggested earlier, implies activities like translation and transposition, quotation and poaching, and play. In researching the [audience-text] relation as improvisation, we can focus on the way particular texts allow the culture to be played, at the modes of engagement privileged by this culture, and at the ways its expressive potential is limited.

The problem is that improvisation often tends to be tactical rather than strategic. When fan communities create institutional structures (fan clubs and other types of 'informed' societies) to reproduce and maintain themselves, they are re-creating themselves as consumers – as the niche markets for repackaged commodities. This allows them greater market influence – but does not deliver control. It can foster a market-dependence which castrates the liberating potential of the improvisation. Even though the direction of improvisation is towards appropriation and transformation, such change is perhaps too easily subverted into style. Quotation, translation, transposition, all sustain a pretence – a focus on the manipulation of images rather than on the strategic significance of the manipulation. By pretending acceptance, their strategic significance is masked, or itself subverted, and the cultural significance of improvisation lost. Attention to what people do, to the ways they manipulate imagery, is a first step in [audience-text] analysis, but not a complete approach. Impersonation is a significant cultural stylistic in consumer culture and as such should indicate that the time is now right for the more difficult task of setting in place research strategies capable of addressing improvisation. In my own research (Nightingale 1992), for example, improvisation was demonstrated in the ways different groups of viewers engage with television broadcasts of live football. In three quite different domestic settings, the telecast was co-opted to perpetuate male dominance within the domestic environment. The improvisation ranged from the re-enactment of broadcast incidents to the delineation of domestic space in imitation of the football stadium, from the privileging of male action to the active exclusion of women from the viewing environment. The broadcast became a pretext for the reassertion of male dominance within the domestic environment – an opportunity to enact the meaning of gender difference.

Commercial exploitation

If openness to commercial exploitation often creates distrust about the nature of the [audience-text] relation, the fear which motivates such academic ambivalence about the [audience-text] relation is, I believe, an old fear, for which there is considerable justification – the fear of separation from access to, or control of, the technologies and the skills for cultural production. Sometimes the fear is articulated to include the cultural competence to enjoy our own national or regional cultural production. The fear, so eloquently expounded in Lefebvre (1971), is a fear that our culture will be reduced to a 'bureaucratic society of controlled consumption' – that cultural life, wit, inventiveness, will be replaced by a tired repetition of the past and be dominated by company hacks out to make a fast buck. The technology of publicity has certainly allowed this possibility ample room for development. When commenting in an academic context on the commercial relevance of interpretive communities, Said (1982) noted the importance to academic publishers of the existence, size, and socialisation of academic interpretive communities. The fan communities documented in the newspaper articles above are 'entertainment industry' equivalents of communities which cannot be understood independently of their money-making potential. Said pointed to their relevance as a type of interpretive community which is widespread and rather like the imagined 'national' communities described by Anderson (1983). Fan communities transform the shared attachment to an ideal of totemic stature into real social relations. Their self-sacrifice reaffirms not just the value of the star but the world which produced the star. In an (Australian) ABC TV discussion (*Couchman* 1991) devoted to the Elvis phenomenon, the studio audience was most animated in giving testimony to the fan community as the global network who justify their caring for each other through their commitment to Elvis. Yet they would not exist as a community without the entrepreneurial complicity of sections of the entertainment industry. The fan clubs are dependent on their own commercial significance.

Some clubs have not had grass roots beginnings, but have been cultivated quite openly by commercial design. The longing for heaven on earth, the desire to create a dream world, was actively exploited by Walt Disney in the establishment of the Mickey Mouse Club. The criteria for membership were always broadly defined, as Walt Disney's definition of the 'real' Mickey Mouse Club member demonstrated. According to Disney, 'everyone who regularly watches the Mickey Mouse Club Television Show is automatically a member of the Mickey Mouse Club and a Mouseketeer First-Class in good standing'. (This quotation is taken from a copy of an internal report viewed at the Disney Archives in August 1992.) Disney established the Mickey Mouse Club to promote the sale of Disney products and to finance his first theme park, *Disneyland*. Familiarity with and enjoyment of Mickey Mouse cartoons promoted a consciousness of itself in this early televisual community. The idea for the club was not completely original. In the 1930s Mickey Mouse clubs had been established as a grass roots activity to complement Saturday afternoon movie-going. The television Mouse Club, by contrast, was designed commercially to finance the establishment of a real but fictional 'nation' (Disneyland) with real fictional 'lands' (Frontierland, Fantasy-land, Tomorrowland), as well as with characteristic modes of dress (ears, Mickey-shaped guitars, etc.), argot (Meece-ker, Moose-ker, Mouseketeers), codes of behaviour (Doddisms – Jimmy Dodd's 'homespun Christian homilies'). This community's leader – Mickey Mouse – was literally a mouthpiece for Walt Disney – his falsetto voice. Walt Disney was the *deus ex machina*, the program's voiced-over narrator: the ventriloquist. Within the program-world, the community was provided with a wide range of opportunities to perform and participate. Everything from imitation to pilgrimage (to *Disneyland*, of course) was advocated. Personal appearances were staged and patronised as enthusiatically as Royal visits to Australia in the 1950s. Through such events the *Mickey Mouse Club* produced and reproduced itself. The program was re-edited into a syndication broadcast between 1962–65 and again in 1975. The Walt Disney Corporation, including the imaginative and corporeal realms it created, thrived. The 'real' Disney fantasy worlds continue to depend on the perpetual flow of media product popularised by the program and its derivatives. In Australia in 1994 this role is performed by *Saturday Disney*, a program which uses Australian presenters to introduce Disney cartoons and to advertise through active promotion, quizzes, and competitions, all Disney theme parks.

In order to solve a corporate financial crisis, an [audience-text] relation was created as a marketing strategy for corporate control of individual activities, tying everyday activity to corporate imagery. The model is echoed by McDonalds and other major fast food conglomerates which rely on the popularity of their self promotion as a corporate idea to justify the logic of the commercial world they create. The Mickey Mouse Club demonstrates the openness to commercial control that is possible with interpretive communities. Its commercial success provides the focus for another type of research, the possibility of another story which has not yet been told. As a member of the generation for whom television was first experienced as the *Mickey Mouse Club Television Show*, I cannot help but remember that the social and cultural questioning of the late 1960s reiterated many of the themes and ideals – fantasy worlds, adventures, desire, a belief in altered states of mind, and happy endings – that also characterised the program. The *Mickey Mouse Club* was a successful marketing device, but it also suggests an as yet untold story. The celebration of cultural homogeneity in the program's manner of addressing its audience as mass market helped consolidate the logic for a later mass revolution among its devotees.

[Audience-text] research facilitates the study of 'interpretive communities' – fleeting and ephemeral entities, seldom grounded in any static geopolitical location or affiliation unless actively promoted, like The Mickey Mouse Club, but which focus cultural improvisation in directions which make discursive sense to those communities. The lack of grounded-ness of such communities has been described by Radway (1988) as 'nomadism'. This description carries with it connotations of communal identity based in ethnicity which are not necessarily a characteristic of interpretive communities where the source of unity frequently involves dedication to an unfinished or an unsatisfactorily finished narrative[2]. At the level of metaphor, however, Radway reminds us that some sort of communality is necessary for jokes to be funny or ideas to be understood.

The [audience-text] relation promises to explain both commercial domination and popular celebration by focussing on the patterns of improvisation developed in popular culture. Since understanding domination is the key to its control, it is important to recognise and to tell the stories of both exploitation and resistance.

Notes

1   In January 1994, I attended an *Elvis Revival* in Parkes, NSW. The impersonation was the culmination of the weekend. The revival began with a 'sound alike' competition, followed by a 'look alike' competition. The next day there was a street parade, where 'sound alikes' and 'look alikes' paraded and busked. A young rock tribute band then played in a local park all Saturday afternoon. On the Saturday night the Impersonator, Eddy Youngblood, performed. By the Sunday, the Revival became bus tours of the region and rock and blues played in the local pubs; celebration of the town and its surrounding countryside outstripped Elvis. The impersonation was the highlight, the culmination of the event, yet it was a public rather than a fan community event. It was the way the Elvis fan community demonstrated its existence and power to the people of Parkes. At the Friday night 'clam bake', around an improvised beach at Parkes's 'Gracelands' reception centre, the community did its best to sound like and look like Elvis. Performances ranged from the committed to the burlesque as a more

poignant, communally significant, sharing occurred. Elvis was performed in a way that only Parkes, NSW, could produce.

2   Recently, I chanced to listen to a radio interview with a spokesperson for the JFK Assassination Information Service, an Australian organisation established to provide information to people fascinated with the assassination narrative. The service is a means to share information and to make contact with similarly obsessed others. The 'audience attachment' here is not to personal style or to character but to the public narrative of the assassination. The community 'performing itself' as an information service can hardly be described as a 'fan club', yet the same desire to solve a public contradiction, to bring about resolution, closure to an unfinished narrative, the desire to replay the 'original' until a satisfactory outcome is produced, places it in the same category as the fan clubs in terms of audience commitment.

References

Anderson, B. (1983) *Imagined Communities*. London: Verso.

Ang, I. (1985) *Watching* Dallas: *Soap Opera and the Melodramatic Imagination*. London: Methuen.

Buckingham, D. (1987) *Public Secrets: 'East Enders' and its Audience*. London: British Film Institute.

Couchman (1991) Television broadcast, June. Australian Broadcasting Corporation.

Fish, S. (1980) *Is There a Text in this Class? The Authority of Interpretive Communities*. Cambridge, MA: Harvard University Press.

Fiske, J. (1987) *Television Culture*. London: Methuen.

Fiske, J. (1993) *Powerplays*. London: Methuen.

Hall, S. (1980) Encoding/decoding, in S. Hall *et al.* (eds) *Culture, Media, Language*. London: Hutchinson.

Harrison, T. (1992) *Elvis People: The Cult of The King*. London: Fount Paperbacks.

Hebdige, D. (1979) *Subculture: The Meaning of Style*. London: Methuen.

Hobson, D. (1982). *Crossroads: The Drama of a Soap Opera*. London: Methuen.

Impersonators (1991) Television broadcast. Sydney: Special Broadcast Service.

Jenkins, H. (1993) *Textual Poachers*. London: Methuen.

Lefebvre, H. (1971) *Everyday Life in the Modern World*, S. Rabinovitch (trans.). London: Allen Lane, The Penguin Press.

Lewis, L. (ed.) (1992) *The Adoring Audience: Fan Culture and Popular Media*. London: Routledge.

Marcus, G. (1991) *Dead Elvis: A Chronicle of Cultural Obsession*. London: Penguin.

Nightingale, V. (1984). Media audiences – media products? *Australian Journal of Cultural Studies*, 2(1): 23–35.

Nightingale, V. (1992) Contesting domestic territory: watching rugby league on television, in A. Moran (ed.) *Stay Tuned! An Australian Broadcasting Reader*. Sydney: Allen and Unwin.

Radway, J. (1988) Reception study: ethnography and the problems of dispersed audiences and nomadic subjects, *Cultural Studies*, 2(3): 358–76.

Said, E. (1982) Opponents, audiences, constituencies and communities, in H. Foster (ed.) *The Anti-aesthetic: Essays on Postmodern Culture*. Port Townsend, Washington: Bay Books.

Sontag, S. (1977) *On Photography*. Harmondsworth: Penguin.

Strasberg, S. (1992) *Marilyn and Me: Sisters, Rivals, Friends*. Toronto: Doubleday, Transworld.

Tulloch, J. and Alvarado, M. (1983) *Dr Who: The Unfolding Text*. London: Macmillan.

Turner, K. (1993) *I Dream of Madonna: Women's Dreams of the Goddess of Pop*. London: Thames and Hudson.

Zizek, S. (1992) *Enjoy Your Symptom! Jacques Lacan in Hollywood and Out*. New York: Routledge.

TUNE IN TOMORROW

Nancy Baym

What forces shape online communities?

Early research suggested that there was only one force that was important
in influencing computer-mediated interaction, and that was the medium.
Although in many ways research has become more sophisticated, the
continuing debates over the nature and worth of the virtual community
belie an ongoing presupposition that there are two types of communities,
one authentic and the other virtual. The distinction rests on the untenable
assumption that the medium through which community is constructed
provides its defining quality. It is true that the medium is essential to the
r.a.t.s. [rec.arts.tv.soaps] story. The removal of geographical constraints
allows people who might otherwise never meet to come into contact. The
asynchronous ongoing structure of Usenet has provided the time for conventions (both generic and normative) to develop as well as the time and
means for people such as Anne, Lexine, Granma, and Lyle to develop
distinctive and recognizable identities. The ASCII text format of messages
allows people to manage (or hide) their identities in ways that might not be
possible offline. Signature files and naming strategies are encouraged and
facilitated by the medium. The newsreader-mandated headers are a major
source of organization and convention, as the soap opera and genre labeling
practices in r.a.t.s. indicate. In more ways than I can summarize here, the

Nancy Baym (2000) Tune in tomorrow, *Tune In, Log On: Soaps, Fandom and Online
Community*. Thousand Oaks, CA and London: Sage, pp. 199–210, 215–18. Reprinted by kind
permission of Sage Publications, Inc.

medium shapes the worlds that grow through its use. However, even if we limit the influences on online community to the medium, that medium still offers several varieties of interaction. To pick just a few examples, the asynchronous, header-organized, interest-specific structure of Usenet is considerably different from America Online's real-time, nontopical, two-line message chat rooms. MUDs and MOOs, where users interact in fictional spaces that might or might not have guiding goal structures, offer still different possibilities and challenges.

But imagining the medium to be the only – or even the most important – influence on online community is shortsighted. The case of r.a.t.s. reveals how many other forces are at play. Hanks (1996) points out the importance of joint projects in his definition of community. In online communities, as in many offline communities, joint projects manifest through the topic around which most discussion revolves. Despite its centrality, topic is a woefully understudied influence on online community. In the case of r.a.t.s., the topic of soaps brings with it a purpose – interpreting – and because soaps are emotional, relational, and talk oriented, the fulfillment of this purpose ideally needs a particular type of environment, one that is welcoming, is supportive, and allows for self-disclosure. The academic mailing lists in which I participate have completely different joint projects; they are concerned primarily with informing, seeking scholarly advice, and clarifying points of domain-specific ambiguity. The only time in these groups that people talk about personal matters is when they have inadvertently sent a message to the list rather than the individual for whom it was intended. These groups do develop distinctive conventions, norms, and personalities, but they do not develop the atmosphere of 'a group of friends' that characterizes r.a.t.s. The Internet's many hate groups, organized in the joint project of promoting White supremacy, are as different from academic and soap groups as these groups are from one another. In short, the topics and purposes around which online communities organize are at least as important as the medium in shaping a group's communication patterns.

Who participates, including the dominant gender of those participants, also is a strong influence on online communities. In the case of r.a.t.s, one finds mostly highly educated American women, most of whom are employed outside the home. The topics they raise, the experiences they share, and the values they bring to the group (including their language patterns) undoubtedly are influenced by this back-ground. Indeed, all participants in any online group bring their offline experiences to bear in some way within the group, even if only to turn those experiences on their head by creating alternative worlds and identities.

The r.a.t.s newsgroup also demonstrates the influence that particular individuals can have in shaping their communities. One reason that r.a.t.s.(a.) has evolved as it has are new posters, who have created new traditions such as the F*Cs (favorite characters on various soaps), the Newbie Sponsorship Program, and the weekly polls. At the same time, one reason that r.a.t.s.(a.) has remained as close to its earlier incarnations as it has are those heavy posters who have remained active. Anne exemplifies the influence that a single person can have on a community. She was one of the very earliest contributors to r.a.t.s. and for over a decade was its most active participant. She began the update genre that has become the group's informative core. Her extremely sociable and welcoming style has helped to set the interpersonal tone for the group and has single-handedly welcomed countless new participants. Her distinctive worth to the community was recognized explicitly when the other participants voted that she receive the Frango Lifetime Achievement Award. Would r.a.t.s. have updates and be friendly without Anne? Probably. Would it be just like it is? Probably not. How would it be different? That is anyone's guess.

Another important influence on online groups is the offline contexts in which participants live the rest of their lives and that permeate the group, a topic to which I will return. What I want to emphasize about all of these influences – the medium, the topic, the purposes, the participants, the individuals, and the offline contexts – is that online communities do not emerge formulaically from their combination. If we had known all about Usenet, had known all about soaps and their social status, and had biographies of each participant, we still would not have been able to predict the social world I have described. Each online community is an ongoing creation, manifested, challenged, and recreated through negotiations that occur implicitly in every message. As people write, they draw selectively on the features of the medium, the joint projects available, their personal histories and experiences, and the group's history in ways that collaboratively coconstruct the values, relationships, identities, and conventions that make a group feel like about who the sender takes the readers and the group to be. Every response affirms or challenges those assumptions. Any group can take new directions at any time because of the influence of a single contributor. As we look closely at more online groups, we likely will find that they share systematic patterns and dynamics, but conceptualizing all online communities as a single phenomenon because they share a medium is like reducing all towns, cities, and villages to a single phenomenon because all of them are built on earth. At this early point in their history, we should be trying to understand the complexity of online groups by examining their differences, not trying to explain them away with their one commonality.

What forces shape online identities?

The issue of identity has garnered more attention than have most other aspects of online interaction. The dominant discourse on the topic, exemplified by Turkle (1995), has argued for understanding online identities as emerging from the combination of offline history and the anonymity of the medium. The case of r.a.t.s. shows us that not all online selves are fantasy beings and that not all online communities are constructed as places to be alternative people. There might be enhanced uncertainty about one another in r.a.t.s., and there might be a great potential for anonymity, but as a whole, the group has developed a norm that prefers relatively straightforward self-representation, manifested in the use of real names, self-disclosure, face-to-face meetings, Web pages with photographs, and so on. No one in r.a.t.s. masquerades as soap characters, for example, unless under the guise of a FAC (favorite *AMC* character), and even then, the person behind the character appears as well. On those rare occasions when people have tried to pull off more fantastic identities, they have been ostracized.[1]

This illustrates one of the more important lessons from r.a.t.s., that online persons are developed in group contexts that offer differing types of resources and value systems for building and affirming identities. Online identities are inherently social creations, situated within the online social whole. In creating identities, people work within the genres of a group's discourse and echo others' voices (both within the group and in entirely different genres). An individual's voice is affirmed and responded to by the others, depending on the values of that group. Those who affirm the communal values are likely to be praised, quoted, and otherwise supported, whereas those who try to present other identities are likely to be disconfirmed, even in systems that have no ways in which to exclude anyone from participating. Despite the range of possibilities, some identities will do better in a group than will others. There is a delicate balance between individuality and the needs of the group in which individual identities are created, and both sides of this tension deserve equal consideration.

How do online communities evolve over time?

The Internet is undergoing changes faster than anyone can foresee. When I began studying r.a.t.s. during the early 1990s, I had to explain to everyone what the Internet was. Now, I usually can get away with a quick explanation of Usenet. Most everyone knows about the Internet, even if, like my 90-year-old grandmother, they think that it works by magic. How do online groups weather the growth of the Internet? What determines how they fare when thousands of new people join their ranks? The r.a.t.s. newsgroup suggests some of the issues and tensions that are likely to emerge. First, it is clear that publicly accessible groups already have lost their status as refuges for the educated elite. The new people coming online include not just well-educated, computer-savvy folks but rather a wide range of more diverse people. As of this writing, most still are White and relatively affluent, but that likely will change over time (one hopes). Even if the Internet of the late 1990s is accessed primarily by a relatively privileged sector of the global population, it already is a more diverse population that it was. As this change occurs, the Internet's groups will have to cope with increasing amounts of difference among participants.

If r.a.t.s. the group Connery (1997) describes, and other mailing lists I have participated in are any indication, then one result of increased diversity will be increased fragmentation as groups spin off into subgroups, sometimes accessible only by invitation. Even within the public domains, subgroups or cliques are likely to form, exacerbating tensions between new participants and longer term ones or those with differing attitudes. The extent to which these groups manage their continual transformations in ways that are satisfactory to most participants will be rooted in the extent to which they are able to agree on a set of core values and then balance the persistence of what they value most with the need to change in ways that new participants will find pleasing.

The r.a.t.s. newsgroup suggests how this can be done – by maintaining and fighting for a clear value structure manifested in multiple conventions while finding ways in which to help new participants understand and feel at ease with the group's conventions. Communicative practice in any group needs to balance tradition and improvisation. The groups best able to grow successfully will improvise new ways in which to incorporate new members while maintaining what they can of their historical continuity. The Newbie Sponsorship Program developed in the *AMC* subgroup, in which all the information one needs to become a competent participant is collected in one Web site and new participants can be paired with more seasoned mentors, might have a few critics but offers a particularly innovative model that other groups might emulate.

How does online participation connect to offline life?

Closely related to the assumption that online community is a single phenomenon is the often-voiced concern that this type of community is bad because it serves as a substitute for the offline lives that its participants would otherwise be having. One fear is that those who cannot build successful identities or social lives offline will turn to the (socially isolated) computer to find a world in which they fit. The stereotype of the social loser who can only make friends online is in many ways quite similar to that of the soap opera viewer who watches because the characters are easier to befriend than are neighbors. A second concern is that increased online interaction will decrease engagement in face-to-face relationships offline (Kraut *et al.*, 1998). Again, these concerns seem to be based in oversimplifications of how people engage the medium that have stood, so far, in place of empirical analysis of the many complex ways in which online communities and offline lives may intertwine. Not only are there no signs that r.a.t.s. is doing so well because its participants have no offline lives, but there also are many signs to the contrary.

We see in r.a.t.s. a wide range of ways in which participation in the group connects to, rather than supplants, offline life. The behavioral norms about how to treat one another come directly from offline life. People in r.a.t.s. can treat one another as friends (e.g., by prefacing a disagreement with a partial agreement and adding the person's name) because this is something that they already know how to do. Participants' interests and concerns of reflect those that matter to them off-line; indeed, the discussions of relational and socioemotional issues so crucial to r.a.t.s. revolve entirely around offline social worlds. Furthermore, people's self-disclosures in r.a.t.s. indicate diverse and full offline lives that are brought into the group, giving it life. Their online identities are congruent with those that they stake out offline. Research in other online contexts also has indicated a continuity between one's online and offline connections to others. Those who are lonely offline seem to remain so online, whereas those who plunge into online interactions also are highly sociable offline (Cody *et al.* 1997; Joe 1997).

The real web of connections between offline and online life that exists in r.a.t.s. stands in sharp contrast to Nguyen and Alexander's (1996) theoretical description of going online, one that exemplifies the dichotomy that many assume. They write,

> The cardinal points and life's materiality disappear into the weightlessness of cyberspacetime. One initially experiences a bodiless exultation that may shortly settle into the armature of addiction. Going online 'flatlines' a person. That is, it immobilizes the body and suspends normal everyday consciousness. (p. 102)

The many ways in which 'normal everyday consciousness' is manifested in r.a.t.s. should put this type of groundless global theorizing to rest. There are more nuanced questions to be asked. If some people do become disconnected from offline life when they go online, we should ask which people these are, in which groups this tends to happen, and what is going on with these people and groups that might promote this type of disjunction. For the rest of us, we should be seeking to understand the many ways in which offline life is brought online rather than imaging that we always (or even often) leave embodied reality behind when we log on.

The offline life that is brought online is complemented by the ways in which online life feeds back into offline life. People in r.a.t.s. learn different ways in which to view relational and emotional issues that they see around them and experience in their own offline lives. When good or bad things happen online, the emotions they create play back into participants' offline lives. To give just one example, the death of Lisa's daughter, an offline experience, was brought online through her self-disclosure and fed back offline to the many people, like me, who never again will view sudden infant death syndrome as something that only happens to other people. The online group also can provide social support for people experiencing difficult times offline, as the proliferation of online support groups demonstrates. Furthermore, relationships that develop online can – and do – move offline, sometimes outlasting their participants' involvement in the groups through which they met. Online worlds develop affective dimensions and experiences, and these feelings, situated in the bodies of group members, do not distinguish between *virtual* and *real*.

How do online communities influence offline communities?

For many pop theorists such as Rheingold (1993), online communities have near utopian potentials in that they free us from physical constraints and allow us to organize by interests, enabling us to find kindred spirits and liberation. From this point of view, online community offers a non-problematic improvement over offline community. At the other extreme are the many dystopian warnings that once we are grouped by interest rather than by geography, we will lose our connections to *real* (i.e., geographically local) community, and these more important communities will suffer as a result. To an extent, these debates result from different uses of the term *community*, a problem that can be averted through more concete descriptions of what we discuss. As Fernback (1997) points out,

Community is a term which seems readily definable to the general public but is infinitely complex and amorphous in academic discourse. It has descriptive, normative, and ideological connotations ... [and] encompasses both material and symbolic dimensions. (p. 39)

The set of connotations that lies at the heart of many critics of online community is exemplified by Doheny-Farina (1996), an advocate of using computer networks to enhance local communities but avoiding them otherwise. He writes,

A community is bound by place, which always includes complex social and environmental necessities. It is not something you can easily join. You can't subscribe to a community as you subscribe to a discussion group on the Net. It must be lived. It is entwined, [is] contradictory, and involves all our senses. (p. 37)

Using a similar model of community, Healy (1997) argues that real community entails more than 'the voluntary association of like-minded individuals' (p. 61).

Central to the skeptics' argument is that we seek community online because we feel its absence offline. Healy (1997) and Stratton (1997) both locate the romance of Internet community in a nostalgia for the homogeneous small town. Stratton writes, 'The American mythologization of the Internet as a community represents a nostalgic dream for a mythical early modern community which reasserts the dominance of the White, middle-class male and his cultural assumptions' (p. 271). Lockard (1997) puts it more bluntly: 'If the offline/Black streets have turned mean, go plug into online/White optic fiber' (p. 228). From this point of view, we should be worried that seeking comfort in White male homogeneity online will have deleterious consequences for morality and ethics in the multicultural geographical world.

Despite their surface appeal, both utopian and dystopian ways of thinking about online communities obscure more issues than they raise. The r.a.t.s. newsgroup might be about as close to the utopian ideal of an online group based on shared interest as there is. It is fun. It offers refuge from the shame of viewing soaps so prevalent offline. People offer genuine support and care for others that they might never meet face-to-face. The group has an affective quality and value system that many of our geographical communities could use. But r.a.t.s. is not a utopia. There are conflicts and cliques. Some people come to disrupt, and old-timers leave disappointed. The idea of the shared-interest community as a utopia ignores the tensions and contradictions that evolve in any ongoing community where new people continually come into a world rich with traditions they did not create. Shared interest need not mean like-minded.

Furthermore, although r.a.t.s. is a warm and loving community based on shared interest, it is not a paragon of White male homogeneity, nor is it disconnected from 'entwined, contradictory, sensual' communities. As we have seen, r.a.t.s. is a realm in which men abide by a value system traditionally associated with women, where women's concerns are centralized and taken seriously, and where diverse viewpoints on some of life's most important matters – things such as how people ought to treat one another – are considered an asset. Online communities can expose people to differences that they would not encounter offline. For example, an Australian participant told me about one of the things he likes most about the group: 'There are so many different people at r.a.t.s.a. [rec.arts.tv.soaps.abc] that I normally wouldn't get to interact with. I'm 23 (male), and it's really great to chat with people with different life experiences and points of view' (Bobby, Viewing notes 1998). If we are going to understand the role that the Internet will play in affecting geographically located communities, then we need to develop more sophisticated understandings of what these online communities entail.

We also will have to develop greater understanding of how people's involvement in online communities influences their involvement in offline communities. A basic assumption behind the fear that online community will damage offline community is that the time spent in online interaction would otherwise be spent building community with our neighbors if we were not online. The fact is that we know very little about what the millions of people who participate in online groups would be doing if they were not online. The r.a.t.s. newsgroup was at its most active between the hours of 9 a.m. and 5 p.m., strongly suggesting that its readers would have been killing time at work if they had not been posting.[2] There also are indications that people who spend time online watch less television. A study conducted by Nielsen Media Research for America Online found that households with connections to the Internet watch 15% less television each week (Viewing notes 1998). It is quite possible that online communities of interest can enhance offline community. For example, the value system promoted in r.a.t.s. might strengthen geographically situated communities. Consider Esther's post, quoted [previously], where she spoke of her own involvement with women's shelters and urged other women to become involved in such work. My own experience was that I met people in my local community through r.a.t.s. who I would not have known otherwise, an experience echoed by other r.a.t.s. participants. Connections formed through the group allowed me to break through the university boundaries among departments, graduate students, and staff, privileging our commonalities over the institutional differences ingrained in the local social structure.

It also is important to understand that the people in r.a.t.s. recognize and articulate the differences between the community and friendships of the group and the community and friendships they experience offline. They do not see them as identical or interchangeable. Even Anne, the heaviest and longest term poster, thinks that the term *community* fits 'only to a certain degree. It does feel like a community, yet it doesn't. It's kind of hard to explain. A group seems better. To me, a community is a group of people all physically in the same area' (Viewing notes 1998).

The r.a.t.s. newsgroup is not perfect, but it is a model of a pretty good online community. It shows that online groups can embrace difference, can embrace women, can be polite, can foster discussion that improves offline life, and can adapt to change without falling apart or becoming too elitist. Whereas r.a.t.s. does little (if anything) to harm offline community, and might in fact benefit face-to-face communities by creating greater interpersonal understanding and tolerance, other groups could have negative consequences for offline communities (hate groups are an obvious example). The medium is not what matters; it is the practices a community promotes that benefit or harm offline community. Our thinking about online communities is not furthered by painting them in simplistic extremes or in contrast to offline community. As Gurak (1997) writes, 'People are already moving back and forth from physical to virtual community; the issue is how to shape and use these new structures' (p. 132). Online communities are not going to go away. If we are worried about a declining sense of community in contemporary life, then we should be thinking in concrete terms about what types of affective involvement and value systems we want in all of our communities and then asking what practice might promote these moralities both online and offline.

Rethinking audience community

This study raises many of the same issues about audience communities as it does for online communities and for similar reasons. Even as it has come to rely on the term *community*, audience research has shied away from the close examination of the discourse through which communities are built, obscuring many important aspects of what these groups involve. The r.a.t.s. newsgroup began as a group of individuals oriented to the same television programs. Through their connection to soap opera texts, they built a range of practices that function to pool information and collaboratively interpret the show. In this sense, r.a.t.s. clearly is an audience. But although this connection to the text is essential, it offers us an inadequate understanding of what it means to be an audience community. Out of the textually oriented practices, r.a.t.s. also developed interpersonal practices and connections that came to be equally (and sometimes more) important to its participants. If we are going to take the term *community* seriously in audience research, then we need to take on the unfamiliar task of examining interpersonal communication.[3] We cannot understand social relationships if we look only at group-text interactions. Being a member of an audience community is not just about reading a text in a particular way; rather, it is about having a group of friends, a set of activities one does with those friends, and a world of relationships and feelings that grow from those friendships. In general, we have far too little understanding of the spontaneous interpersonal interaction and social relations that make an audience a community, although these interactions are crucial to being a fan and incorporating mass media into our everyday lives. The Internet allows us an unprecedented (although not the only) route into these communities.

How does the internet change what it means to be an audience?

The Internet did not invent fan groups; they were thriving long before computers existed. On the other hand, the Internet has changed them, and for those with Internet access, it has changed what it means to be a fan. The full ramifications that the Internet will have on other mass media remain to be seen, but a few implications are apparent from r.a.t.s. First, the Net has allowed audience communities to proliferate. Where geography might not have allowed the critical fan mass to let a community coalesce, the removal of that boundary lets fans of even the most obscure shows, films, bands, and the like find one another. As fans access one another with greater regularity and frequency, interpretations of the media are increasingly collaborative. Indeed, being a member of an audience itself is becoming an increasingly social practice. The Internet also allows fans to participate in audience communities at their own comfort levels. Those who are not interested in attending fan conventions or collecting every product can read online groups as frequently or rarely as they like. Thus, the Internet makes audience communities more common, more visible, and more accessible, enabling fans to find one another with ease, regardless of geography, and enhancing the importance of the interpersonal dimensions of fandom.

The Internet also makes audience communities more visible for mass media producers, who can log on anytime to get instantaneous feedback. As Harrington and Bielby (1995) note, there is no systematic evidence that soap producers are consistently monitoring the Net. On the other hand, there is a good deal of evidence (most of which is collected in the r.a.t.s.a. FAQ [frequently asked questions]) that they are well aware of it and that some writers, actors, crew, and other behind-the-scenes personnel are reading and participating in r.a.t.s. and other online groups. Producers and writers of other shows have been far more explicit about engaging their online communities. How the online discussions will feed back into media texts remains to be seen, but it is clear that, at least in the case of soaps, the writers might be wise to pay some attention to what these fans are saying. As soap ratings are slipping, these fans are sending strong and consistent messages about what they do and do not like in the medium.

The Internet also has begun to shift the balance of power between media producers and consumers in a number of ways that the industry might rightly find disconcerting. The producers remain in control of the scarce resource of airwaves, but online, fans can create sites as impressive as can the major studios. The World Wide Web has become filled with fan-authored sites. Whereas ABC has a site for each of its soaps, the shows' fans have created many sites for those soaps, often for particular characters on those soaps, and fans can visit those fan-created sites as easily as she or he can visit the network-created sites. This is one example of what we see throughout the discussion in r.a.t.s.; the Internet gives fans a platform on which to perform for one another, and their informal performances might please fans more than the official ones do. Fans also amuse one another with fan fiction, writing their own soap episodes and story lines that are collected and posted to Web sites. As media converge more and more, and as more and more audience members go online, the absolute control of producers over their products might erode further. And if it does not, then fans might well develop alternative products that gain greater audiences. Scholarship so far has barely scratched the surface of the interplays between media producers and online fans.[4]

Studying communities through practice

One goal of this book has been to show the utility of the practice approach for research on both online and audience community. Close examination of the routinized ways in which such communities organize their social lives allows us to see them as wholes while simultaneously viewing the details and dynamics that lead to their constant evolution. We can see their social relationships, identities, value systems, and ongoing tensions as well as the strategies that participants use to maintain and negotiate their structure. Practice can serve as an organizing framework through which these communities can be examined and compared.

The analysis of r.a.t.s. also suggests some areas that practice theorists might pursue in other communities as well. There has been a strong focus in practice research on the cognitive. Chaiklin and Lave (1993), for example, tout practice theory as a way in which to ground cognitive theory in social context. Miller and Goodnow (1995) point out that there have been relatively few developmental studies that take a practice approach to affect compared to those that focus on cognition. Ortner's (1984) argument (on which Miller and Goodnow draw) that the motivational and affective side of practice is relatively undeveloped compared to the cognitive remains true as of this writing. Practice in r.a.t.s. certainly can be understood in cognitive terms. The questions of how members learn the group's norms and develop the types of knowledge and ways of thinking that allow them to be competent members clearly involve cognition. But r.a.t.s. practice also illustrates the importance of the socioemotional in organizing community. People in r.a.t.s. are not just working with how to think, they also are negotiating how to feel, both in this community and in the others they inhabit. The strong emphasis on humor in r.a.t.s. shows us the extent to which emotive elements can be essential to shaping and negotiating a community's core values. Elaborating the affective dimensions of practice also will allow us to better develop the connections between practice as situated cognition and practice as embodied experience.

As a community of interest rather than a geographical culture or subculture, r.a.t.s. also raises the issue of how different communities intersect through practice. People on r.a.t.s., like all of us, move between multiple communities, importing and exporting practices along the way. Our understanding of all communities will be enhanced by understanding not just how they operate as coherent wholes but also how they interact with other wholes. As we come to live in an ever-expanding array of specialized communities, the issue of how those communities interweave is crucial to understanding culture. This is an issue that the practice approach is particularly well suited to address.

Toward a convergent future

Our lives are increasingly mediated by technology. Our senses of self, our relationships with others, and our communities all are shaped by our daily interactions with and through machines. Online communities and audience communities are two outgrowths of this transformation. As media proliferate and converge, we can only assume that both types of community will increase in prevalence and influence. Anderson (1983) argues that all communities beyond the primal face-to-face are imagined, a process enabled by mass media. Rather than asking whether these new types of communities are authentic, he suggests that we look instead to 'the style in which they are imagined' (p. 6). I suggest that one way in which to understand the imagination of community is through close examination of one of the most primal forces that ties people together – interpersonal interaction. It is in the details of their talk that people develop and maintain the rituals, traditions, norms, values, and senses of group and individual identity that allow them to consider themselves communities. Rather than judging from the outside, we need to listen closely to what members of new media communities have to say to one another and to those who ask. Only then will we understand their diversity and the opportunities and challenges they offer.

Notes

1   One example of this involved an *All My Children* participant who claimed that the character Aunt Phoebe was in fact his aunt. The fact that fictional aunts do not have real nephews was not lost on the other participants, who quickly ridiculed him out of the group.
2   The well-publicized study conducted by Kraut *et al.* (1998), which produced the finding that people became increasingly depressed as their Internet connection time increased, relied on a sample with many high school students using the Internet at home. The fact that these r.a.t.s. participants are primarily adult working women participating from their workplaces of the Internet and the caution we should have about claims that collapse all users and uses.
3   This goes both ways. Scholars of interpersonal communication could benefit from considering the roles that mass media play in the construction and maintenance of our relationships and social groupings as well.
4   See Clerc (1996) for a particularly good scratching regarding *The X-Files*.

References

Anderson, B. (1983) *Imagined Communities: Reflections on the Origin and Spread of Nationalism*. London: Verso.

Chaiklin, S. and Lave, J. (eds) (1993) *Understanding Practice: Perspectives on Activity and Context*. Cambridge: Cambridge University Press.

Clerc, S. (1996) Estrogen brigades and 'big tits' threads: media fandom online and off, in L. Cherney and E.R. Weise (eds) *Wired Women*. Seattle, WA: Seal.

Cody, M.J., Wendt, P., Dunn, D. *et al.* (1997) Friendship formation and creating communities on the Internet: reaching out to the senior population. Paper presented at the annual meeting of the International Communication Association, Montreal, May.

Connery, B.A. (1997) IMHO: authority and egalitarian rhetoric in the virtual coffeehouse, in D. Porter (ed.) *Internet Culture*. New York: Routledge.

Doheny-Farina, S. (1996) *The Wired Neighborhood*. New Haven, CT: Yale University Press.

Fernback, J. (1997) The individual within the collective: virtual ideology and the realization of collective principles, in S.G. Jones (ed.) *Virtual Culture*. Thousand Oaks, CA: Sage.

Gurak, L.L. (1997) *Persuasion and Privacy in Cyberspace: The Online Protests over Lotus Market Place and the Clipper Chip*. New Haven, CT: Yale University Press.

Hanks, W.F. (1996) *Language and Communication Practices*. Boulder, CO: Westview.

Harrington, C.L. and Bielby, D.D. (1995) *Soap Fans: Pursuing Pleasure and Making Meaning in Everyday Life*. Philadelphia: Temple University Press

Healy, D. (1997) Cyberspace and place: the Internet as middle landscape on the electronic frontier, in D. Porter (ed.) *Internet Culture*. New York: Routledge.

Joe, S.K. (1997) Socioemotional use of CMC: self-disclosure in computer-mediated communication. Paper presented at the annual meeting of the International Communication Association, Montreal, May.

Kraut, R., Patterson, M., Lundmark, V. *et al.* (1998) Internet paradox: a social technology that reduced social involvement and psychological well-being? Preliminary draft, http://homenet. andrew.cmu.edu/progress/HN.impact.10.htm

Lockard, J. (1997) Progressive politics, electronic individuals, and the myth of virtual community, in D. Porter (ed.) *Internet Culture*. New York: Routledge.

Miller, P.J. and Goodnow, J.J. (1995) Cultural practices: toward an integration of culture and development, in J.J. Goodnow, P.J. Miller and F. Kessel (eds), *Cultural Practices as Contexts for Development* (New Directions for Child Development, no. 67). San Francisco, CA: Jossey Bass.

Nguyen, D.T. and Alexander, J. (1996) The coming of cyberspacetime and the end of the polity, in R. Sields (ed.) *Cultures of Internet: Virtual Spaces, Real Histories, Living Bodies*. Thousand Oaks, CA: Sage.

Ortner, S.B. (1984) Theory in anthropology since the sixties, *Comparative Studies in Society and History*, 26(1).

Rheingold, H. (1993) *Virtual Communities*. Reading, MA: Addison-Wesley.

Stratton, J. (1997) Cyberspace and the globalization of culture, in D. Porter (ed.) *Internet Culture*. New York: Routledge.

Turkle, S. (1995) *Life on the Screen: Identity in the Age of the Internet*. New York: Simon & Schuster.

Viewing notes (1998) *Soap Opera Weekly*, 8 September.

15 | STORIES OF PLACES AND WAYS OF BEING

Annette N. Markham

Terri
Mediation, and access to it, is empowerment;
I physically crave it

I was surfing on the Web one night, mostly wasting valuable time, when I happened upon an intriguing online journal called *Women and Performance Quarterly*. At first, I was drawn to it by the title of Issue 17, *Sexuality and Cyberspace*. The specific article titles pulled me further in, along with fascinating graphics and eerie moving artwork. I glanced through the articles, thinking about various issues of embodiment, gender, and cyberspace. 'Performing the Digital Body – A Ghost Story,' by Theresa M. Senft; 'Turing, My Love,' by Matthew Ehrlich; 'On Space, Sex, and Stalkers,' by Pamela Gilbert. The next time I looked up, two hours had passed.

I was fascinated, needless to say, and on impulse I wrote an email message to the guest editor, Theresa M. Senft, complimenting her on this wonderful collection of essays and asking her if she would like to participate in my study. Several weeks passed, and I assumed the absence of a reply meant, 'No, thanks.' Actually, Terri wanted to say 'Yes, of course!' but, as she explained later, she had experienced a systems crash. We eventually found a space in our schedules to talk in my and Beth's room at Diversity University.

Annette N. Markham (1998) Stories of places and ways of being, *Life Online: Researching Real Experience in Virtual Space*. Walnut Creek, Lanham and Oxford: Alta Mira Press, pp. 191–9, 210–16. Reprinted by kind permission of Alta Mira Press.

Terri says, 'Okay. How shall we start?'

You say, 'well, let me give you some official sounding pre-interview stuff:'

Terri exclaims, 'okie dokie!'

You say, 'I guarantee that I will not ever reveal your address/name/location. I also guarantee that I will delete any references that might give a reader clues about where you live, who you are, or where you work.'

You ask, 'You can disconnect from this interview at any time and I will not bother you again. Do you mind if I archive this conversation for later analysis and possible publication?'

Terri says, 'sounds good. but you also have my permission to use my identity for anything I say. I'm fine being on record; record away.'

You exclaim, 'Thanks. And can I just say that I have been looking very forward to meeting you. You are a fantastic writer!'

Terri exclaims, 'you are such a sweetie. If you tell me I am rich and thin, too, we can get married!'

Markham laughs!

Terri works for Prodigy, an online service provider, where she writes a column called 'Baud Behavior.' She's also a doctoral candidate at New York University's Department of Performance Studies; a prolific writer in various online arenas; a guest editor of *Women and Performance Quarterly*; a reviewer for the feminist journal *SIGNS*; an active member of the WELL and ECHO, two of the best-known communities online; and a dominatrix in another online service. To put herself through college, she worked as a phone-sex operator. (*Incidentally, she's also a wonderful, open, and engaging person. I feel lucky to have met her.*)

Of all the people I interviewed, Terri was the most candid about her experiences in both online and offline contexts. When I asked her again recently if she wanted me to use her real name, she responded immediately, 'I have this weird belief that since the Net is a space of writing, people should 'own their own words.' Unless, of course, they request you grant them anonymity. But I have no anonymity, for I am a brazen hussy.'

Terri is also highly reflexive about her identity and performance of self in various contexts, which makes sense given her research interests in feminist theory, performance studies, and technology. In addition to talking with me in a formal interview, Terri gave me access to several essays she had written or participated in as well as to her website. Some of the conversation below is supplemented by these resources, all of which are included in the bibliography.

*

'What does the Internet mean to you?'

Terri said, 'I'm assuming you don't want a technical answer here, let me think.' After a moment, her answer appeared on my screen. 'Truthfully? The Internet gave me guts. It allowed me to write people I had never met to ask them to read my book. It allowed me to realize my dream of NEVER wearing pantyhose to a job. It has helped me understand that I can move anywhere and still be connected to my friends and lovers. I know the phone can do those things too, but the phone means very very different things to me than the net.'

I asked, 'What about the net makes it so unique or different (say, from the phone, or face-to-face conversation)?'

Terri replied, 'I really believe that online experiences (for me) are similar to offline, with this one major exception – online life has a paper trail. I try to capture every long conversation I have online. I find myself reading over what just happened. I like that feeling. I wish I was videotaping my offline life for examination. It would save me therapy bills! haah!'

Markham laughs!

'Can you imagine?' Terri asked.

'Yes. I can imagine how quickly I'd end up in therapy trying to examine and analyze my every move ... yikes!!!'

Immediately, Terri responded, 'I'm already there, so for me, it would be like mother's little helper, I swear.'

I laughed aloud. 'The image cracks me up! You know, it would be the basis of a great novel called *Terri's Little Helper*.'

'Yeah,' Terri said, 'It could be directed in the film version by woody allen, starring some nutty young chick ...'

*

When the interview began, I assumed we would be talking about Terri's online experiences as they *related to* her regular life. I soon realized we were actually talking about Terri's life, period. For Terri, life online is not a reflection of, a reproduction or, or a simulation of real life or even offline life. Online and offline are two different modalities in which living one's life just happens. Roughly, one is based in text and the other is based in the body. But these distinctions blur significantly for Terri, not just because she spends a great deal of time online, but also, as she says, because 'cybernetics is a condition, not a life-style choice. If you are disabled, use a sex toy, utilize telephone messaging services, are chemically dependent in any way, if you have sent e-mail or keyed a bank ATM lately, then you are, yourself, a cyborg – a body containing both organic and technological components.'

As well as collapsing many of the distinctions between technology and humans to talk about identity, Terri also focuses on identity as the effects of ongoing performances rather than as a stable state. She writes, 'There has been a recent impulse ... that suggests that online life is the ideal spot to experiment with hypothetical identity-making. This line of thought ... carries a wrong assumption that only an online textual body is performative, whereas a biological body at the end of the terminal is stable. ... Online or off it, identity and gender are complicated performances' (Senft 1997: 7. Terri elaborates on these issues in her other writings.)

Not only is Terri's computer a natural extension of her body, her connections with others through the computer are a normal, meaningful part of her everyday life. After all, if we perform identity, gender, sexuality, and community, it doesn't make much sense to privilege one particular performance over another. As she describes her various online roles, I realize that issues of technology and the body inevitably infiltrate every aspect of her life. Put differently, when she is online, Terri is neither living in words nor trying to escape the idea of the body to be with others in some existential way. Rather, Terri performs embodiment through the text, in a visceral way.

'When my mother died, I found it difficult to talk to people – on the phone, in person, anywhere. That was when I got introduced to a cybersex community called Cyberoticom, where I was Jane Doe. Jane Doe, on cyberoticom, was this spoiled little rich girl, something I never was. She would do any kind of wild thing sexually, as long as there were yummy gifts at the end.'

The first time she went online, Terri recalls, she had an explicitly sexual encounter before the night was over. In her online community, she freely shares stories of her various sexual performances online: 'I go back to Echo to report my AOL sex antics ... My favorite part of the experience is when I climax on line, typing 'yesssssssssss' and everyone claps ... I think I'd really like it if after my real-life orgasms, I got an applause track played.'

I asked, 'How would you describe your self online?'

Terri paused a moment, then said, 'Well, it depends on where online. Like, I am different here than I would be in a spazzy fun conference on Echo, or who I would be as a NYC 'outsider' on the San Francisco based

WELL, or how I would be when I am posting to an academic listserv, cuz Gawd knows who reads those things.'

I grinned, knowing exactly what she meant. I sometimes felt strange writing in vastly different voices to different audiences.

Terri added, 'And I am definitely different now than when I am running the 'Obey Me' room at America Online, working as an online dominatrix. All of these are 'me,' you know?'

'Wow,' I said, in my usual unimaginative way. 'I'm sure I'd get confused. But I know what you mean. I enact these same sorts of multiple roles all day, every day ... online and offline.'

'Yeah.' Terri agreed, 'It's like we expect to be a singular being, and every moment of our life, we're proven wrong. When I first joined Echo, I was advised to be 'myself,' and I couldn't really figure out what on earth that was. Was I supposed to be a graduate student, a sex worker, a bisexual woman, a family cancer survivor, a person who suffered from depression, or what? In time, I have learned to 'be' all of those things online, but there is a time and a place for each of these manifestations of personality.'

A moment later, Terri concluded, 'I don't think I've ever met anyone who had 'one self.' '

'I agree,' I said, 'But here's another question I've been grappling with. We all live multiple manifestations of personality, as you say. But sometimes the mediated (computer) contexts make me seem almost distinct from my self at times. I'm not being clear, I'm sure. I guess I'm asking: Do you think your sense of self as a person online is fundamentally distinct from your sense of self offline?'

'Hmmmmm. I feel far more vulnerable offline. That is the most honest way I can describe it. Sometimes vulnerability is great! Sometimes it's crippling, and I like muting it when necessary.'

'What do you mean, muting it?'

'Going online to mute the vulnerability I feel offline. At this point in my life, I'll suppress expressing stuff if it makes 'me' uncomfortable. But at the same time, I'm not ashamed of my life, you know? And because I am physically separated from other people online, I have no trouble revealing all kinds of other things about myself, within the text.'

'On the other hand, one thing I conceal online is my physical presence: my body, my home, my voice, my health.'

Markham nods

'Terri,' I asked, following a thought, 'Why do you feel vulnerable offline?'

There was a long pause, and then Terri replied, 'Everyone has their own story about this. Mine goes like this – I was a textbook abused child, which is to say I was beaten and yelled at repeatedly through childhood. To cope I learned to speak quickly and well. As a result, I am damn near overbearing in person. I experience the phone as a very visceral thing, grain of the voice and all that. Probably why I like and understand phone sex so much. But things feel too raw on the phone for me sometimes, I crave mediation, physically crave it.'

Terri continued, 'I crave mediation because of the abuse I suffered for years in the name of 'familial immediacy'. I didn't even get to have a lock on my bedroom door as a child. For me, mediation, and access to it, is empowerment. So being online allows me to choose my level of immediacy. It gives me the power to mediate my own presence.'

'How so?' I prompted.

'My thoughts are here, on this screen, and for now, that is enough. You can't hear if I am sobbing, or if I am off my medication, or anything. This makes me feel safe for now.'

Interesting, I thought to myself. When I think of 'safe' I think of being anonymous, part of the crowd, not singled out. But Terri doesn't seem to be referring to this kind of safe. She is referring to separating the presence of others from herself physically.

Terri verified my thoughts a moment later, 'I don't think 'real' need be synonymous with 'available for anyone, all times and in all ways.' Women have been synonymous with the body and immediate presence for all history, look where it gets us. No thanks. I far prefer choosing my level of immediacy.'

*

As we continued to talk about the performance of self in online contexts, I realized Terri was talking about control in a very different sense than the other participants. I had met many other users who said they felt empowered by the Internet because it gave them more of a voice, it made them more confident, or it allowed them to talk to people they might not otherwise feel comfortable talking with. I assumed that Terri was talking about power in much the same way. However, for Terri, empowerment means she can control directly the *form* and *degree* of the connection. Through online communication, Terri can limit the level of intimacy, and control the extent to which relationships are mediated.

This makes sense. Any of us who are raised without privacy or power might physically crave it as well. And like Terri, while sitting at our terminals with the capacity to make or break walls between self and other at will, we might feel 'tremendously powerful.'

Interestingly, Terri does not worry about the online presentation of self. She does not attempt to control her online appearance or persona, but allows it to emerge spontaneously, through conversational interactions with others. Yet at the same time that Terri does not try to control the presencing of self, she does seek to control the absence of self, as well as the presence and absence of others.

In other words, Terri wants to be able to disconnect from Other whenever she chooses to. Of course, this is more possible online than off because it is easier to shut off the computer and instantly rid yourself of the other's presence (or 'mute' the other, as Terri says), than to walk away from a physical person, or to try to lock a door with no locks to keep abusive family memebers away. This measure of control is at least part of the reason she prefers to exist online.

Online or offline, our selves are constructed throught multiple performances and responses to those performances. We can imagine that some of our performances are more authentic or meaningful than others; we might like to erase certain performances, repeat others, create new patterns. As I talked with Terri, though, it occurred to me that she doesn't seem to suppress or privilege any performances of her self, online or offline. They are all meaningful components of existence. As she says, 'they are all me, you know?'

However, Terri consciously separates the contexts in which the performances take place, whether these contexts are online or offline. This is a crucial move; for her, understanding self as it is performed in one context can help her perform in other contexts. As Terri notes, she often gets too comfortable in one context or the other, which makes her realize she needs to find more balance:

'Two months ago, I would have said that I am most comfortable with the virtual version of me. Now, I am realizing that when I am more comfortable with myself online than off, this is a sign that I am retreating from the flesh, if that makes any sense. In some ways, online life is too comfortable for me.

'This is not necessarily a bad thing: online life has taught me all kinds of new ways to re-imagine myself in the physical world. But now, I am trying to use my physical experiences (vulnerability, sexuality, mortality and the like) to broaden my online persona, and I have to say that it is a much more difficult project, at least for me.'

Terri appears to have accepted online and offline experiences as part of the performance of everyday life. Although they might be different experiences, and each mode of experience may offer different advantages, technology is as natural as any other means of expressing and enacting identity. In effect, Terri is not only rejecting my question 'Is it real?' but she is simultaneously rejecting a traditional way of thinking about how identity gets constructed in the first place. And in most of her discourse, everything about 'being' is inevitably also about performance.

I think it is important to note that Terri was one of the few people I met online who actually acknowledged that being online is not such a great thing; rather, it marks an impossible attempt to escape the body.

You say, 'Do you think 12 hours online per day is a lot?'

Terri says, 'Yes, I do! I am beginning to feel like the online equivalent of a stockbrocker with his shoulder permanently disfigured (cuz he's the one with the phone all the time and holds it up to his ear with his shoulder).'

You ask, 'Good imagery. ... I wonder what appendage is disfigured (disfigured for you, that is)?'

Terri says, 'my posture has completely fallen apart in the last few years due to hunching over the screen. I am also displeased by the arrival of what can only be called Computer Butt.'

Markham grins understandingly

Terri asks, 'I am hoping its a phase, you know?'

You ask, 'the computer butt or the being online so much?'

Terri exclaims, 'hahaha both!'

Terri says, 'like, we fell in love with online stuff and binged on it, and soon we'll realize that we simply MUST exercise and such in order to live full healthy lives.'

You ask, 'would you spend more or less time online if you could?'

Terri says, 'sitting at the terminal, with so much going on, makes me feel tremendously powerful. I could give a shit about large-scale corporate power, but now I see its seductiveness for people like my brother (who works for an investment house)'

Terri says, 'But, no, I wouldn't spend less time online. Instead, I would figure out how to spend *more* time exercising, singing ... physical things that DON'T require other people.'

You ask, 'What do you mean, physical things that don't require other people?'

Terri says, 'Well, because so much of my life is connected to being online all the time, and because of grad school, I feel like I have MORE than enough human contact, you know. What I DON'T create is time to be alone, NOT in a book, NOT in a conversation, NOT writing, but doing something like running, or singing, or (gads) meditating...'

Markham grins, thinking of her own life

Terri says, 'It just doesn't take much for life to turn into a version of 'Codependent No More,' you know? It gets wearisome.'

I knew what she was talking about, especially when I looked at my own life of breathing filtered air and always walking on concrete. Perhaps after one incorporates technology to such an extensive degree, one feels the urge to get connected to the planet again. We get plugged in, we think it's everything, and then we need to get offline to live healthy lives because our backs are sore, our butts have grown soft, and our posture is atrocious. Our eyes hurt from the glare of the screen, we suffer repetitive stress syndrome in our hands and wrists, and we lack vital nutrients because we spend all our time inside, sitting at the computer, forgetting that we need to nourish our bodies.

So Terri is currently somewhere in New England, painting houses for a living. She'll do a few things online, but for the most part, she's getting connected in a different way.

In sum...

During this study, I spent hours and days sitting in my office chair, engaging contexts created primarily through words, accomplishing conversations through the exchange of messages. In many ways, because I felt so isolated from my own body during this time, I felt compelled to think of cyberspace as essentially disembodied. Yet, as I sat silently, alone in front of my computer, I watched people, including myself, compose themselves through word choices, sentence structures, graphic accents, typos, and eloquent phrases. Responding to responses, we wove dialogic understandings of each other, sometimes connecting, sometimes deciding it was best to move on.

All we have in text-based Internet spaces are texts. The multiple effects of our texts, like the effects of our behaviors and actions in the physical world, cannot be known. We just guess and try to communicate the best we can in each particular situation. For instance, the participants wrote to me, I sketched images in my mind about their appearance, age, race, etc., using templates I derived from my own life experiences. I have no way of knowing whether my (non) imagination matched their physicality, but this is not so important. In text-based spaces, self is constructed through dialogue and thus is more embodied by the text than by the body. To complicate this physical uncertainty, I also could have no way of assessing the 'truth' of their texts. After a few weeks of second-guessing the honesty of their words, I realized that, online or offline, all of us make sense of our experiences and tell the stories of our lives in self-centered and self-understood ways. Truth is an elusive term in any context; however, because truth is always tentative online, it doesn't make sense to dwell on it too much. It's really more about faith and acceptance.

Studies of online communication should include the texts of people who constitute these social spaces. This medium offers unique ways of expressing the self and constructing social reality. The *process* of building relationships and social structures, though, is thoroughly dialogic; online cultures exist because people interact with each other through writing, over time. Just as the text cannot capture the nuance of the voice, the voice cannot capture the nuance of the text. Because of this, researchers (*myself included at the top of the list*) must be willing to study online contexts in their own contexts, without trying to impose alternative categories, false dichotomies, a priori assumptions and templates. And of course, once the researcher is *willing* to discard these, she must be *able* to do so, which is a much more difficult task of rearranging one's frame of reference, I'm afraid.

Real is that which is experienced or that which is known

I learned from talking to these people that being is not related to some abstract concept like 'real' or 'virtual.' Life is much too complex for that. They did not question the reality of their experiences. Instead, they took for granted that being online is as real as being offline – all experience is real. These are their real lives, not some simulation. Even when these participants distinguish sharply between that which is real and that which is otherwise, their descriptions remain solidly grounded in their experiences.

In Matthew's case, for instance, real means nothing more or less than being offline. He does not describe online living as different than being offline. Online only means you have accessed more information. For Jennifer, going online is real in the sense that other people's texts are really there, and a person's text is a substitute for their voice or bodily presence. Mist also experiences her Internet experiences as real, but at the same time, she does not let them interfere with 'more meaningful contexts.' For Mist, there are real and more (meaningfully) real aspects of experience.

Beth considers all experiences real, online and offline. For her, authenticity of self is a reality represented in text. But when it comes to knowing

Other, the text is not enough; it is not a sufficient means of knowing what is *really* real. For Sheol, life online is as meaningful as life offline, perhaps more so. The realities of online life are a matter of degree; different contexts online express different levels of reality.

Terri doesn't ponder the issue of reality. She's more concerned with how technology and the body are implicated in determining what is real. Online or offline, every aspect of self and being is an effect of performance. Hence, the reality of self and other is not a useful categorization tool because it is a shifting activity, not a given state.

For Sherie, the text represents more than just a means to create identity and self; the text is the very embodiment of self. Online and offline realities are separate, very different aspects of reality.

A person's experience of computer-mediated contexts may be startling, profound, and unique. However, this does not necessarily mean online experiences are more or less real than other life experiences. In this technological age, if we want to use the term *reality* as a useful descriptive category, it must be reconsidered and expanded to encompass multiple experiences that may or may not be connected to the physical world. In addition, we need to remain grounded in our explanations of cyberspace. Online, self, others, and social realities are constructed through the exchange of texts, which can occasion a euphoria that we can transcend the social realities our physical bodies occupy. This is a tantalizing but exaggerated perspective. The potential to experiment with experiences and self-expression can be a refreshing escape from the pressures of living in societies that mostly constrain us; but as most of these users articulate, the reality of online life cannot be separated from offline life, no matter how much we might wish it could be. Kept in perspective, however, both are valuable contexts for experiencing life.

Framing experience as a tool ... place ... way of being

When I first decided to put these people in categories along a continuum from less-to more-connected to online experiences and technologies, I didn't really think the continuum was progressive, where people moved along it from one end toward the other; I anticipated that people would shift around on the continuum as they shifted through contexts. I made this presumption, of course, because it reflected my own experience at the outset of the study. However, as I continue to talk with people about their online experiences, I am realizing that the continuum is marked by significant differences in vocabulary and ways of describing and talking about self, other, and experiences.

For example, those participants who consider the Internet primarily as a *tool* (Matthew, Jennifer, and Mist) all used the term *information* as an important way of making sense of online communication. Michael, who considers the Net a real place, never mentioned the word, but he talked of going there, hanging out, chatting, spending time. On the other hand, of those participants who frame cyberspace as a place to live or a way of being (Sheol, Beth, Terri, and Sherie), only Sheol made a point to talk about information and that was due mainly to his life goal to control information as a hacker. Thus, for those who experience the Internet more ontologically, their online relationships constitute the most meaningful aspect of their experiences.

Perhaps I picked up on certain vocabularies because I had placed them in these categories, but I don't really think so. Only now – as I tied these interviews together – did I begin to notice any trend among their discourses. Interestingly, I sensed a connection between the way people framed their online experiences and their understanding of their sense of self through the body. Most participants who consider the Internet to be a place or a way of being talked about issues of embodiment. This makes sense, because the more connected one feels to online experiences, the more those feelings loop back to the embodied self. To go to the Internet simply to access information is to envision it as a tool, not a place; but to go to be with others implies a place to be, and this necessarily implicates a sense of embodiment.

For instance, the three women who frame their experiences as a place, or a way of being, seem simultaneously to deny and privilege the body. For Beth, cyberspace offers a way to keep men away from her body so they don't try to judge her self based on her bodily presence. For Sherie, the body is flesh, and even if it cannot be escaped, it can be avoided; yet, ironically, throughout the interview, the body was central to the discussion. For Terri, the self is not questionable and the body itself is not the problem. Rather, it is others' access to her body that she worries about. Like Beth, Terri wants to control the extent to which people can touch her, but for different reasons. Beth wants to remain a virgin; Terri never wants to be abused again. These women have found some measure of success in achieving their goals through their online lives, but they are plagued by the embodied self. Terri understands this and is trying not to run away from her embodied self. She understands that ultimately there is no way to escape embodiment so she is working to accept, not deny, the fact of her bodied existence.

For Matthew, Jennifer, and Mist, the embodied or disembodied self is not a salient distinction or subject of discussion because online technologies are tools, not places. Technology facilitates research and enables one to communicate farther. Going online means turning on the computer, just as one would pick up the phone. They know of other people who experience cyberspace as more of a place, but they consider these people extreme.

Michael considers the Internet a place where he can get to know others and expand his community of friends. He is stable in his physical understanding of the world, however; embodiment online is the same as embodiment offline. Armed with this conviction, Michael can actively participate in a community where every member wears an animated mask. He believes that, under each mask, he will find the authentic and true person. Online and offline places may look and operate differently, but they are both places where real people go to get to know one another.

Through online communication, self can control bodies

Online technologies extend our physical capacities in many ways and offer the potential for greater control over the flow of information and the presentation of self. When we connect to the Internet, we can access seemingly endless amounts of information. We can search through many types of online groups and lurk to see what they say and do before we decide to participate. As Matthew notes, the Internet allows us to communicate with colleagues, friends, and family in bits and pieces during our spare time, writing and editing messages we might send now, later, or never. As an augmentation of the self that is situated outside the body, online communication technology offers a powerful means of control over the text, over the performance of self through the text, and control over Others' capacities as well. In general, the participants in this study expressed through our conversations a desire and tendency to control the contexts through which they live their lives.

Key to the process of controlling the context is separation from the physical body. With the body comes a host of uncontrollable aspects of the context. For Matthew and Mist, the voice just talks, and they can't edit the words that come out of the head in face-to-face conversations nearly as well as they can in the textual environment of cyberspace. For Jennifer, seeing the conversation allows her to be more attuned to it, more able to adjust it (and adjust to it). In this way, she can more effectively control the course of conversation and the relationship that emerges from it.

Beth and Sherie do not feel the need to control the text. Each just lets her texts speak her thoughts directly, but they both emphasize that online communication allows them to present certain aspects of the self and omit others, specifically those related to bodied being. In this way, Beth's and Sherie's physical distance from the text is vital to sustaining a belief that a more authentic self can be presented online.

For Sheol, as well, physical separation from the context is a vital means of control. Sheol is not trying to omit his body because he feels it interferes with the authentic expression of self, however. Rather, he wants to control successfully the flow of information as it passes through the network, which requires the absence of presence; indeed, it potentially keeps him out of jail.

In contrast, Terri considers her body to be precious. It is a part of her self that no one is allowed to approach without expressed permission, and online communication provides an essential means of controlling the access others have to her body. When Terri craves solitude, separation of the body from online contexts enables her to shut down the connection whenever she chooses to be free of even the disembodied presence of the Other.

For all these people, control is primarily perceived both as an outcome (product) of the self's communicative efforts and as a performative act (process) that can be directed toward the self or Other. If the body is physically separated from the context, as it is online, the extent to which the other can control self is diminished. Hence, the other isn't something to worry about. (*Until something happens to make you question that assumption, like getting hacked, or being stalked, or having another online persona control your physical ability to control your online character [see Julian Dibbell 1996].*) For these users, control is unidirectional. Control is wielded by the user of the tool, the one writing the text, the one writing the script for the performance – a distinctly non-interactive, non-transactional view of communication.

This notion of control is somewhat illusory. Online, we begin to exist as a persona when others respond to us; being, in this sense, is relational and dialogic. As Laing (1969) explains, our identity cannot be completely abstracted from our identity-for-others, our identity-for-ourselves, the identities we attribute to others, the identities we think they attribute to us, what we think they think we think they think, and so on (p. 86). We thus might believe we control the presentation of self through vivid descriptions, careful editing, and constant self-monitoring, but we are always relating with others in this ongoing construction of self – others whose responses are not always calculable. Even so, these participants believe they have a high degree of control, which seems to satisfy them. Perhaps the illusion of control is sufficient.

Interestingly, for all these participants, the body is still the center of being, whether they want to believe this or not. Whether they talk explicitly of their bodies, or choose to flee the reality of their bodies, their experiences still are located in the place where they live the most visceral parts of their lives, the body. No matter how much Sherie wants to talk of 'being the text,' her words make it clear that her point of reference is her embodied experience. Her body still plays a central role. For others less anxious to de-center the self, the body and its senses and feelings are crucial ways to verify the authenticity of the online Other. Sheol, for instance, knows his online experiences are real because they are very emotional, and when significant things happen online, he feels the emotion in the body, which lends cre-dence or authenticity to his experience. And even though Jennifer accepted Brian's proposal of marriage before they ever met face-to-face, meeting each other as physical bodies was the crucial next step, without which marriage would have been impossible for them.

Everywhere I went online, I saw the body as a privileged site for experience. It is, after all, where we live as breathing organisms. As these persons continue to experience their lives (as mediated through computers), they are shifting the grounds of their own being; or at least I am shifting the grounds of my own being, which makes me suspect they are as well.

The question I am trying to answer is not 'What is virtuality, as compared to reality?' Perhaps it is not even 'What is real?' Perhaps I am asking, 'What does it mean to be? And how – if at all – is virtuality altering our under-standing of being?' These people may not be resolving these questions in definitive ways, but they are playing out different possibilities knowingly and unknowingly, getting answers in various ways and in various contexts.

We now have the technological capacity to interact and exist in multiple contexts at the same time. Because our experience of this technology is new, we are only just beginning to ask ourselves how we can accomplish these multiple modes of experience or ways of being and what the possibilities and consequences may be. A professor down the hall says online commu-nication seems a more interactive form of the novel. Beth says everyone should have this technology, especially older people, so they can connect with others even as their bodies force them to stay in a confined physical place. Sheol says it has changed his life 'forevermore.' Mist says she can't imagine what the world would be like without it. Gargoyle, a programmer I met, says it is the most significant thing ever to happen to humans. My online friend Scooter says it is consuming, and all of us will have to be completely online before we realize what it's doing to us.

The more I talk about these issues with others, online and offline, the more mundane the entire question seems to become ... after all, we exist. Things change. New contexts emerge, and with each new context, we struggle to frame our experiences of it in meaningful, self-reflective ways.

This one seems just another part of life, another place to 'grow old with others,' as my friend Bill likes to say.

References

Dibbell, J. (1996) A rape in cyberspace: or how an evil clown, a Haitian trickster spirit, two wizards and a cast of dozens turned a database into a society, *Village Voice*, 21 December: 36–42.

Laing, R.D. (1969) *Self and Others*. New York: Pantheon.

Senft, T.M. (1997) Introduction: performing the digital body – a ghost story. *Women and Performance Quarterly* [online journal] 17. www.echonyc.com/~women/Issue 17/ (retrieved May 1997)

GAMERS AS CO-CREATORS

ENLISTING THE VIRTUAL AUDIENCE – A REPORT FROM THE NETFACE

John Banks

In this chapter, I offer a description of recent initiatives deployed in the computer game industry to engage and interact with online gamers in ways that potentially move beyond the limitations – methodological and theoretical – identified by Gillard. This chapter is very much positioned and written from the very midst, the netface, where these issues are being engaged and grappled with. It is an ethnographic report from a participant-observer at Auran, a computer game development company based in Brisbane, Australia. Like many other computer game developers and publishers, Auran has been actively engaging with online fans who coalesce around game products that are undergoing development and retail release. Auran has been actively thinking through the complex set of issues, problems and opportunities that emerge from managing relationships with online gamer fans.

What follows is not so much a case study as a reflection on a process of engagement. It has emerged from a combination of PhD research and my experience as a company employee from mid-2000. The research commenced back in late 1997 and was focused on the emerging culture of online computer gaming but, as I followed and was guided by the actors involved, it became a study of the relationship among online PC gamers, game development companies and game publishers. In late 1997, I

John Banks (2002) Gamers as co-creators: enlisting the virtual audience – a report from the netface, in Mark Balnaves, T. O'Regan and Jason Sternberg (eds) *Mobilising the Audience*. St Lucia, Queensland: Queensland University Press, pp. 191–6, 199–211. Reprinted by kind permission of Queensland University Press.

established a research relationship with Auran. I was led to Auran by a growing group of fans forming around *Dark Reign*, a then forthcoming real-time strategy game coproduced by Auran and Activision and published in September 1997 by Activision. The fans were in the process of establishing websites focusing on *Dark Reign*. The sites included game preview content and news such as descriptions of game features, screenshots. A significant feature of *Dark Reign* is support for online multi-player gameplay. Players could join games via the Activision servers and compete online against others, including team games of two against two and four against four.

In 1997, support for online multi-player games was an emerging trend in the PC game industry. Titles such as the first-person shooter *Quake* established their commercial success from their uptakes and extensions as online multi-player experiences. A rich and active online fan culture built up around these titles. These activities included forming teams (clans) for competition against other teams. Clans would have dedicated websites, challenging others and boasting of their victories. This has recently extended to a genre known as MMORPG (massively multi-player online role playing games). Titles such as *Everquest* can only be played online and have been very successful.

A further important feature of the emerging online game culture is fan-created content – extensions and additions to the game software (described as 'mods' or 'add-ons'). Game development companies release for download from their websites or include with the retail release software package game editing tools to be used by skilled and creative players to produce new material for the game. These tools generally require a relatively high level of computer software and graphic art skill to be used effectively. They are essentially the software tools that the game designers and artists use to produce the retail release title. This content includes skins or textures that change the graphics of elements in the game – for example, the dress and look of the player's character or avatar – and new levels and scenarios; through to complete modifications that verge in some cases on being almost completely new games, or at least a significantly new set of features that add to the player's enjoyment and the possibilities of game play.

This fan-based 'producerly' activity could all too easily be read within the tradition of cultural studies as a mundane example of resistant audience practice. Are gamers functioning here as 'textual poachers' (Jenkins 1993)? Aren't they taking the products of capital and reworking them according to their own agendas, pleasures and enjoyments? Are our very notions of audience – the texture, landscape and relationality – being transformed by the emergence of these 'producerly' practices?

The very way that we pose these questions can predispose us towards particular methodologies and frameworks for producing and constructing responses. Additionally, we should keep in mind that our responses and interpretations do not just stand outside these networks, but play a role in building and making them. Our interpretations are part of the very materials from which these networks are made.

Many of the questions assume something – an entity, object or subject that we can clearly lable and define as 'gamer', 'fan', 'audience', 'consumer', 'producer', 'academic' and 'corporation'. But these are not entities so much as relations: circulating dynamics, processes that define moments or conjunctions in a heterogeneous network of relations that do from time to time coalesce into more or less stable patterns of activity or practice. For example, the "I" of this chapter is not simply an academic researcher. He is also an active game fan and regular consumer of game products and an employee of a game production company in the dual position of online community relations manager and project director. For its part, Auran is not a singular, homogeneous object but is constructed from multiple materials, subjectivities and positions. Defined by a complex set of heterogeneous relations and materials, Auran encompasses a broad range of knowledge practices: programming, digital art creation, marketing, website creation and management, engineering, project management, administration, cultural and new media studies. It is a vehicle for attracting venture capital and is therefore caught up in a network of relations with other corporations (game publishers, etc). It is partly defined by relations with gamer fans in a range of quite complex ways. However, this relationship with fans is also shaped by a complex series of internal interactions, tensions, negotiations and compromises.

In my position as online community relations manager, I am often positioned within the company as an advocate for and representative of the fans. I seek the release of information and content from development teams. For their part, development teams are often reluctant to release information and material (such as screenshots) too early in the development cycle. Project directors raise the concern that if, for technical and design reasons, significant changes are made subsequent to a public announcement, Auran and the development team will be criticised by fans who perhaps do not always fully understand and appreciate the game development process. They generally prefer detailed game feature information and screenshots to be released when the project is reasonably close completion. They also have justifiable concerns about meeting feedback requests from the fans, particularly requests for feature additions and modifications while the game is still in development. Developers and projects managers worry about "feature-creep" and see it as potentially threatening the stability, quality and deliverability of a software development project.

However, to assume that gamers and the corporation stand in an exterior relationship – on one side the producer and on the other side the consumer or audience – would be a mistake. For a start, many – if not most – of the designers, artists and programmers who work at Auran are also themselves game fans. Many of them participate activley in the fan networks that form around particular game title and genres on the Internet. These gamer-employees bring with them skills, practices and cultures that are very much influence by their activities as gamers. These practices in turn influence and impact upon Auran at the most basic level of work place practices.

Furthermore, a key expectation of hard-core gamers is that game companies will now actively listen to, engage with and support the fans that form around game titles. This understanding of the game development process both pre-and post-retail release is brought into the industry by game designers, programmers, artists, website development teams, CEOs and marketing departments who, as gamers, are also participants in the online culture of gamer fans. Fans expect that game companies will provide forums in which they can express their views and opinions about games in development and games released. Fans expect to be increasingly involved in the game production process. Fans expect game companies to release editing tools and support the fans community's efforts to create additional content for the game. In short, a hard-core gamer fan expects that game development companies will build a collaborative relationship with them.

Consequently, the focus here will be on the "netface" – the relationships and networks that are the process of being constructed and managed (by game developers, published and fans). It will focus on the efforts that Auran has been making around a product currently in development, *Trainz*, to enlist the passions and commitments of fans in extending the online networks that is to contribute towards the popular (and therefore commercial) success of *Trainz* upon its retail release in late 2001.

...

Auran and *Trainz*

When I first commenced my employment, Auran was in the early stages of developing a new product, *Trainz*. It is a virtual model railroad simulation. Players will be able to collect authentically detailed 3D models of locomotives and rolling stock. It will also allow players to drive the trains through fully 3D train line landscapes from the engineer's cab-view perspective. Finally, on first release, it will include *Surveyor*, an editor that enables players to create layouts. Using *Surveyor*, players will be able to manipulate the landscape and place objects such as trees, buildings, track, bridges, tunnels, etc. *Surveyor* will also be modular, meaning that players will be able to join their layouts together. Auran believes that player activity in creating layouts will be very important to the success of *Trainz*. We envisage that player-created layouts will be available for download from *Trainz* fan websites. Furthermore, the modularity of its layouts will encourage the formation of online virtual model rail clubs. Additionally, the open-architecture design of *Trainz* will facilitate the ability for end users to import the 3D models that they create into *Trainz*. (The game does not include the software required to create additional 3D content. Instead, Auràn is relying on the extensive diffusion of 3D software-modelling packages such as 3D Studio Max to create the 3D content such as locomotives or buildings.) From the very early stages of the *Trainz* design, it was planned to develop a product that was very open to end user modification and extension.

My brief for *Trainz* was to support and encourage the formation of an active fan community around the product and the Auran *Trainz* website (www.virtualtrainz. com). The decision to establish a website as a vehicle for facilitating dialogue with the online train and rail fans was taken in August 2000, at a very early stage of development. Designed to promote *Trainz*, the website included an overview of the features that it was planned would be supported. The site was also supported with a forum where visitors could post questions and comments about *Trainz*. For example, we started threads asking questions such as: What locomotives would people like to see included with *Trainz*? We also actively engaged in open-ended and extended dialogue with the fan participants about the reasoning behind various design features. The feedback from the forums and email exchanges with train and rail fans would then be regularly discussed in *Trainz* development team meetings. Auran's willingness to design and support a website that actively encouraged and facilitated feedback with our potential customers and fans was also enhanced by the fact that the online services manager, Rachael Nixon, had educational qualifications that included study in the discipline of media and cultural studies. Nixon appreciated and understood the new player-created 3D locomotive models into it would need to be relatively end user-friendly. A decision was made to commit considerable development resources to ensuring that *Surveyor* would be relatively user-friendly – that an average gamer would be able to use and enjoy the editing tools to create *Trainz* layouts.

As we anticipated, in the first few months after the launch of the *Trainz* website, Auran was approached by a number of train and rail enthusiasts interested in the possibility of creating third-party content for the game – particularly 3D models of locomotives and trackside accessories such as buildings. The Auran decision to support the ability to import into the game models created in recognised 3D modelling programs, such as 3D Studio Max, enabled individuals to produce models for *Trainz* from an existing software base. This allowed individuals such as 3Drailhound, who hosts a website, *3D Train Stuff* (www.3dtrainstuff.com/) to dedicate their site to producing additional models for both *Trainz* and *Microsoft Train Simulator*. Throughout 2001, as the popularity of both *Microsoft Train Simulator* and *Trainz* increased, individuals and teams interested in producing third-party content for *Trainz* rregularly approached us.

There is an increasing trend for fans to consider commercially releasing their add-on content. For example, the *3D Train Stuff* team proposes to release models for both *Trainz* and *Microsoft Train Simulator* for purchase via its website. Marc J. Nelson, a talented 3D artist, has formed a team of train and Rail Sim fans around the website (http://3drains.com), and also plans to commercially release models for download. Auran has developed relationships with these groups and intends to support their efforts by producing additional content for *Trainz*. Throughout the development of the game, Auran has regularly entered into extended dialogues with fans who are interested in pursuing the possibility of creating additional content for the program.

Early in 2001, Auran decided to formalise this arrangement by inviting a group of the most active and passionate fans to participate in a *Trainz* third-party content and beta program. This program, conducted within the terms of a non-disclosure agreement that all participants enter into, will involve releasing the *Trainz Surveyor* editing tools to the participants prior to the retail release of *Trainz*. with *Microsoft Train Simulator* would be quite difficult to use and require relatively high skill levels that may well be beyond the average model train enthusiast.

In the promotion of *Microsoft Train Simulator*, Microsoft was stating that the end product would have an open architecture and ship with an editor that allowed players and third parties to create their own routes and import other models (for example, locomotives, rolling stock, buildings, etc.) into *Microsoft Train Simulator* that they had made with a 3D Software package such as 3D Studio Max. In short, much like their flight simulator line product lines, around which a range of third parties and fans produced additional content (aircraft, flight routes, airports, etc), Microsoft hoped that a similar third-party and fan content network would form around *Microsoft Train Simulator*.

Now the *Trainz* designers decided that the locomotive models in *Trainz* should be authentically detailed. This required high polygon count models. A relatively high-end processor and 3D capable video card are required to optimally run a game with high polygon models in a 3D environment. It was not technically feasible to then attempt to place these models within the context of lengthy and detailed prototype rail routes. The decision was therefore made to scale the *Trainz* routes or layouts to be of a size larger than a typical model railroad layout but significantly less than a full-scale prototype route.

The *Trainz* development team also believed that highly detailed smaller scaled layouts would support an end user-friendly editor. The time and resources required to effectively model a prototype route in detail would be considerable and out of the reach of an average train enthusiast with a moderate level of computer skills. Technically, then, the aim of the *Trainz* design is to place in the hands of train and model railroad enthusiasts a collection of highly detailed models, and a set of software editing tools that they can use to create their own layouts.

Throughout late 2000 and early 2001, Auran received a considerable degree of criticism from the passionate train simulator fans that this perceived change in design direction was not what they wanted or expected from a train-rail software game. This criticism was particularly levelled by Vern Moorhouse via posts to the *Trainz* website forum, emails to Auran and commentary posts on his *Trainsim* website. We entered into lengthy exchanges with Vern and other members of the *Trainz* online fan community, seeking to explain and justify the design direction of *Trainz*. From this point, to clarify expectations of what *Trainz* would be, we started to describe *Trainz* as a virtual model railroad and emphasised the ability of players to create layouts with user-friendly tools. From early 2001, Microsoft also commenced its marketing ramp-up to retail release. This involved increasingly enlisting the existing online train and rail fans into its network. For example, Moorhouse was invited to visit Kuju in England for a preview of *Microsoft Train Simulator*. He then posted his favorable views of *Microsoft Train Simulator* on his website. A number of the fans were flown to the United States for 'Fanstock', an annual event in which the owners of leading fan sites for forthcoming Microsoft games are invited to exclusive previews of the titles in development.

During this period, the pre-release hype for *Microsoft Train Simulator* was considerable. Microsoft was promising that the simulation's open architecture would support the ability for end users to create their own prototype routes and export models that they had created into the game. They were shipping with the game the very tools that the Kuju development team had used to make *Microsoft Train Simulator*. But the actual tools used by development teams generally require a high degree of skill and so do not include a particularly user-friendly interface. However, these tools would be of use to professional development teams in creating commercial add-on packs for *Microsoft Train Simulator*. Consequently, we at Auran anticipated that gamers would find using the *Microsoft Train Simulator* editor a frustrating and time-consuming process rather than an enjoyable activity – thus providing a market niche for *Trainz* with this section of the market. Throughout the ramp-up to the release of *Microsoft Train Simulator*, Microsoft released very little preview content regarding the editor. Additionally, at this stage it was difficult to counter the speculations of the fans as we were not yet in a position to release previews of *Surveyor* and we wanted to see what the *Microsoft Train Simulator* editor delivered.

In the lead-up to the launch of *Microsoft Train Simulator*, Auran issued a press release that announced we would be supporting *Microsoft Train Simulator* by releasing locomotive models that could be imported into and used with the Microsoft simulator. In August 2001, we added a *Microsoft Train Simulator* Add-On Pack area to the *Trainz* website and released a free download of a locomotive model that could be imported into *Microsoft Train Simulator*. It was announced that the *Microsoft Train Simulator* Add-On Packs featuring Auran-produced models would be available for purchase via an online e-commerce system over the next few months.

When *Microsoft Train Simulator* was released in June 2001, the comments and reviews that appeared on train simulator fan websites immediately confirmed the *Trainz* development team's judgment that the editor would not be end user-friendly. Fans were very quickly learning that the editor required a considerable learning curve and was difficult to use. At the time of writing (August 2001), very few fan-produced routes had been released for download on the fan websites. However, a number of talented fan 3D artists had managed to create locomotive models that they had successfully imported into *Microsoft Train Simulator* and made available for download from their websites.

The online fans' response to the difficulties and frustration encountered with using the *Microsoft Train Simulator* editor reinforced Auran's decision to release a user-friendly editor and to support the fans' efforts to create layouts for *Trainz*. By June 2001, *Surveyor* had reached a stage where we could effectively demonstrate its ease of use to fans. It was crucial at this stage to convince the somewhat sceptical fans who were actively participating on the *Trainz* forum that *Surveyor* was user-friendly. A core group of particularly passionate fans were regularly posting their views, opinions, questions and criticisms on the *Trainz* forum and also entering into email dialogues with us. These individuals, emerging as opinion leaders in the *Trainz* online fan community, were largely based overseas, in the United Kingdom, the United States and Canada. However, one of this group, 3801 (the nickname this person uses on the *Trainz* forum), resides in Canberra in Australia. 3801 had established a reputation with the online fans as a knowledgeable train and rail enthusiast, as well as a tentative and constructively critical supporter of the *Trainz* project. We contacted 3801 (we had already been involved in regular email exchanges with him) and invited him to visit the Auran offices in Brisbane for a preview of *Surveyor*. He accepted the offer and was very impressed with the features and user-friendly interface of *Surveyor*. He immediately identified the potential that *Surveyor* offered to the average gamer for creating their own layouts and predicted that, immediately following the release of *Trainz*, many layouts would be available for download from *Trainz* fan websites. He suggested that we may well see virtual model railroad clubs emerge, based on the sharing of layouts.

3801 sought permission to post his impressions of *Surveyor* on both his personal website and on the *Trainz* forum. Auran granted permission with the understanding that certain confidential technical issues could not be publicly commented on, and that he should feel free to express any criticisms that he had of *Surveyor*. His posts about *Surveyor* were very favorable, claiming that it not only met but exceeded Auran's claims for it as a powerful and user-friendly tool. 3801's posts generated considerable interest in and enthusiasm for *Trainz*. Part of his visit to Auran included gaining his input into and participation in Auran's plans to release *Surveyor* and the *Trainz* software generally to a group of the more active and passionate *Trainz* fans for beta testing and feedback purposes. In brief, as described earlier, Auran plans to release the software (at this stage under the terms of a non-disclosure agreement) to a select group of approximately 20 fans who will then use it to create layouts and provide feedback to the *Trainz* development team. We envisage that an outcome of the beta program will also be the creation of layouts that will be made available to purchasers of *Trainz* when it is released.

Subsequent to 3801's visit, we have commenced our ramp-up to the release of *Trainz*. This has included releasing preview in-game screenshots and movies of the game on the website. This includes an episodic series of movies demonstrating how *Surveyor* can be used to create layouts. Combined with the recent release of the free locomotive download for *Microsoft Train Simulator* and the announcement of our plan to release add-on packs for *Microsoft Train Simulator* in the near future, the preview material is attracting rapidly increasing traffic to the *Trainz* website. Forum activity and emails seeking further details about *Trainz* have significantly increased over the past few weeks. One of the challenges confronting Auran is managing and maintaining our level of interaction with a rapidly growing fan community, particularly in the period immediately prior to and just after retail release. We have established an expectation with the community that this interaction will continue. However, we are finding that the core community of active and passionate fans is assisting us by answering many of the questions raised by new visitors to the forum.

At the time of writing (August 2001), we are in the process of finalising the details of our beta test program that we anticipate will provide invaluable feedback to the *Trainz* development team. Auran is also entering into discussions with fan groups who are exploring the possibility of turning their activities into commercial ventures.

In this chapter, I have barely scratched the surface of the complex and heterogeneous materials that constitutes the network of relations that defines *Trainz*. For example, technological objects, processes and sites such as the website, email, chat, the working and design of the software I have simply identified with the noun *Surveyor*. I have not even touched on the story of *Surveyor*, involving as it does the daily work practices of the designers, programmers and artists. The work of the Auran online services team which builds and maintains the technological infrastructure and processes that support the interactions among the fans and between the fans and Auran is also not visible in this account. Added to this is the complex series of commercial transactions and negotiations with software publishers and model railroad companies without which *Trainz* would not emerge into sustainable material existence. I could go on, adding to the series of materials, actors, interactions and relations that constitute and are developing in the process of building *Trainz*. Such technologies and processes do not stand outside the network determining the social relations; they are part of the very materials that constitute the network. Likewise, the gamer as audience and as co-creator does not stand outside this network of relations; they emerge as a moment from them.

The relationship between Auran and the *Trainz* fans also emerges from this network of relations. This dynamic suggests that gamers are increasingly co-creators. As we have seen, they are a vital element in the network that defines *Trainz*. The fate of *Surveyor* and the potential for *Trainz* to grow into a successful online game network, enrolling the attention, passion, energy and dollars of other gamers, very much depends on what the fans will do with *Surveyor* when they have it in their hands. How will they transform it? How will *Surveyor* transform their activities as online gamer fans? Will they take it up and play with it to extend the *Trainz* network? Who is doing the enrolling and who is the enrolled in this process? The answer very much depends on who is doing the asking and what their position in the network is. The gamer as co-creator is a social moment and a potential which emerges from this dynamic and materially heterogeneous network.

Does this emergence of a new gamer audience with potentially more active practices indicate a shift in power between producers and consumers of new media product? Are, for example, the game development companies increasingly sharing control with the end users – the players? Is this shift of control moving into the production process itself? How are the development companies and the fans seeking to manage and exploit these emerging relationships? How are academic researchers positioned by and within these relations? What are the implications and uptakes of these shifts to our understanding of audience in the context of new media such as computer games? Do these trends suggest an even closer engagement and relation between gamers and game development companies? Or is it simply 'business as usual', with the activities of consumers being increasingly seduced and incorporated within the networks of corporate capital? It has been beyond the scope of this chapter to answer all these questions, but this report from the netface shows that the provider-audience relation is an increasingly complex and multifaceted one.

Reference

Jenkins, H. (1993) *Textual Poachers: Television Fans and Participatory Culture.* London: Methuen.

17 INTERACTIVE AUDIENCES?

Henry Jenkins

'You've got fifteen seconds. Impress me.'

An advertisement for Applebox Productions depicts the new youth consumer: his scraggly dishwater blonde hair hangs down into his glaring eyes,
his mouth is turned down into a challenging sneer, and his finger posed over
the remote. One false move and he'll zap us. No longer a couch potato, he
determines what, when, and how he watches media. He is a media consumer, perhaps even a media fan, but he is also a media producer,
distributor, publicist, and critic. He's the poster child for the new interactive audience.

The advertisement takes for granted what cultural studies researchers
struggled to establish throughout the 1980s and 1990s – that audiences
were active, critically aware, and discriminating. Yet, this advertisement
promises that Applebox productions has developed new ways to overcome
his resistance and bring advertising messages to this scowling teen's
attention. The interactive audience is not autonomous, still operating
alongside powerful media industries.

If the current media environment makes visible the once invisible work of
media spectatorship, it is wrong to assume that we are somehow being
liberated through improved media technologies. Rather than talking about
interactive technologies, we should document the interactions that occur
amongst media consumers, between media consumers and media texts, and

Henry Jenkins (2002) Interactive audiences? in D. Harries (ed.) *The New Media Book*. London: British Film Institute, pp. 157–70. Reprinted by kind permission of the British Film
Institute.

between media consumers and media producers. The new participatory culture is taking shape at the intersection between three trends:

1 New tools and technologies enable consumers to archive, annotate, appropriate, and recirculate media content.
2 A range of subcultures promote Do-It-Yourself (DIY) media production, a discourse that shapes how consumers have deployed those technologies.
3 Economic trends favoring the horizontally integrated media conglomerates encourage the flow of images, ideas, and narratives across multiple media channels and demand more active modes of spectatorship.

It would be naive to assume that powerful conglomerates will not protect their own interests as they enter this new media marketplace, but at the same time, audiences are gaining greater power and autonomy as they enter into the new knowledge culture. The interactive audience is more than a marketing concept and less than 'semiotic democracy'.

Collective Intelligence

In *Collective Intelligence*, Pierre Levy offers a compelling vision of the new 'knowledge space', or what he calls 'the cosmopedia', which *might* emerge as citizens more fully realize the potentials of the new media environment. Levy explores how the Web's 'deterritorialization' of knowledge might enable broader participation in decision-making, new modes of citizenship and community, and the reciprocal exchange of information. Levy draws a productive distinction between organic social groups (families, clans, tribes), organized social groups (nations, institutions, religions and corporations) and self-organized groups (such as the virtual communities of the Web). He links the emergence of the new knowledge space to the breakdown of geographic constraints on communication, of the declining loyalty of individuals to organized groups, and of the diminished power of nation-states to command the exclusive loyalty of their citizens. The new knowledge communities will be voluntary, temporary and tactical affiliations, defined through common intellectual enterprises and emotional investments. Members may shift from one community to another as their interests and needs change and they may belong to more than one community at the same time. Yet, they are held together through the mutual production and reciprocal exchange of knowledge. As Levy explains:

Not only does the cosmopedia make available to the collective intellect all of the pertinent knowledge available to it at a given moment, but it also serves as a site of collective discussion, negotiation, and development. ... Unanswered questions will create tension within cosmopedic space, indicating regions where invention and innovation are required.[1]

Online fan communities are the most fully realized versions of Levy's cosmopedia, expansive self-organizing groups focused around the collective production, debate and circulation of meanings, interpretations and fantasies in response to various artifacts of contemporary popular culture. Fan communities have long defined their memberships through affinities rather than localities. Fandoms were virtual communities, 'imagined' and 'imagining' communities, long before the introduction of networked computers.[2] The history of science fiction fandom might illustrate how knowledge communities emerged. Hugo Gernsbeck, the pulp magazine editor who has been credited with helping to define science fiction as a distinctive genre in the 1920s and 1930s, was also a major advocate of radio as a participatory medium. Gemsbeck saw science fiction as a means of fostering popular awareness of contemporary scientific breakthroughs at a moment of accelerating technological development.[3] The letter column of Gernsbeck's *Astounding Stories* became a forum where lay people could debate scientific theories and assess new technologies. Using the published addresses, early science fiction fans formed an informal postal network, circulating letters and amateur publications. Later, conventions facilitated the face-to-face contact between fans from across the country and around the world. Many significant science fiction writers emerged from fandom. Given this history, every reader was understood to be a potential writer and many fans aspired to break into professional publication; fan ideas influenced commercially distributed works at a time when science fiction was still understood predominantly as a micro-genre aimed at a small but passionate niche market. This reciprocality between readers, writers and editors set expectations as science fiction spread into film and television. *Star Trek* fans were, from the start, an activist audience, lobbying to keep its series on the air and later advocating specific changes in the programme content to better reflect its own agendas. *Star Trek* fandom, in turn, was a model for other fan communities to create forums for debating interpretations, networks for circulating creative works and channels for lobbying the producers. Fans were early adopters of digital technologies. Within the scientific and military institutions where the Internet was first introduced, science fiction has long been a literature of choice.[4]

Consequently, the slang and social practices employed on the early bulletin boards were often directly modeled on science fiction fandom. Mailing lists focused on fan topics took their place alongside discussions of technological or scientific issues. In many ways, cyberspace is fandom writ large. The reconstitution of these fandoms as digital enclaves did not come without strenuous efforts to overcome the often overtly hostile reception that fan women received from the early Internet's predominantly male population. Operating outside those technical institutions, many female fans lacked computer access and lacked technical literacy. Heated debates erupted at conventions as fans were angered at being left behind when old fan friends moved online. At the same time fan communities helped many women make the transition to cyberspace; the group ensured that valued members learned to use the new technologies.[5]

Nancy Baym has discussed the important functions of talk within online soap fandom: 'Fans share knowledge of the show's history, in part, because the genre demands it. Any soap has broadcast more material than any single fan can remember.[6] Fans inform each other about programme history or recent developments they may have missed. The fan community pools its knowledge because no single fan can know everything necessary to appreciate the series fully. Levy distinguishes between shared knowledge (which would refer to information known by all members of a community) and collective intelligence (which describes knowledge available to all members of a community). Collective intelligence expands a community's productive capacity because it frees individual members from the limitations of their memory and enables the group to act upon a broader range of expertise. As Levy writes, within a knowledge community, 'no one knows everything, everyone know something, all knowledge resides in humanity'.[7] Baym argues:

> A large group of fans can do what even the most committed single fan cannot: accumulate, retain, and continually recirculate unprecedented amounts of relevant information. ... [Net list] participants collaboratively provide all with the resources to get more story from the material, enhancing many members' soap readings and pleasures.[8]

Soap talk, Baym notes, allows people to 'show off for one another' their various competencies while making individual expertise more broadly available. Fans are motivated by epistemaphilia – not not simply a pleasure in knowing but a pleasure in exchanging knowledge. Baym argues that fans see the exchange of speculations and evaluations of soaps as a means of 'comparing, refining, and negotiating understandings of their socioemotional environment'.[9] Fan speculations may, on the surface, seem to be simply a deciphering of the aired material but increasingly, speculation involves fans in the production of new fantasies, broadening the field of meanings that circulate around the primary text. For example, in the early 1990s, alt. rec.arts.twin-peaks, a group devoted to discussing David Lynch's cult mystery/soap opera series, sought to 'break the code and solve the crime', that is, to successfully predict future revelations about the Laura Palmer murder and thus to arrive at the 'truth' of the series.[10] But as each member mobilized and interpreted the series 'evidence', they introduced a range of different potential narratives, centring on alternative assumptions about 'who done it' and how Laura's death fit within larger schemes. Their ability to recognize previously undiscovered narrative possibilities enlarged their pleasure in watching *Twin Peaks* and the group actively recruited new members to expand the range of interpretations. This collective exchange of knowledge cannot be fully contained by previous sources of power – 'bureaucratic hierarchies (based on static forms of writing), media monarchies (surfing the television and media systems), and international economic networks (based on the telephone and real-time technologies' – which depended on maintaining tight control over the flow of information. The dynamic, collective and reciprocal nature of these exchanges undermines traditional forms of expertise and destabilizes attempts to establish a scriptural economy in which some meanings are more valuable than others.[11] The old commodity space was defined through various forms of decontextualization, including the alienation of labor, the uprooting of images from larger cultural traditions, the demographic fragmentation of the audience, the disciplining of knowledge, and the disconnect between media producers and consumers. The new information space involves multiple and unstable forms of recontextualization. The value of any bit of information increases through social interaction. Commodities are a limited good and their exchange necessarily creates or enacts inequalities. But meaning is a shared and constantly renewable resource and its circulation can create and revitalize social ties.

How computers changed fandom

For Levy, the introduction of high-speed networked computing constituted an epistemological turning point in the development of collective intelligence. If fandom was already a knowledge culture well before the Internet, then how did transplanting its practices into the digital environment alter the fan community? The new digital environment increases the speed of fan communication, resulting in what Matthew Hills calls 'just in time fandom'.[12] If fans once traded ideas through the mails, they now see the postal service as too slow – 'snail mail' – to satisfy their expectations of immediate response. Hills explains, 'the practices of fandom have become increasingly enmeshed with the rhythms and temporalities of broadcasting, so that fans now go online to discuss new episodes immediately after the episode's transmission time or even during ad-breaks perhaps in order to demonstrate the 'timeliness' and responsiveness of their devotion'.[13] Where fans might have raced to the phone to talk to a close friend, they can now access a much broader range of perspectives by going online. Hills worries that the broadcast schedule may be determining what can be discussed and when. This expectation of timeliness complicates the global expansion of the fan community, with time lags in the distribution of cultural goods across national markets hampering full participation from fans that will receive the same programme months or even years later. International fans often complain that they are additionally disadvantaged because their first time experience of the episodes is 'spoiled' by learning too much from the online discussions. The digital media also alters the scope of communication. Fandoms centring on Asian popular culture, such as Japanese anime or Hong Kong action films, powerfully exploit the Internet's global reach. Japanese fans collaborate with American consumers to ensure the underground circulation of these cultural products and to explain cultural references, genre traditions and production histories.[14] Anime fans regularly translate and post the schedule of Japanese television so that international fans can identify and negotiate access to interesting programmes. American fans have learned Japanese, often teaching each other outside a formal educational context, in order to participate in grassroots projects to subtitle anime films or to translate manga. This is a new cosmopolitanism – knowledge sharing on a global scale.

As the community enlarges and as reaction time shortens, fandom becomes much more effective as a platform for consumer activism. Fans can quickly mobilize grassroots efforts to save programmes or protest unpopular developments. New fandoms emerge rapidly on the Web – in some cases before media products actually reach the market. As early participants spread news about emergent fandoms, supporters quickly develop the infrastructure for supporting critical dialogue, producing annotated programme guides, providing regular production updates, and creating original fan stories and artwork. The result has been an enormous proliferation of fan websites and discussion lists. Kirsten Pullen estimates, for example, that as of June 2000 there were more than 33,000 fan websites listed in the Yahoo! Web Directory, dealing with individual performers, programmes and films.[15] One portal, Fan Fiction on the Web, lists more than 300 different media texts that have generated at least some form of fan fiction, representing a much broader array of genres than previously suspected.[16] As fandom diversifies, it moves from cult status towards the cultural mainstream, with more Internet users engaged in some form of fan activity. This increased visibility and cultural centrality has been a mixed blessing for a community used to speaking from the margins. The speed and frequency of communication may intensify the social bonds within the fan community. In the past, fans inhabited a 'week-end only world', seeing each other in large numbers only a few times a year – at conventions.[17] Now, fans may interact daily, if not hourly, online. Geographically isolated fans can feel much more connected to the fan community and home-ridden fans enjoy a new level of acceptance. Yet, fandom's expanded scope can leave fans feeling alienated from the expanding numbers of strangers entering their community. This rapid expansion outraces any effort to socialize new members. Online fan discussion lists often bring together groups who functioned more or less autonomously offline and have radically different responses to the aired material. Flame wars erupt as their taken-for-granted interpretive and evaluative norms rub against each other. In some cases, fans can negotiate these conflicts by pulling to a metalevel and exploring the basis for the different interpretations. More often, the groups splinter into narrower interests, pushing some participants from public debates into smaller and more private mailing lists. Levy describes a pedagogical process through which a knowledge community develops a set of ethical standards and articulates mutual goals. Even on a scale much smaller than Levy's global village, fandoms often have difficulty arriving at such a consensus. Andre MacDonald has described fandom in terms of various disputes – between male and female fans, between fans with different assumptions about the desired degree of closeness of the producers and stars, between fans who seek to police the production of certain fantasies and fans who assert their freedom from such constraints, between different generations of fans, and so forth.[18] MacDonald depicts a community whose utopian aspirations are constantly being tested against unequal experiences, levels of expertise, access to performers and community resources, control over community institutions, and degrees of investment in fan traditions and norms. Moreover, as Nancy Baym suggests, the desire to avoid such conflicts can result in an artificial consensus which shuts down the desired play with alternative meanings.[19] Networked computing has also transformed fan production. Web publication of fan fiction, for example, has almost entirely displaced printed zines. Fanzines arose as the most efficient means of circulating fan writing.[20] Fan editors charged only the costs of reproduction, seeing zines as a vehicle for distributing stories and not as a source of income. In some fandoms, circuits developed for loaning individually photocopied stories. In other cases, readers and editors came to see zines as aesthetic artifacts, insisting on high quality reproduction and glossy colour covers. Fans have increasingly turned to the Web to lower the costs of production and to expand their reading public. Fans are also developing archives of older zine stories, helping to connect newer fans with their history. The higher visibility of fan fiction on the Web has inspired many new writers to try their hand and spread the practice to new fandoms, yet older fans complain of the lack of editing and nurturing of emerging talents. In several cases, fans have organized themselves to map out alternative story arcs and to script their own episodes when series were cancelled or took unwelcome turns. Digital technologies have also enabled new forms of fan cultural production. Elena Garfinkle and Eric Zimmerman have documented the emergence of Kitsekae or digital paperdolls, that can be dressed and undressed by the user and programmed to perform simple actions. The Kitsekae become vehicles for erotic play and fantasy – primarily among anime fans.[21] Similarly, game fans have produced short animated films using game engines, developed to enable *Quake* enthusiasts to record and replay their game play. Fans call these new works machinema after a Japanese word that refers to puppetry.[22] Game avatars become, in effect, puppets that enable fan artists to tell their own stories. The scrapbook function in *The Sims* has similarly enabled new forms of fan fiction, as fans play the game in order, to create the images necessary to illustrate their stories. In some cases, they also develop 'skins' designed to represent favourite television or comicbook characters. Fan artists have been part of the much larger history of amateur film and video production. George Lucas and Steven Spielberg, were themselves amateur film-makers as teenagers, producing low-budget horror or science fiction movies. *Star Wars*, in turn, has inspired super 8 film-makers since its release in the early 1970s. As the video cassette recorder became more widely available, fans re-edited series footage into music videos, using popular music to encapsulate the often unarticulated emotions of favourite characters.[23] As fan video makers have become more sophisticated, some fan artists have produced whole new storylines by patching together original dialogue.

The World Wide Web is a powerful distribution channel, giving what were once home-movies a surprising degree of public visibility. Publicity materials surface while these amateur films are still in production, most of the films boast lavish movie posters, and many of them include downloadable trailers to attract would-be viewers impatient with download times. *Star Wars* fans were among the first to embrace these new technologies, producing at last count more than 300 Web movies.[24] These fan film-makers have used home computers to duplicate effects that Lucasfilm had spent a fortune to achieve several decades earlier; many fan films create their own lightsabre or space battles. Some of these fan film-makers have received offers for professional projects or had their films screened at international film festivals. When Amazon.com offered videos of one favourite amateur *Star Wars* production, *George Lucas in Love*, it outsold *The Phantom Menace* during its first week in circulation. Amateur film culture has already made an impact on the commercial mainstream. Spike Jonze, the director of *Being John Malkovich*, for example, got his start making amateur films within the skateboard subculture. Similarly, MTV's *Jackass* took its inspiration from the Web-based distribution of amateur stunt films, while *Celebrity Death Match* adopts an aesthetic remarkably similar to action figure cinema. In the future, amateur productions may initiate many innovations in popular culture which gain higher visibility as they are pulled into mainstream media, much as the fans appropriate and recirculate materials from commercial culture.

Knowledge culture meets commodity culture

Levy distinguishes between four potential sources of power – nomadic mobility, control over territory, ownership over commodities, and mastery over knowledge – and suggests a complex set of interactions and negotiations between them. The emergent knowledge cultures never fully escape the influence of the commodity culture, any more than commodity culture can totally function outside the constraints of territoriality. But knowledge cultures will, he predicts, gradually alter the ways that commodity culture operates. Nowhere is that transition clearer than within the culture industries, where the commodities that circulate become resources for the production of meaning: 'The distinctions between authors and readers, producers and spectators, creators and interpretations will blend to form a reading–writing continuum.'[25]

Creative activity, he suggests, will shift from the production of texts or the regulation of meanings towards the development of a dynamic environment, 'a collective event that implies the recipients, transforms interpreters into actors, enables interpretation to enter the loop with collective action'.[26] Room for participation and improvisation are being built into new media franchises. Kurt Lancaster, for example, has examined how commercial works (including computer, role-playing and card games) surrounding the cult science fiction series *Babylon 5* facilitate a diverse range of fan performances, allowing fans to immerse themselves in the fantasy universe.[27] Cult works were once discovered; now they are being consciously produced, designed to provoke fan interactions. The producers of *Xena*, for example, were fully aware that some fans wanted to read Xena and Gabrielle as lesbian lovers and thus began to consciously weave 'subtext' into the episodes. As Levy explains, 'The recipients of the open work are invited to fill in the blanks, choose among possible meanings, confront the divergences among their interpretations.'[28]

To be marketable the new cultural works will have to provoke and reward collective meaning production through elaborate back stories unresolved enigmas, excess information, and extratextual expansions of the program universe.[29] There has been a marked increase in the serialization of American television, the emergence of more complex appeals to programme history, the development of more intricate story arcs and cliffhangers, over the past decade. To some degree, these aesthetic shifts can be linked to new reception practices enabled by the home archiving of videos, net discussion lists and Web programme guides. These new technologies provide the information infrastructure necessary to sustain a richer form of television content, while these programmes reward the enhanced competencies of fan communities. Television producers are increasingly knowledgeable about their fan communities, often courting their support through networked computing. *Babylon 5* producers J. Michael Straczinski went online daily, responding to questions about his complex and richly developed narrative, sometimes actively engaging with flame wars with individual fans as well as conducting what he saw as a continuing seminar on the production of genre television.[30] While Straczinski sought to be more accessible to fans, he found it difficult to shed his authority or escape a legal and economic system designed, in part, to protect corporate interests from audience appropriation. His lawyers warned him that he would have to leave the group if there was danger that he would be exposed to fan speculations that might hold him hostage to potential plagiarism suits. While Straczinski is perhaps unique in the degree of his exposure to fans, other producers have shown a similar awareness of online fan discourse. For example, when the WB Network postponed the season finale of *Buffy the Vampire Slayer* in the wake of the Columbine shootings, producer Josh Whedon made a notorious public call for Canadian fans to 'bootleg that puppy' and distribute it via the Web to American viewers. Fans, in turn, rallied to Whedon's defence when the Religious Right launched a letter-writing campaign against the introduction of a lesbian relationship involving series regulars.[31] By contrast, *Survivor* producer Mark Burnett engaged in an active disinformation campaign to thwart audience efforts to predict the winner of its million-dollar competition, burying false leads in the official website awaiting discovery by fan hackers. When long time World Wrestling Federation announcer Jerry Lawler was fired, he brought his side of his disputes with Vince McMahon directly to online fans. For many media producers, who still operate within the old logic of the commodity culture, fandom represents a potential loss of control over their intellectual property. The efforts of the recording industry to dismantle Napster demonstrated that the traditional media companies were prepared to spend massive sums in legal action against new forms of grassroots distribution.[32] Television producers, film studios, and book publishers have been equally aggressive in issuing 'cease and desist' letters to fan websites that transcribe programme dialogue or reproduce unauthorized images. If new media have made visible various forms of fan participation and production, then these legal battles demonstrate the power still vested in media ownership.

The horizontal integration of the entertainment industry – and the emergent logic of synergy – depends on the circulation of intellectual properties across media outlets.[33] Transmedia promotion presumes a more active spectator who can and will follow these media flows. Such marketing strategies promote a sense of affiliation with and immersion in fictional worlds. The media industry exploits these intense feelings through the marketing of ancillary goods from t-shirts to games with promises of enabling a deeper level of involvement with the programme content. However, attempts to regulate intellectual property undercut the economic logic of media convergence, sending fans contradictory messages about how they are supposed to respond to commercial culture.[34] Rosemary Coombes and Andrew Herman have documented intensifying legal and political skirmishes between corporate lawyers and consumers. Many fan webmasters post their 'cease and desist' letters in order to shame the media industries: shutting down grassroots promotional efforts results in negative publicity.[35] Often, the conflict boils down to an issue of who is authorized to speak for a series, as when a Fox television executive justifies the closing of *Simpsons* fansites: 'We have an official website with network approved content and these people don't work for us.' Levy sees industry panic over interactive audiences as short-sighted: 'by preventing the knowledge space from becoming autonomous, they deprive the circuits of commodity space ... of an extraordinary source of energy'. The knowledge culture, he suggests, serves as the 'invisible and intangible engine' for the circulation and exchange of commodities.[36] The online book dealer, Amazon.com, has linked bookselling to the fostering of online book culture. Readers are encouraged to post critical responses to specific works or to compile lists of their favourite books. Their associates programme creates a powerful niche marketing system: Amazon patrons are offered royalties for every sale made on the basis of links from their sites. Similarly, the sports network, ESPN, sponsors a fantasy baseball league, a role-playing activity in which sports fans form teams, trade players and score points based on the real-world performance of various athletes.[37] Attempts to link consumers directly into the production and marketing of media content are variously described as 'permission-based marketing', 'relationship marketing' or 'viral marketing' and are increasingly promoted as the model for how to sell goods, cultural and otherwise, in an interactive environment. As one noted industry guide explains, 'Marketing in an interactive world is a collaborative process with the marketer helping the consumer to buy and the consumer helping the marketer to sell.'[38] Researchers are finding that fandom and other knowledge communities foster a sense of passionate affiliation or brand loyalty that insures the longevity of particular product lines.[39] In viral marketing, such affiliations become self-replicating as marketers create content that consumers want to actively circulate among their friends. Even unauthorized and vaguely subversive appropriations can spread advertising messages, as occurred through Internet spoofs of the Budweiser 'whazzup' commercials.

Building brand loyalty requires more than simply co-opting grassroots activities back into the commodity culture. Successful media producers are becoming more adept at monitoring and serving audience interests. The games industry, which sees itself as marketing interactive experiences rather than commodities, has been eager to broaden consumer participation and strengthen the sense of affiliation that players feel towards their games. Lucas Arts has integrated would-be *Star Wars* gamers into the design team for the development of their massively multi-player online game. A webpage was created early in the design process and ideas under consideration were posted for fan feedback.[40] Maxis, the company that managers the *Sims* franchise, encourages the grassroots production and trading of 'skins' (new character identities), props and architectural strucutres, even programming code. Sims creator Will Wright refers to his product as a 'sandbox' or 'doll house', where consumers can play out their own stories. Ultimately, Wright predicts, two-thirds of *Sims* content will come from consumers.[41]

It remains to be seen, however, whether these new corporate strategies of collaboration and consultation with the emerging knowledge communities will displace the legal structures of the old commodity culture. How far will media companies be willing to go to remain in charge of their content or to surf the information flow? In an age of broadband delivery, will television producers see fans less as copyright infringers and more as active associates and niche marketers? Will global media moguls collaborate with grassroots communities, such as the anime fans, to ensure that their products get visible in the lucrative American market?

From jammers to bloggers

In his 1993 essay 'Culture Jamming: Hacking, Slashing and Sniping in the Empire of Signs,' Mark Dery documented emerging tactics of grassroots resistance (media hacking, informational warfare, terror-art and guerilla semiotics') to 'an ever more intrusive, instrumental technoculture whose operant mode is the manufacture of consent through the manipulation of symbols'.[42] In Citizens Band Radio slang, the term 'jamming' refers to efforts to 'introduce noises into the signal as it passes from transmitter to receiver'. Dery's essay records an important juncture in the history of DIY media. Over the past several decades, emerging technologies – ranging from the photocopier to the home computer and the video cassette recorder – have granted viewers greater control over media flows, enabled activists to reshape and recirculate media content, lowered the costs of production, and paved the way for new grassroots networks.

Many of the groups Dery describes, such as Adbusters, ACT UP, Negativeland, The Barbie Liberation Army, Paper Tiger Television and the Electronic Disturbance Community, would happily embrace his 'culture jammer' banner. Yet Dery over-reached in describing all forms of DIY media as 'jamming'. These new technologies would support and sustain a range of different cultural and political projects, some overtly oppositional, others more celebratory, yet all reflecting a public desire to participate within, rather than simply consume, media. Dery, for example, distorts the fan community concept of 'slash' when he uses it to refer to 'any form of jamming in which tales told for mass consumption are perversely reworked'. Culture jammers want to opt out of media consumption and promote a purely negative and reactive conception of popular culture. Fans, on the other hand, see unrealized potentials in popular culture and want to broaden audience participation. Fan culture is dialogic rather than disruptive, affective more than ideological, and collaborative rather than confrontational. Culture jammers want to 'jam' the dominant media, while poachers want to appropriate their content, imagining a more democratic, responsive and diverse style of popular culture. Jammers want to destroy media power, while poachers want a share of it. Returning to this same terrain at the end of the decade, it is clear that new media technologies have profoundly altered the relations between media producers and consumers.

Both culture jammers and fans have gained greater visibility as they have deployed the Web for community building, intellectual exchange, cultural distribution and media activism. Some sectors of the media industries have embraced active audiences as an extension of their marketing power, have sought greater feedback from their fans, and have incorporated viewer generated content into their design processes. Other sectors have sought to contain or silence the emerging knowledge culture. The new technologies broke down old barriers between media consumption and media production. The old rhetoric of opposition and co-optation assumed a world where consumers had little direct power to shape media content and where there were enormous barriers to entry into the marketplace, whereas the new digital environment expands their power to archive, annotate, appropriate and recirculate media products. Levy describes a world where grassroots communication is not a momentary disruption of the corporate signal but the routine way that the new media system operates: 'Until now we have only reappropriated speech in the service of revolutionary movements, crises, cures, exceptional acts of creation. What would a normal, calm, established appropriation of speech be like?'[43] Perhaps, rather than talking about culture jammers, we might speak of bloggers. The term 'blog' is short for weblog, a new form of personal and subcultural expression involving summarizing and linking to other sites. In some cases, bloggers actively deconstruct pernicious claims or poke fun at other sites; in other cases, they form temporary tactical alliances with other bloggers or with media producers to ensure that important messages get more widely circulated. These bloggers have become important grassroots intermediaries – facilitators, not jammers, of the signal flow. Blogging describes a communication process, not an ideological position.

As Levy writes:

> The new proletariat will only free itself by uniting, by decategorizing itself, by forming alliances with those whose work is similar to its own (once again, nearly everyone), by bringing to the foreground the activities they have been practicing in shadow, by assuming responsibility – globally, centrally, explicitly – for the production of collective intelligence.[44]

Bloggers take knowledge in their own hands, enabling the successful navigation within and between these emerging knowledge cultures. One can see such behaviour as co-optation into commodity culture in so far as it sometimes collaborates with corporate interests, but one can also see it as increasing the diversity of media culture, providing opportunities for greater inclusiveness, and making commodity culture more responsive to consumers. In an era marked both by the expanded corporate reach of the commodity culture and the emerging importance of grassroots knowledge cultures, consumer power may now be best exercised by blogging rather than jamming media signals.

Notes

1   Pierre Levy (1997) *Collective Intelligence: Mankind's Emerging World in Cyberspace*. Cambridge: Perseus, p.217.
2   The phrase 'imagined community' comes from Benedict Anderson (1991) *Imagined Communities: Reflections on the Origin and Spread of Nationalism*. New York: Verso. Levy op cit., p. 125, introduces the concept of an 'imaging community'.
3   A fuller account of Gemsbeck's role in the development of science fiction fandom can be found in Andrew Ross (1991) *Strange Weather: Culture, Science and Technology in the Age of Limits*. New York: Verso. For a fuller account of contemporary literary SF fandom, see Camile Bacon-Smith (2000) *Science Fiction Culture*. Philadelphia: University of Pennsylvania Press.
4   Sherry Turkle (1984) *The Second Self: Computers and the Human Spirit*. New York: Touchstone. provides some glimpse of the centrality of science fiction in that early hacker culture, as does my study of *Star Trek* fans at MIT in J. Tulloch and H. Jenkins, (1995) *Science Fiction Audiences: Watching Doctor Who and Star Trek*. London and New York: Routledge.
5   Susan J. Clerc (1996) Estrogen brigades and 'big tits' threads: media fandom online and off, in Lynn Cherney and Elizabeth Reba Weise (eds) *Wired Women: Gender and New Realities in Cyberspace*. Seattle: Seal.
6   Nancy Baym (1998) Talking about soaps: communication practices in a computer-mediated fan culture, in Cheryl Harris and Alison Alexander (eds) *Theorizing Fandom: Fans, Subculture, and Identity*. New York: Hampton Press.
7   Levy, op cit., p. 20.
8   Baym, op cit., pp. 115–16.
9   Ibid., p. 127.
10 Henry Jenkins (1995) 'Do you enjoy making the rest of us feel stupid': alt.tv.twinpeaks, the trickster author and viewer mastery, in David Lavery (ed.) *Full of Secrets: Critical Approaches to Twin Peaks*. Detroit: Wayne State University Press.
11 For a useful discussion of the ways that the Net is challenging traditional forms of expertise, see Peter Walsh, That withered paradigm: the Web, the expert and the information hegemony, http://media-in-transition.mit.edu
12 Hills, M. (2002) *Fan Cultures*. London: Routledge.
13 Ibid.

14 For an overview of anime and its fans, see Susan J. Napier (2001) *Anime from Akira to Princess Mononoke: Experiencing Contemporary Japanese Animation.* New York: Palgrave.

15 Kristen Pullen (2000) I-Love-Xena.Com: creating online fan communities, in David Gauntlett (ed.) *Web.Studies: Rewiring Media Studies for the Digital Age.* London: Arnold. See also Sharon Cumberland, Private uses of cyberspace: women, desire, and fan culture, http://media-in-transition.mit.edu

16 Fan Fiction on the Net, http://members.aol.com/KSNicholas/fanfic/slash.html

17 The phrase 'Week End Only World' is discussed in the concluding chapter of Henry Jenkins (1991) *Textual Poachers: Television Fans and Participatory Culture.* New York: Routledge.

18 Andre McDonald (1998) Uncertain utopia: science fiction media fandom and computer mediated communication, in Cheryl Harris and Alison Alexander (eds) *Theorizing Fandom: Fans, Subculture, and Identity.* New York: Hampton Press.

19 Nancy Baym (1999) *Tune In, Log On: Soaps, Fandom and Online Community.* New York: Corwin.

20 Stephen Duncombe (1997) *Notes from Underground: Zines and the Politics of Alternative Culture.* New York: Verso.

21 Elena Garfinkle and Eric Zimmerman (1998) Technologies of undressing: the digital paperdolls of KISS, in Katie Salens (ed.) *Beyond the Object*, Zed.5, Center for Design Studies, Virginia Commonwealth University.

22 Katie Salens (2001) Scattergun edit: telefragging monster movies, in Bart Cheever and Nick Constant (eds) *Dfilm.* Cambridge: MIT Press.

23 For a fuller discussion of fan video practices, see *Textual Poachers*. For a larger context on amateur media production, see Patricia R. Zimmermann (1995) *Reel Families: A Social History of Amateur Film.* Indianapolis: Indiana University Press.

24 Henry Jenkins (2001) *Quentin Tarantino's Star Wars?*: digital cinema, media convergence and participatory culture, in Bart Cheever and Nick Constant (eds) *Dfilm.* Cambridge: MIT Press.

25 Levy, op cit., p. 121.

26 Ibid., p. 123.

27 Kurt Lancaster (2001) *Interacting with Babylon 5: Fan Performances in a Media Universe.* Austin: University of Texas Press.

28 Levy, op cit., p. 125.

29 Amelie Hastie (2001) Proliferating television in the market and in the know, Console-ing Passions, Bristol, 6 July.

30 Lancaster, op cit., p. 26. See also Alan Wexelblat, (2002) An auteur in the age of the Internet, in Henry Jenkins, Tara McPherson and Jane Shattuc (eds) *Hop on Pop: The Politics and Pleasures of Popular Culture.* Durham: Duke University Press.

31 Allison McCracken (2001) Bronzers for a smut-filled environment: reading fans reading sexual identity at Buffy.com, Console-ing Passions, Bristol, 6 July.

32 David Spitz (2001) *Contested Codes: Toward a Social History of Napster*, Masters thesis, Comparative Media Studies Program, MIT.

33 See, for example, Eileen Meehan (1991) Holy commodity fetish, Batman!': the political economy of a political intertext, in Roberta Pearson and William Uricchio (eds) *The Many Lives of the Batman: Critical Approaches to a Superhero and His Media*. New York: Routledge.

34 This formulation of the issue was inspired by Sara Gwenllian Jones (2001) Conflicts of interest? The folkloric and legal status of cult TV characters in online fan culture, Society for Cinema Studies Conference, Washington DC, 26 May.

35 Rosemary Coombes and Andrew Herman (2001) Defending toy dolls and maneuvering toy soldiers: trademarks, consumer politics and corporate accountability on the World Wide Web, presented at MIT Communication Forum, 12 April.

36 Levy, op cit., p. 237.

37 For example, see Amy Jo Kim (2000) *Community, Building on the Web: Secret Strategies for Successful Online Communities*. (Berkeley, CA: Peachpit Press).

38 Don Peppers (1999) Introduction, in Seth Godon, *Permission Marketing: Turning Strangers into Friends, and Friends into Customers*. New York: Simon & Schuster, p. 12.

39 Robert V. Kozinets (2001) Utopian enterprise: articulating the meanings of Star Trek's culture of consumption, *Journal of Consumer Research*, June http://www.journals.uchicago.edu/JCR/journal/

40 Kurt Squire, Wars galaxies: a case study in participatory design, *Joystick 101*, www.joystick101.org, forthcoming.

41 Personal interview, April 2001.

42 Mark Dery (1993) *Culture Jamming: Hacking, Slashing and Sniping in the Empire of Signs* (Open Magazine Pamphlet Series, 1993) http://web.nwe.u-fl.edu/~mlaffey/cultiam1.html

43 Levy, op cit., p. 171.

44 Ibid., pp.36–7.

INDEX

MEDIA AND AUDIENCES

Ross and Nightingale

- How has the concept of 'the audience' changed over the past 50 years?
- How do audiences become producers and not just consumers of media texts?
- How are new media affecting the ways in which audiences are researched?

The audience has been a central concept in both in media and cultural studies for some considerable time, not least because there seems little point exploring forms of increasingly global communication in terms of their content if the targets of media messages are not also the focus of study. This book ranges across a wide literature, taking both a chronological as well as thematic approach, in order to explore the ways in which the audience, as an analytical concept has changed, as well as examining the relationships which audiences have with texts and the ways in which they exert their power as consumers. We also look at the political economy of audiences and the ways in which they are 'delivered' to advertisers as well as attending to the ratings war being waged by broadcasters and the development of narrowcasting and niche audiences. Finally, the book looks ahead to the future of audience research, suggesting that new genres such as 'reality TV' and new ICTs such as the Internet, are already revolutionizing the way in which research with audiences is taking place in the 21st century, not least because of the level of interactivity enabled by new media.

Contents

Series editor's foreword – Introduction – Early theories of audience – Measuring and moulding audiences – News, politics and public opinion – The cause and effect debate – Fan audiences – Audiences and cultural action – Audience research in the 21st century – Glossary – Bibliography – Index.

288pp   0 335 21166 6 (Paperback)   0 335 21167 4 (Hardback)

CRITICAL READINGS: MEDIA AND GENDER

Cynthia Carter and Linda Steiner (Eds)

- How is gender constructed in the media?
- To what extent do media portrayals of gender influence our everyday perceptions of ourselves and our actions?
- In what ways do the media reinforce and sometimes challenge gender inequalities?

The *Media and Gender Reader* provides a lively and engaging introduction to the field of critical media and gender research, drawing from a wide menu of exciting and important international scholarship in the field. Featured here is the work of authors studying a wide array of entertainment, news, grassroots and new media texts, institutions and audiences from a diverse range of conceptual and methodological approaches. The topics featured include, among others, gender identity and television talk shows, the commercialization of masculinity, historical portrayals of women in advertising, representing lesbians on television, the cult of femininity in women's magazines, gender and media violence, the sexualization of the popular press, racist sexual stereotyping in Hollywood cinema, women in popular music, media production and the empowerment of women, soap opera audiences, girl gamers, the impact of media monitoring, pornography and masculine power, and women's historical relationship to the Internet. It will have international appeal to readers in the Humanities and Social Sciences, especially in Mass Communication, Communication Studies, Media Studies, Cultural Studies, Women's Studies, Gender Studies, Journalism Studies and Sociology.

Contents
Series editor's foreword – Acknowledgements – The contested terrain of media and gender: editors' introduction – Part one: Gendered texts in context – Readings 1-5 – Part two: (Re)Producing gender – Readings 6-10 – Part three: Gendered audiences and identities – Readings 11-15 – Index.

288pp   0 335 21097 X (Paperback)

CRITICAL READINGS: SPORT, CULTURE AND THE MEDIA

David Rowe (Ed)

This is a carefully selected anthology of important and contemporary work dedicated to understanding the relationships between sport, culture and the media. It is both a stand-alone work and a useful accompaniment to the editor's highly praised book *Sport, Culture and the Media: The Unruly Trinity*.

The book covers both how media sport is produced and the ways in which it can be interpreted. It is divided into two related sections:

'Media Sport Construction: History, Labour, Culture and Economics' addresses such important topics as globalization, media convergence, the corporate contest for broadcast rights, the making of sports pages and broadcasts, and the staging of mega-media sports events like the Olympic Games.

'Media Sport Deconstruction: Readings, Forms, Ideologies and Futures' is concerned with issues including nationalism, gender, sexuality, ethnicity and race in sports television, the press, fiction and new media.

Readers will, therefore, gain a comprehensive grasp of the cultural significance of media sport.

Contents

1990s America' – Women, sport and globalization: competing discourses of sexuality and nation – Representations of football in baseball literature: The lyric Fenway, the prosody of the Dodgers, and are you ready for some football? – Sport as constructed audience: a case study of ESPN's The eXtreme Games – Convergence: sport on the information superhighway – Internet coverage of university softball and baseball web sites: the inequity continues – Further Reading – Index.

c374pp   0 335 21150 X (Paperback)   0 335 21151 8 (Hardback)

openup
ideas and understanding
in social science

www.**openup**.co.uk

Browse, search and order online

Download detailed title information and sample chapters*

*for selected titles

www.**openup**.co.uk